SMART TALK®

FOR ACHIEVING YOUR POTENTIAL®

5 Steps to Get You from Here to There

D0013079

Lou Tice

PACIFIC
INSTITUTE
PUBLISHING

The publisher offers discounts on this book when ordered in bulk quantities. For more information, write, call or fax:

Pacific Institute Publishing
1709 Harbor Ave. S. W.
Seattle, WA 981026
Phone 206.628.4800
Fax: 206.587.6007
www.thepacificinstitute.com

Editorial/design/production: Executive Excellence
Revised Edition Editorial/design/production: Pacific Institute Publishing

Library of Congress Cataloging-in-Publication Data (original version)

Tice, Louis E.
Smart Talk for Achieving Your Potential: 5 Steps to Get You from Here to There / Louis E. Tice
  p. cm.
ISBN 0-9634917-9-2

1. Motivation.   2. Education.   3. Success.   II. Title.

Printed in Canada   CIP
10 9 8 7 6 5 4 3   95-069759

ISBN 978-1-930622-07-4 (Revised 2005 Edition)

Designed by Courtney Cook Hopp
Printed by Friesen Corp.

To Diane,
my wife, companion, and lifetime business partner,
I dedicate this book. She has provided inspiration, love,
support, and courageous feedback, for which I am
profoundly grateful.

What they're saying about

SMART TALK®

FOR ACHIEVING YOUR POTENTIAL®

"In this book, Lou Tice shares the keys to building winning teams – including the visualization and affirmation of common goals."

— Pete Carroll, Head Football Coach
University of Southern California Trojans

"Lou Tice has masterfully constructed teachings for everyday life to address all the complex challenges we face in our personal and professional lives. This gem is the human tour guide to understanding and greater fulfillment!"

— Myrna Bentley, President/CEO
Concentra Financial – 2004's Best Managed Company in Canada

"While you may have heard many of the concepts before, Lou makes these principles easy to understand and immediately applicable and relevant to everyday life.... It taught me how to live my life more fully."

—Tom Stevens, 2006 President
National Association of REALTORS®

"Lou Tice's book is state of the art in continuous personal and professional leadership development. By following his five-step process, every person can improve the quality of his or her life."

— Major General Bernard Loeffke, USA (Ret.)

"Mr. Tice's concepts bridge cultural and language barriers and affirm the inherent potential of people to achieve their goals."

—Yoshiki Paul Otake, Founder and Chairman Emeritus
AFLAC – Japan

"Lou Tice has condensed a wealth of research into easily accessible programs. The Pacific Institute's training has been one of the best recruitment and retention tools we have, and Lou's work has been instrumental in helping our employees achieve their potential personally and professionally."

—Ken Smithmier, CEO
Decatur Memorial Hospital

"The principles of Lou Tice and The Pacific Institute are well founded concepts that have enabled me to raise my expectations to become the cabinet secretary of the New Mexico Department of Transportation. In addition, our employees are utilizing these same tools to build an innovative, efficacious organization for the 21st century."

—Rhonda G. Faught, P.E., Cabinet Secretary
New Mexico Department of Transportation

"Lou Tice's concepts have significantly changed the culture of Indiana Business College and have touched the lives of every employee and every student, both professionally and personally. Our new organizational aim, "We change lives, one student at a time" is a testimony to our recent success as we've seen our 12-campus enrollment double within the past five years. I recommend this book to anyone or any organization that seeks to improve themselves. It's awesome!!"

— Ken Konesco, President/CEO
Indiana Business College

"This book presents basic truths that can make you immediately more effective in your personal and professional lives."

— Dr. Cecil Bell, Chairman, Department of Management and Organization
School of Business, University of Washington

"In this readable book, Lou Tice teaches us how to progress in this very material world without succumbing to the prevailing ethic, which is, at best, pragmatic and, at worst, downright cannibalistic. Bravo!"

— Warren Bennis, Distinguished Professor of Management,
University of Southern California Marshall School of Business

"The principles Lou Tice teaches benefit me personally and professionally. I apply them to optimize my own potential, and to achieve peak performance in our organization."

— Dr. Kathleen M. Hawk-Sawyer, former Director
Federal Bureau of Prisons

"Whether you're looking for immediate help or for lasting improvement in performance and relationships, this book is pure gold."

— John MacLeod, former Head Basketball Coach
University of Notre Dame and the NBA's Phoenix Suns

"Understanding the concepts of 'Smart Talk' has fundamentally changed the course of my life. As we have provided the curriculum to thousands of people in our organization, our effectiveness has improved dramatically, so we now regularly "dare to dream" and make those dreams our new realities."

— Donald G. Western
Vice President, Specialty Industries Division, Caterpillar

"Lou Tice shares the approaches, processes and techniques that help create efficacious people, winning teams and highly successful organizations. This is a must read for any leader."

— Rod L. Bussell
Vice President, Mining and Construction Division, Caterpillar

Also Available from The Pacific Institute

*   *   *   *

BOOKS:

Smart Talk for Achieving Your Potential (Spanish Edition), by Lou Tice

Personal Coaching for Results, by Lou Tice

Leadership is a Performance Art, by Pete Carroll and Lou Tice

Cultures of Excellence, Lou Tice and Dr. Glenn Terrell (Eds.)

The Ministry of Leadership: Heart and Theory, by Dr. Glenn Terrell

The Spirit of Leadership, by Dr. Robert J. Spitzer, S.J.

From Warrior to Healer, by Maj. Gen. Bernard "Burn" Loeffke, USA (Ret.)

VIDEO:

Family Enrichment Video Library

Foundation for Personal and Professional Development

How to Make Retirement a New Adventure[TM]

AUDIO:

Mastering Your Potential®

MULTIMEDIA:

Investment in Excellence–Today® *(CD-Rom)*

For information on personal and organization applications,
call 1-800-426-3660
(USA and Canada) or check us out on the web at
www.thepacificinstitute.com

If you are planning for
a year
                    sow rice,

If you are planning for
a decade
                    plant trees,

If you are planning for
a lifetime
                    educate people.

—Chinese proverb

Acknowledgments

S ince *Smart Talk* was first published in 1995, thousands and thousands of books have found their way to all four corners of the globe. It has been an exciting project, and I am proud and humbled at how well the contents have been received. Ten years in constant publication is quite the accomplishment!

As in any endeavor, one never does anything completely alone. Since *Smart Talk* is a primer for the education we teach, I must first thank those scientists and psychologists on the front lines of research, upon whose work my work is built:

- **Dr. Albert Bandura,** distinguished professor of psychology at Stanford University and recently voted one of the top four contributors to the field of psychology in the 20th Century. I owe much of my knowledge of social cognitive theory to his research, as it sets the foundation of much of what we teach at The Pacific Institute.

- **Dr. Martin Seligman,** distinguished professor of psychology at the University of Pennsylvania, has influenced my thinking in many ways, not the least of which is his exhaustive and mindset-changing research on optimism and pessimism.

- **Dr. Gary Latham,** distinguished professor of psychology at the University of Toronto, whose important research on goal-setting is central to what we teach.

- And the research and writings of **Dr. Warren Bennis,** distinguished professor of business administration at the University of Southern California's Marshall School of Business, have been invaluable to my understanding of leadership.

To Ken Shelton, my thanks for his editorial and organizational skills in the preparation of this manuscript. I must also acknowledge my many friends and associates around the world, my faithful colleagues at The Pacific Institute, and the millions around the world we have served through our *Investment in Excellence*® program. By sharing their feedback and friendship, they have helped immensely to make our work possible.

Contents

Preface

Smart Talk for Achieving Your Potential
by Lou Tice

IN writing this book, I want to help you achieve more of your potential so that you can improve yourself, your marriage, your family, your company, your community, and the world around you.

The best way I know to help you improve the quality of your life and the performance of your team or company is to help you improve your self-talk. As you learn the process of Smart Talk, you learn how to take yourself and your organization from where you are to where you have the potential to be.

You may already be a peak performer, or you may be a discouraged learner, an embattled parent, a confused or abused child. You may have suffered through divorce or the death of loved ones. You may be chronically unemployed and on the verge of giving up.

Whoever you are, I already know this about you: You were not born to be a victim or loser. You have immense potential, and you can build a better world for yourself and others.

"Build a better world," said God.
And I answered,
"How? The world is such a vast place,
And so complicated now,
And I'm small and useless;
There's nothing I can do."
But God in all His wisdom said,
"Just build a better you."
     —Anonymous

As you read this book, I hope you'll say to yourself, "I could be more, do more, and have more. I'm going to start with myself, with my own self-talk, and build out from there."

1

This isn't the only way; but it is one good way. Once you learn the process, you can figure out the *here* and *there,* the *why* and *how* of your own life.

I'll use myself and my wife, Diane, as examples. Of course, we aren't the only models or, necessarily, the best models for you. We don't want you to say, "My gosh, they're spectacular. Look at what they're doing. They're too far ahead of me. I don't see myself ever doing that."

And so we'll share the struggles we've had over the years so you can connect with us. When you see where we started, you'll see that you're better prepared than we ever were. When you hear some of the dumb things that I've done in my life and yet overcome them to get where I am, you'll laugh and move forward with confidence.

When I left my job at Kennedy High School in Seattle to start my business, I had $1,000 in the bank and nine children to feed. In an attempt to drum up business, I would put on free previews in different places. I once asked a person to appraise my presentation and to tell me how I could improve. So this person came and watched me and later said, "Where did you get that suit?" He said, "You look like a crumpled professor."

Well, it was my best suit; in fact, it was my only suit.

Upon hearing this feedback, Diane immediately went out and bought me a new suit, a brown polyester suit. If you dropped a match on it, it would melt.

Shortly thereafter, I was invited to speak at a breakfast meeting at the Washington Athletic Club, to an exclusive group of boosters. I showed up wearing my new suit, but I was trying to pretend that I'd had the suit for years. I gave my speech, and afterward I talked with Gene Juarez, a leader in the business community. He complimented me on my *new* suit. I thought to myself, "How did he know it was new?"

A few minutes later, I excused myself and went to the restroom. As I was washing my hands and combing my hair, I noticed that I still had the size label and the price tag on my sleeve!

I've done lots of dumb things like that. In fact, after I had gone through the brown suit, Diane bought me two seersucker suits, one with stripes and one with checks. One summer day, I got up very early to fly to Boise, Idaho, to introduce Boise Cascade to our new video-based training program. This was an important presentation, as we had invested a lot of money in making these videos and needed to make a sale to sustain our young company.

I was totally focused on making a winning presentation, but I could tell that they weren't impressed. Afterward, they thanked me politely and sent me on my way.

At the airport in Boise, I asked my colleague, Brian Casey, "What do you think, Brian? Why weren't we successful?"

He said, "Lou, have you looked at yourself in the mirror today?"

For the first time all day, I saw what I had put on in the darkness that morning—the pants from one of those seersucker suits and the jacket from the other! I'll tell you what: if anybody ever looked like a hayseed, I did. Those stripes and checks clashed something terrible.

Brian added, "Here you are trying to impress these people with achieving your potential, and look at you."

When you know where Diane and I started, you will say, "If Lou Tice can somehow influence leaders of the military, business, industry, education, and government with price tags on his sleeves and ill-matched suits, imagine what I could do using this process."

As you read this book, please remember where we started. I want you to relate to us and then go on to do bigger and better things with your life. You should be inspired to say, "I can do better. I can take it even further. I'm already in a better position than Lou Tice ever was."

I want you to connect with us on that level and see how you can grow to new levels. I hope to start a fire inside, a purpose like you've never had in your life. That will add tremendous depth and meaning, but it's got to be *your* purpose. My task is to help draw the purpose out. I won't give you the purpose. But I intend for you to find the purpose for the rest of your life.

I want to help you light the fuse that will cause explosive growth in yourself and in your work and community. I also encourage you to expose people in leadership roles who are mean, spiteful, immoral, self-serving, and manipulative. You'll set a much better example for people so they'll quit following false leaders. In your work, you'll see that there's a better way to live and lead, and you'll show the way.

Three Basic Principles

In my life, I am guided by three basic principles: I want to be authentic, progressive, and effective.

• *Authentic* is to always be who I am, and not change because I'm with you one moment and my wife the next. If I'm always wondering what others would want me to be, I will try to manipulate and get what I need out of them. I am who I am, win or lose. That's authenticity. And if you reject me or if I'm not capable, I won't pretend to be something that I'm not. I've just got to be who I am. I encourage you to be who you are.

• *Progressive* means to improve who you are. If who you are is not effective enough, if it's not good enough, that's okay. Now you've got to progress and grow. Progressive means every day you're getting better. You affirm, "I'm getting better every day." The process of affirmations is the key to the whole learning and teaching process, the key to getting from here to there. Your *here* and *there* change, but the process remains the same.

• *Effective* suggests that you do the right things, the important things, not just the urgent or pressing things. How do I become a more effective human being, a better father, a better leader, a better teacher? How do I grow? Being effective implies that you know where *there* is. Do you know where *there* is? Where are you going? Some *theres* are better than others. I've tried a lot of them. But when we're talking about becoming effective, we're talking about setting and achieving goals— the process of taking thoughts and building reality as best we know it. That's what it's all about, too: taking an idea and making it substance.

I started this process 30 years ago, when I was in my 20s. I was always trying to get from *here* to *there*. Rarely have I traveled in a straight line; but from the detours and diversions, and from my failures, I have learned a few things.

Now, I want you to take these developmental principles and know where you're going and what you want to do with this information. Take it and ask, "How will this help me get where I want to be?" "How will this enable me?"

Examine what might be stopping you now from moving on. Set the vision of why you're here and what you want to do with your life and why you want it.

You want more personal growth, family development, business development. But on a much deeper and long-term level, you want happiness, enrichment, service, persuasion, influence, and love.

All of us are interested in *making a difference* by progressing from one goal to the next goal to the next goal and not getting stalled between goals as we go along. We want many different things, but primarily we want to make a contribution, make a difference, do the things we set out to do successfully. Why do we want it? We want to impact others around us—whether those be people who work with us or family or people who are close to us, taking the gifts that we have and making them useful.

I realize that by changing myself and my own thought process, I can improve the relationships with my family and workplace and, in turn, grow exponentially to where I can make the world a better place by making simple changes in myself.

This process is not something that I've invented. No one invented it. It's part of human nature. Now you want to apply it, stretch it, direct it where you want it to go.

Don't expect me to be perfect. Diane is near perfect, but I'm not even close. I'm still in the process of growing, still in the process of trying to undo where I'm stuck. I do better than I did a few years ago. But I'm still a work in progress.

You, too, are a work in progress. Together, using Smart Talk, we can get where we want to go.

Introduction

ONCE I travelled to Fort Campbell, Kentucky. At the airport, I was met by two young pilots who were assigned to fly me to Fort Campbell in a Blackhawk helicopter. Although it was dark, these pilots flew the helicopter 150 miles an hour, 150 feet off the ground. I was scared to death. But these pilots were wearing special glasses that allowed them to see as if it were daylight. Seeing with the glasses also allowed them to travel very fast, even at night.

The principles in this book will be your special glasses. When you know how to use them, they will completely change your view of life. They will illuminate not only your self-imposed barriers, but also your inner resources and unlimited potential. They will help you take the biggest strides of your life toward fulfillment of your goals. With these special glasses, you will see new aspects of vision and reality, perception and belief, high performance and success. With the power of your new sight, you will see the way to become more fully yourself.

You might say, "He's talking 'pie in the sky.' This may be possible for somebody else, but it can't be for me." Yes it can, if you remain open-minded, aware of possibilities, alert to options. Don't lock on too quickly that "this can't be" or "that won't work." For the moment, withhold your judgment; otherwise, you'll become too "realistic." Once you put on the special glasses, you'll see how to *transcend* current reality, how to *transcend* sensibility, how to *transcend* linear logic, how to *transcend* your current culture and environment. With this special sight, you will change the beliefs that are holding you back, and move toward where you want to go in life.

Of course, I can't give you the answer to every problem in your life, but in this book I will give you a five-step process for changing your life and improving your organizations. The five steps correspond to the five sections of the book.

A Five-Step Process

From the start, I want the process to be clear in your mind. You need to see the interrelationships of the five steps of this natural growth process on personal and professional levels.

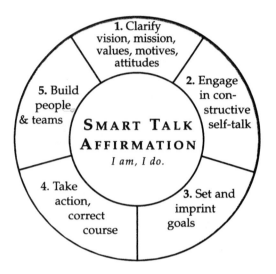

The Core: *Affirmation.* In this context, affirmation means the exercise of faith and belief in your inherent potential, imagined ideal, desired result, and set goal. You affirm them as if they were presently realized in your life. Affirmation applies to every step: You apply positive, proactive thinking to create visions, shift attitudes, see options, seize opportunities, expand comfort zones, and build teams and organizations.

Step 1. Clarify Vision, Mission, Values, Motive, Motivation, Attitudes

Step 2. Apply Creative Thinking, Positive Self-Talk

Step 3. Define Targets and Imprint Goals

Step 4. Take Action, Make Course Corrections

Step 5. Build Others, Improve Organizations

To illustrate these steps, I'm including the five-part story of Diane's battle with cancer. Each part serves to introduce one of the five sections of the book.

Now by adding a couple of concentric rings to this diagram, we can see how the five steps apply equally to families, teams, organizations, and societies. By building a better you, you become a person who can build a better world.

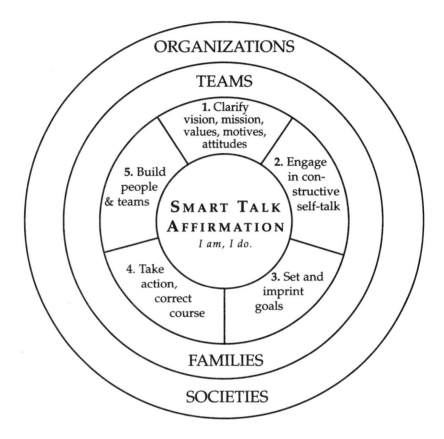

Know in advance that I'm going to challenge you. You won't be spoon fed, and it won't be easy. You may struggle to figure out what I'm writing about. But once you get it and apply it, you'll pass it on to others. You'll build teams. You'll realize your dreams.

Some people believe that creation is over. Some believe that the future is merely a projection of the past and present. I think the world is constantly evolving, and that human beings are co-responsible with God for that creation and evolution.

If you want a better marriage, a better family, a better school, a better community, a better government, and a better future, you need to live a better life. If you want to build a better world, start by building a better you.

Will you accept personal responsibility for the changes you need to make? If so, you are ready to read this book and apply the principles. What I have is a *blueprint for positive change and growth.* However, assimilating this blueprint is only the first step. Believing that a book can change your life is just as big a trap as believing that circumstances completely control you. It is simply another way of shifting the locus of control to something outside of you. If you're not careful, you can become a great contemplator who lays back and says, "I can see how this could work." Yet, contemplation without action is meaningless frustration. The real adventure is *applying* these concepts to your life daily.

The concepts are organized to enable you to change your thinking and behavior *as you read.* As you absorb these concepts you will experience the sort of "Aha!" feeling you get when you discover, for the first time, something that was already obvious. And you will continue to feel these "Aha!" feelings throughout your life. You will constantly be telling yourself, "Look at that! How did I ever miss seeing it?"

I started teaching these concepts in high school, and today I teach them to the highest-ranking members of government and the military; to strife-torn people in foreign countries; to caretakers and inmates of correctional systems; to educators and students; to factory workers, farmers, administrators, laborers, and athletes; to the health, welfare, and political system—and to many others.

These principles have made a difference to me economically, socially, environmentally, and personally by allowing me to gain greater influence at higher levels and to help people create solutions to their most pressing needs. At my company, we talk about dealing in miracles: "It would be a miracle if you could get labor and management to work together"; "It would be a miracle if you could reduce the recidivism of criminals"; "It would be a miracle if you could develop a sensible way to get people off of welfare"; "It would be a miracle if you could improve the quality of our educational system."

And I say to myself, "That's what we should attack." With the information in this book, you can work miracles in your own families, communities, companies, teams, and organizations: "It would be a miracle if we could get our people more jobs"; "It would be a miracle if I could get my friend off drugs"; "It would be a miracle if we could get our parents to stop screaming at each other"; "It would be a miracle if the kids picked up their clothes." Miracles happen; in fact, you can cause them to happen.

Two lines in Henrik Ibsen's *Peer Gynt* talk about a "reckoning" at life's end and the use or squandering of our potential: "We are thought; you should have formed us. Legs to run with; you should have given us."

All the thoughts, ideas, and dreams that we have in our life are worthless—unless we give them legs. In this book, I want to help you bring form to your ideas, and give "legs" to your thoughts and dreams.

This will be an action book. I hope to inspire you to action, to life-long action, on your goals. I don't want you to quit and give up. I'll give you a model and a process. I'll tell you what drives you and how you can keep going and why you should keep going. I'll show you that you don't need to compete with other people; you don't have to try to be the best in your profession. You simply identify your own ideals, goals that you want to accomplish: what you want for yourself, your family, your community. You don't need to be on top, or the richest person in town—unless that's what you want.

What matters is making the world around you a better place. What matters is creating happiness-producing events for your children and for yourself, for your community.

Imagine yourself in prison for 30 years. Then someone comes along and says, "By the way, you didn't need to stay in jail. You imprisoned *yourself*. You chose to be your own judge and jury. You sentenced yourself to unhappiness. You sentenced yourself to a life of poverty, or mediocrity, or to being an ineffective person. The key to the cell door was always in your pocket. At any time, you could have unlocked the door and walked out free."

In a very real sense, that's what this book is all about. I'm saying, "Look, the key is in your pocket. All you have to do is unlock the door and walk out free."

DIANE'S STORY

A Note of Introduction: *Diane's journey is a vivid and beautiful example of the five-step process. Diane moves from the state of being confronted with one of the most serious forms of cancer to an end result of great physical and mental health. She does so while continuing to be involved in the business and coordinating the building of a 15,000 sq. ft. lodge. Each unit tells her story as it relates to the five-step process of "getting from here to there."*

Part I: A Real Mid-Life Crisis

LOU: In July a few years ago, our family celebrated Diane's 50th birthday. She was happy, vibrant, upbeat. She had devoted so much of her time over the years to doing things for her family, and for others, that she hadn't taken enough time for herself. She was eagerly anticipating that opportunity.

Every year, after her birthday, Diane goes for a complete physical. Because she had just turned 50, her doctor recommended that she also see a gynecologist. She decided she would. Afterwards, Diane forgot all about the test. Quite frankly, she considered it routine. Then suddenly, in September, our lives changed forever.

DIANE: To me, my 50th birthday was a halfway point in my life. I was looking forward to, and planning for, the second half. I thought, "Now I can begin. The kids have all grown and our company is building, so now I'll have time to do all the things I want to do." I was ready to enjoy my next 50 years.

I have a firm faith in God and His presence within me. And I believe that the strength in my life comes from within, not from other people outside myself. I believe in the immortality of my soul. But I never thought too much about these beliefs until one afternoon, a week after my tests, when I received a call at home from the doctor who had done my tests. In a shaky voice, he said, "I have the results of your test." I said, "Oh, good." I assumed everything was fine. Then he said, very abruptly, "You definitely have uterine cancer. It's in the third stage, and there are only four stages. So you'll have to have a total hysterectomy right away. And, of course, I will assist at the surgery." I was stunned. I held the phone away from my ear, looked at it, and thought, "Like hell, you will."

I was upset about the cancer, but I was so angry with the way this man told me about it that I automatically resisted him. To me, his cold, matter-of-fact tone was saying, "You don't stand a chance. But I'll do you the favor of assisting in your surgery anyway." I thought, "No, you won't. Who do you think you are?" So I hung up and called my regular doctor and told him I was enraged at the way this other doctor had broken the news. I said, "It was so inappropriate. He didn't prepare me. He didn't even ask if anyone else was there with me. What if I had taken it badly? I might've fainted dead away on the floor."

Of course, it never occurred to me to faint. I just thought, "I am not going to let a doctor determine *my* future. Especially *this* doctor." I found out later, in my own research, that many people don't react assertively with doctors. They tend to believe everything that doctors say, and blindly follow their advice. I am not in awe of doctors—maybe because I've had serious ailments in the past. That attitude turned out to be an important factor in my recovery process.

This event makes you realize where the locus of control really is. You decide very quickly whether you're going to determine your own life, or sit back and say, "Yes, doctor"—or, for that matter, "Yes, teacher," "Yes, boss," "Yes, family," "Yes, everybody else but me." Psychologically, when confronted with a serious threat, people will either flee, fight, or just give in. Reflecting back now, I can say that because of the inappropriate way I found out about my cancer and because of my self-confidence and my beliefs, I subconsciously decided to fight. And I'm glad it happened that way because it solidified, in my mind, my belief that we are all responsible for our own lives.

Though I do have a firm faith in God's strength within me, I know I must also do my part and use my free will responsibly.

LOU: Even though Diane had taken a devastating hit, she was already visualizing the recovery. Immediately, she started screening out threats and filtering in important information. Instead of thinking, "I'm dying. Doctor, tell me what to do," she was thinking, "There's no way this doctor will participate in my surgery." Because Diane had that assertive, "I'm going to fight" attitude, the important information—that this guy was a locked-on thinker who locked out options—screamed right through. So Diane *knew* that he should not be involved in her case.

By deciding that this doctor would not participate, and also that she would fight, Diane made the first important decision in her battle to recover. To get a second opinion, she visited a highly regarded surgeon. He, too, recommended surgery as the best first step. But Diane researched further. She considered not just the operation, but the *total process of recovery*. Only after she reviewed the opinions of respected surgeons from the best cancer centers in the world did she decide that surgery was the proper way to go for the first step.

But with this unnerving intrusion into our lives, and all the uncertainty, I felt it was important to relax and have some fun first. So we agreed that it would be a good idea to get away for a few days before the surgery. We went to our ranch in the Cascade Mountains with two close friends, and we had a wonderful weekend. We didn't discuss the operation or the uncertainty: We conducted ourselves normally, having fun with people we liked. That, too, is part of our curriculum: When you are under duress, you can control the dissonance by staying in your comfort zone and conducting your affairs as normally as possible.

After the relaxing weekend, Diane felt more assured. The following Thursday, she checked into the hospital in Seattle, and the surgery was scheduled for Friday afternoon. I had already begun a four-day seminar for about 200 people, so I needed to focus on that, too. On Friday, after I finished teaching the afternoon session, I went to my hotel room to await the call from the doctor at the hospital. I had a troubling feeling. Events were out of our hands for the moment, and I had never been in this traumatic situation before. I felt terribly uneasy.

My self-talk was both positive *and* negative. I had faith that the operation would be successful and that Diane would be fine. But I also worried, "Well, what *if*?" It was like, "I don't *want* to hear the results. But I *need* to hear the results because I want it to be good news. But I'm afraid if I hear the results, it will be *bad* news." My self-talk was telling me to avoid the truth, but knowing I needed to hear the truth, I finally said, "I'll just sit here and wait. And I'll stop worrying. Whatever comes, I'll be ready for it."

You never really know if you are ready to handle a tragedy or disaster. I thought I could handle this, but my anxiety kept triggering doubt. An inner voice was urging me, *"Avoid this call!"* It was interesting, especially during a seminar weekend, to find out that I had a powerful urge to avoid the truth. I had to remind myself: "You can't control events. But you can control your reaction to events."

Finally, the doctor called with a *good news, bad news* report. He said, "We got all the cancer we could see. But we know it's broken loose in her system because we found a tumor on her bladder." He explained that Diane's cancer was in an advanced stage; that she would need chemotherapy and some follow-up radiation treatments; and that, even with treatment, the chances for long-term survival were not good. That hit me right between the eyes. I thought, "Oh God. How do I tell Diane?"

Late Friday, instead of attending the reception at the seminar, I decided to go straight to the hospital to see Diane. I decided to walk the mile or so from the hotel to the hospital because I needed that time to gather myself and prepare what I wanted to say. I wanted to find the right way to tell Diane the truth, and still convey my love, my faith, my hope.

When I left the hotel room, my self-talk was, "Focus your intent," but I was still too nervous to properly prepare what I wanted to say. While waiting for the elevator, I remember imagining what my life would be like without Diane. "We've been together since we were 16. We've never missed a Christmas together, or a Thanksgiving, or a birthday. For 36 years, our goal-setting has been so closely tied that even though we're two separate people, with separate identities, we feel as though we have one mutual destiny."

For an instant, I felt that if the elevator doors somehow opened into an empty shaft, it would be all right if I just fell in. I knew that our kids were provided for, and were old enough to take care of themselves, so what difference would it make? I didn't feel desperate or frightened. I had this easy, peaceful, "I quit. I'll go with her" feeling. I'm sure other people have felt this way in similar circumstances, but I had never felt anything like it before—and I never thought I would. See, you can't anticipate feeling that way.

Walking to the hospital, I started to cry because I still didn't know how to tell Diane. I thought, "Do I give up or do I fight?" Normally, my intent would be to fight. For me, that meant all-out war. I didn't care if I had to give up everything—our business, our home, all we had. But the important decision was Diane's. She had to have the same intent.

Continued on page 65.

STEP 1:
Clarify Vision, Mission, Values, Motives, Attitudes

EACH new start brings some butterflies, but that's normal and healthy. Professional golfer Greg Norman learned to play the game by reading articles and books written by master golfer Jack Nicklaus. At his first Masters tournament, Norman found himself paired with his mentor, Nicklaus. On the first tee, Norman smashed the ball 300 yards right down the fairway. Jack then hit the ball 300 yards down the fairway.

As the two men walked down the fairway, Jack asked, "Greg, how did you feel as you stood at that first tee in your first Masters? Did you feel excited? Did you feel tight? How did you feel?"

Greg Norman said, "Jack, I was scared to death, my knees were shaking. I was nervous."

And Jack said, "Don't you love that feeling?"

I love that feeling—of having a fresh start at a new level—and you will love that feeling, too, when you decide to start living life at a higher level.

In this section, you will find three chapters that get at the roots of high performance—vision, mission, values, motives, motivation, and attitudes.

We need to know who we are, where we are, and where we're going.

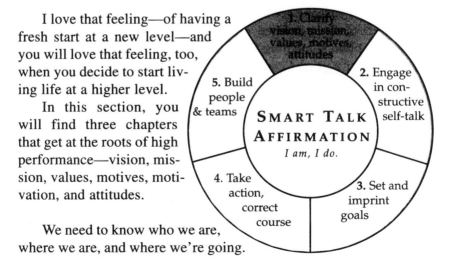

1. Clarify vision, mission, values, motives, attitudes

2. Engage in constructive self-talk

3. Set and imprint goals

4. Take action, correct course

5. Build people & teams

SMART TALK AFFIRMATION
I am, I do.

Knowing and accepting the *here*, the current reality, is just as important as imagining and assimilating the *there*. If we don't know who and where we are, we lack the courage to face current reality. We get stuck. Our current reality, rather than being our *baseline* on a performance improvement track, becomes our *lifeline*—our life story, and perhaps the life story of our children and grandchildren, employees and associates.

What is the process of taking an idea and projecting the possibilities? What is the process of taking an idea and building a building or starting a family, or organizing a party, or growing a company, or improving a community?

Chapter 1 deals with vision and mission. You will never accomplish all that you dream, but you will seldom accomplish anything that you don't envision first. So, think in terms of ideals; compare your ideals with your current reality; establish what you want; find models of what you want to become; and visualize yourself achieving your desired end result.

Chapter 2 deals with motives and values. I encourage you to reach for your quest, assess values, establish a value system, determine your motives. Ask tough questions of yourself to assess your values. Determine your hierarchy of values and prioritize your investments of time, energy, and money. Having a clear sense of mission will make all the difference.

Chapter 3 deals with getting your attitude right. Once you set a goal for yourself, you probably won't accomplish it until you *want* to accomplish it, and you have a strong *want to* reason attached to it. You likely won't change if you wait for a *sign* or some other outside stimulus.

No process can guarantee success, but Step 1 increases the odds that you can build something from an idea. By knowing and applying the process, you can take charge of your future. You can build a better community, a better family, a better company.

c h a p t e r   1

THE *HERE* AND THE *THERE*

I want to give you all you need to get from where you are now (from *here*, this present moment) to *there* (where you want to go). I want to get you from *here* to *there*. To do that, you first need to understand that you're in the belief business.

The Belief Business

What you achieve is largely a matter of what you believe; in fact, you might say: *believe equals achieve.*

Some 20 years ago, I was a teacher and football coach at Kennedy High School in Seattle. But what I learned from a brilliant visiting professor at the University of Washington changed my way of thinking, and my life.

The first goal I set for myself was to use the information I'd learned to help people and to improve organizations.

"Oh, so you want to change the system?" was the response.

"Yes, that's right."

"Well, how long have you been a consultant?"

"Never."

"Do you have a doctorate degree or any experience?"

"Nope."

"Where did you do your field work?"

"Nowhere."

"Well, then, what are your qualifications?"

"Quite frankly, none."

So, what made me think I could achieve this goal? My affirmative belief that my current reality was not an accurate reflection of my inherent potential.

Your reality is the same size and shape as the container you hold it in. If you confine your creativity, your imagination, your future to the small con-

19

tainer of your current reality, your thinking will be dominated by negative self-talk and your actions will be confined to your current comfort zone.

What if you let your *reality* grow without containment? You may think, "That sounds too simple." It's not simple; it takes a firm understanding and application of certain principles. But it's possible, and worth the effort.

Your current reality is not fixed. You can learn how to see beyond who you are at the present moment and transcend your present circumstances to attain your goals. I don't mean that you should deny present reality, because recognizing reality is an important step in the process of change. But don't be *fixed* by your present state. The universe is not fixed. Creation is not fixed. You are not fixed. You can learn how to choose your future, how to create it, how to invent it now.

If you believe that your current reality is fixed, you get trapped in your own mistaken sense of "This is the way it is." You think, "It's always been this way, and it will always be this way." But the present is not permanent.

Remember Sir Isaac Newton? His view was that God created a perfect world—with just one exception: *people*. People were considered basically sinful. They were always trying to ruin a good thing. The idea was: "If God created a perfect world, then why are you trying, with all of your imagination and creativity, to *change* it? You'll screw things up."

Some of you were raised and conditioned by parents who felt that way. Some work for bosses who think this way. Some have teachers who feel that everything should stay the way it is. "We don't want any of your bright ideas, thank you. In fact, we discourage any new ideas you have."

Two centuries later, Alfred North Whitehead, a philosopher and mathematician, saw a dynamic world, not a fixed one. He saw a world in which people are co-creative agents with God. To him, creation is ongoing, as are the lives of human beings. They aren't fixed, or stuck; they are always in motion.

If you share that view—as I do—then what do you think about people who say, "Well, I'll lay back and let God, or Fate, or Destiny, or Nature, or the Powers That Be, direct my life for me?" What will their lives be like? "Okay, if I'm a bum, I guess it's meant to be. If I'm lazy, or can't control this terrible temper, it isn't my fault. If I'm wallowing in debt and never pay my bills, that's just the way it is."

What a wonderful excuse for not being accountable or responsible for your own life! What a simple way to cement yourself into a fixed reality and never change!

High-performance people live in a Whiteheadian world. For them, present reality is only temporary. Instead of saying, "Well, I guess this is the way it is," they build a *new* reality every day. They don't sit around cursing Fate, or wishing for change, or hoping their lottery number comes up. They create change for *themselves.*

You were probably conditioned to believe that you were either *born with it* or *born without it.* You've heard people say, "She's a born leader" or "He's a born loser." In other words, you either "have what it takes," or you don't.

After taking an I.Q. or aptitude test, you were informed, "You aren't very good at this, and you're only average at that." Those notions become beliefs, even though those tests measure only what you *have* learned, not what you *can* learn. They measure what you *have* been, not what you *can* be. If you accept the test results as *the truth* about yourself, you tend to act like the person you believe yourself to be. As long as you hold that belief, you remain trapped or limited by it.

You may also be blocked by the beliefs that others have about you— or about your age, skin color, ethnic background, or vocation. If I'm your leader, parent, teacher, coach, or manager and believe that you don't have what it takes, I'll set up situations that prevent you from being all that you can be.

When you feel blocked by the beliefs you or others have about you, think of the bumblebee. When aeronautical engineers examine the bumblebee, measure its wing span, compute its body weight, and note its oversized fuselage, they conclude that there is no rational reason why a bumblebee can fly. But the bumblebee doesn't know this. It doesn't know that its wing span is too short, or that its fuselage is too heavy to sustain flight. So it flies anyway.

Remember Dick Fosbury, the Olympic high jumper who introduced "The Fosbury Flop"? He was the first international competitor to go over the bar backwards. Back then, coaches told their kids, "Don't watch this guy. He's a freak." These days, *everybody* goes over backwards. ***Remember: if you change the way you think, you change the way you act.*** And barriers in your life begin to fall.

Before 1954, everybody *knew* you couldn't run a mile in under four minutes. Then Roger Bannister crashed through the barrier. Within the next four years, the four-minute barrier was shattered more than 40 times. Why? Runners now knew that it could be done.

A few years ago, the minimal standard for qualification for the NCAA high jump Nationals was six feet, ten inches. But since too many people qualified, officials raised it to six eleven. The same number qualified. They said, "We have to weed some of them out"—and they raised it to seven feet. The same numbers qualified. They raised it to seven one and then seven two, thinking, "That'll definitely stop them"—but the same number qualified.

If we change the belief, the performance follows. If you change the belief, you can change the way you run your life; the way you run your company; the way you run your family. *You* build the barriers. It's often only the *belief* that makes something so.

As Shakespeare wrote, "There is nothing either good or bad, but thinking makes it so."

See the *why* and *what*. Don't worry now about *how*. Ordinary people do things in ordinary ways. They follow rules; they wait in line; they come and go in well-established patterns; they get stuck in ruts and routines.

One day I decided that ordinary wasn't good enough for me, so I went right after my vision. Based on my current reality, and how far my vision was from that reality, I might have thought, "How can I possibly make an impact?" I didn't know *how* I would do it; I just knew that I would invent a way to achieve my goal.

You can't cunningly plan yourself into your ideal situations. When you set a goal, you immediately feel compelled to ask, "How do I do it? How can I get it?" And you start planning. But from where I started, there was no plan that could possibly have put me into my present situation. It took something else.

It took a willingness to let myself get off the old track and to leap-frog my present reality. The idea of leap-frogging present reality might seem like magic to you. When you watch a magician do an amazing card trick, you see the end result, not the process. You don't see the magician slide the card up his sleeve. It looks amazing because you can't see the *how*.

Once when I was a high school teacher and coach, I needed to raise money for the school athletic program. After considering several ideas, I decided to get 20 kids to fight each other in a boxing tournament. I figured that they were going to fight anyway, so why not sell tickets.

Well, I sold most of the tickets, but five days before fight time I still didn't have a boxing ring, boxing gloves, or referee. People were starting to say, "Lou, forget this crazy idea, and give the money back." I couldn't, I'd spent some of it for advertising.

At that time, I was teaching a night class of adults. I mentioned my problem to the class, and one person said, "You know, I used to be a boxer when I was in the army."

I said, "Oh."

He said, "And I've got a friend who runs a boxing club here in Seattle."

I said, "Really. You don't suppose your friend could find me a boxing ring?"

He gave me the guy's phone number, and I called it when I got home about 10:00 that night. The man said, "I'm sorry, I can't help you, but my friend has a boxing club, and he rents his ring out." I called that guy next, and he said, "Yes, I'll rent it to you, for $50."

I said, "I'll take it, but don't bring the boxing ring if you can't find me a referee."

He said, "Okay, I'll referee the fights."

I said, "For the same price?"

He said, "Yep."

I said, "Well, there's no sense in bringing the boxing ring or coming to referee if you don't know where I can get some boxing gloves."

And the guy said, "What do you have?"

I said, "I have the tickets sold and the kids ready to fight. By the way, if you have any headgear and drinking bottles and a bell, you'd better bring those things, too."

I had no idea where I would find a boxing ring and referee when I set the goal and sold tickets. Many people need to know where the resources are at the time they set the vision or goal, and that's why they achieve so little in life.

Don't be too concerned with *how* you're going to be what you want to be in the future; you'll learn how to create and invent the process along the way. You're creative, intuitive, and powerful inside—you're a creative genius. But you've got to allow yourself to get off the old track.

Right now, I want you to be more concerned with *why* and with *what*. If you get that right, you will invent the *how*.

The best way to control your future is to invent it. How do high-performance people invent their future? How do they get off the old track? How do they leap-frog their current reality and drop themselves into their vision? By fixing on the vision, the mission, the affirmation, and initially ignoring the *how*.

To transcend current reality, you can't be too concerned with the *how*. Otherwise, you'll shrink your vision. If you can't logically, realistically tell yourself how to reach your goal based on what you think you can do at the moment, you will deny what you're capable of doing in the future because it seems unrealistic. "Oh, it's just a pie-in-the-sky dream anyway." "Where will the customers come from?" "Where will I get the money?" "Who will help me?" "I'm not qualified. I need a degree first."

You will invent a hundred rationalizations to keep you from doing what you want to do. You will tell yourself that your goal is out of reach, and then you'll back it up to where it seems more realistic, more attainable, more comfortable. Even then you might take *years* to achieve that goal— and you might never use your vast creative potential to make a better life.

Don't be a linear thinker. If you remain a logical, linear thinker, you'll buy one of those planners or organizers, and then you'll plan the next three months based on how capable and creative you are at the present moment. That's old thinking. The old linear, cause-and-effect thinking, the old method-orientation, is outdated. You need to go on hunches and follow a direction that, at first, may seem impractical and insensible. You need to take giant leaps, not baby steps. At first, don't worry about *how*. Don't worry about an efficient, straight-line, mistake-free course of action. You'll invent it along the way.

For example, one time when Diane and I still lived in our first house, we were driving in the car with our children from the Oregon coast to Seattle. Diane and I had just come out of teaching high school, and we didn't have much money. But we let the kids think about what they wanted in their ideal home.

They wrote down 170 things on a list. They listed everything from ice cream makers to eagles to sunken garbage cans so they didn't need to pick up the garbage every time the dog knocked it over. They listed a jukebox, a slot machine, a swimming pool, their own bedrooms, etc. We wrote all the items down and visualized the place.

Now, we weren't very affluent at the time, but within a few months, we found a home with 66 of the features on our list, including the ice cream maker, the jukebox, and the pool table. And then we put the list away.

Ten years later, Diane found it and was surprised to see that all 170 things now appeared because we had built a ranch. The kids had wanted horses, cows, chickens, and other things we couldn't have in the city, but with our ranch, we had completed the list without ever referring to it. We had programmed our minds with such clarity that we didn't need to constantly focus on our dream list. By visualizing and assimilating those things we wanted in our minds, we eventually made it happen in a very natural way.

I'm convinced we can be and do and have what we really want in life. It's just a matter of deciding what we really want. In fact, I think that it's easier for us to obtain what we really want than to settle for compromise. That is because we won't go after what we casually want with nearly as much energy, drive, and excitement as we will muster to pursue something that we really want.

Start with the end result. To be a high-performance person, you must first decide what end results you want. Exactly what do you want for yourself? What career? What income? What community? What home? What spiritual life? What relationships? You must create a vivid mental picture of the end results you want. Once you imprint that vision in your mind, you will become very creative to find information that you can use to help achieve it.

Your vision must be more than just a vague desire, such as, "I want to do good for mankind." There are thousands of ways to do good. You must focus vividly on something specific. Ordinary people just wish for things. They never focus their desires into specific visions and missions. I encourage you to discard wishes; they're destructive. Nobody's rushing to grant your wishes. You need to make things happen for yourself.

The end result needs to be developed in your mind so what you say is, "I've got an idea." That's all. "I've got an idea." "I've got an idea of how I want my family to be. I've got an idea of what I want my income to be. I've got an idea of the home I want. I've got an idea of the cake I want to bake. I've got an idea of what I want the party to look like. I've got an idea."

You've got to have an idea or ideal, vision or mission. It's just a matter of making constructive use of your imagination. It's all in your mind, in your imagination. You construct a future in your mind before it ever occurs. For example, you have an idea of a future dinner, movie, or party. Or, you imagine the product you're going to make, the organization you're going to build, the trip you're going to take. It's as simple as that.

Open up your secret garden. I'm now giving you permission to dream and to open up this secret life inside your head. I'm telling you: "What you imagine is something you could make happen in the real world." You don't have to *get real* any more. You don't have to be bound by practicalities; you can have these dreams.

You may feel both excited and filled with anxiety at this prospect. I know because I've felt that way many times. Many of the challenges that I face produce feelings of anxiety, but it says to me, "Well, that's okay, that's normal."

You should be feeling that way. That's a positive sign. You don't have to listen to those voices that say, "Don't try; go back."

Remember: Who you are and where you're going in life are dynamic, not static. Right now you may know more of what you don't want; for example, you may know that you don't want to be poor, sick, or stupid. But ask yourself another question: "What do I want? If I don't like who I am, what I do, or what I have, how do I want it?" That's a positive way to focus your goals for the future.

When people say to me, "yes, but," I'm reminded of a guy named Johnny Harris. Johnny was four years on death row. At one time, he was only nine days away from hanging. While in prison, he hated other people so much that he put nine people at the same time in the infirmary with broken jaws. However, his life sentence was cut because of a self-defense judgment, and he was released on a technicality.

Two years later, after going through our program, he won the "God Speaking Through Man" Award of the National Unity Church of Truth, with Dr. Carl Menninger of the Menninger Foundation as a co-recipient for humanitarian acts.

So don't tell me you've got a tough case. You are so capable with not nearly as many blocks to your success as people like Johnny Harris.

The only thing that's going to stop you is your lack of vision, lack of mission, old patterns, old habits, old excuses and beliefs that are inappropriate.

Look, if a high school teacher with a bunch of kids to feed can quit his job and, by vow of being authentic and progressive and effective and being mission driven, growth driven, and goal directed, do what Diane and I have done, what's your excuse? I'm nothing exceptional. I see myself as ordinary, just an ordinary person doing extraordinary things.

Think in Terms of Ideals

Each one of us must think and work in ideals. What's an ideal? It's an image, picture, or vision that exists presently only in your mind. An ideal is very simple, not complex. You look at current reality, the way things actually are at the present moment—the way you live now, the way you dress, your work, your health, your community, and the state the world. You look at current reality, and you say to yourself, "What would be the ideal for me? What would be the ideal way to treat my spouse and children? What would be the ideal work for me? What would be the ideal month, week, day?"

Let yourself be free of *reality* for a moment. Let yourself picture this ideal without worrying whether you know how to get there or how to do it or even know what it entails. Just draw a beautiful, simple picture of how it might be, and then keep that picture in mind.

I know that's difficult in day-to-day life, hanging on to your ideal and not getting pulled back into the reality of the moment. But don't get trapped by how much money you have or how effective or ineffective you are, or how powerful or powerless you are at the moment. In one sense, it doesn't make any difference. You must think in ideals first.

Thinking in terms of ideals may be new for many of you, because you're trapped in your present reality and can't get out. You're trapped in a mental prison of your own making. And when you're immersed in a present reality, you tend to think you *know the truth* about it. But someone coming in from the outside can better think in ideals because they're not caught up in the realities of your life.

In my current roles as a consultant, coach, mentor, speaker, husband, father, grandfather, and business owner, I'm often coming into other people's lives and organizations from the outside. I'm not experiencing all of what they are experiencing, and so it's relatively easy for me to think in ideals, to inspire them to think in ideals, and to provide them with a process to reach the ideal.

I advise them: "Think in ideals, even when all about you is insanity and denial."

Some people reply, "You don't know me. You come here talking fantasy, with no foundation in reality. Why think in ideals? Nothing in my life is ideal. Why set myself up for disappointment?" I respond: "I'm just asking you to have an idea of what could be. I'm inviting you to work in ideals and to be courageous and confident enough to believe you can pull it off. Establish what you want at the moment. I don't care what you want. Figure out what you want. Your wants will change down the road. But if you can focus on what you want now, and know why you want it, you will likely achieve it."

I then invite them to affirm: "I know what I want. I know why I want it. I listen to people who have helpful information, and apply it to something that's real to me."

You want to reach for something. You want to grow as a person, as a family, as a company. You want to become more. More of what? That's what I keep asking myself: "What do I want to become? What do I want to do?" Often it's no big deal—something simple for my family or for my business associates or for myself.

My ideals have taken me around the world. In Spain, I visited the home of Miguel Cervantes who wrote *Don Quixote de la Mancha*. One theme of that book is the conflict between the real and the ideal. Our dreams, ideals, and quests give us a sense of what we might become. But after Quixote embarked on his quest, some thought him to be a maniac. Likewise, we might appear to others to be crazy—and that perception becomes reality, to them.

To make the ideal real, you've got to pick out something in your mind that you want to reach for—your impossible dream. What do you want for yourself and others? What do you want for your community, your family, your friends?

Many of us are taught to have a *realistic* point of view. Our friends might tell us, "Forget your ideal. Not everyone will like you. You'll have your critics and enemies. You'll never achieve what you imagine." And if you are weak, you might accept their negative affirmations as reality.

I have a more positive philosophy in my life. My own self-talk is the most powerful affirmation. My intent is to positively talk to myself and influence the talk around me. I find that to be very hard. It's hard to keep from being pulled down with all the negative talk around me and to help people become more positive without being perceived as someone who doesn't understand what reality is. Because that's what I get when I try to turn things around to a positive way. People say, "He's living in a dream world" or "He doesn't understand what it's really like." That's not true. I do understand, but to them I sound like a dreamer, an idealist, a Quixote.

Your quest will take some form of commitment on your part. Others will challenge you when you share your ideals. They might say, "Since so many people and things in this life are unfair and unjust, why try? Why believe? Why hope and dream?"

I can't talk to you in terms of my ideals. You must identify your ideals, starting from where you are. And as you grow, your *there* will keep getting bigger and better and greater. That's the natural process— the journey of getting *there* from *here*.

Three years from now, at another starting point, you might say, "I want to get there." You have to determine the new *there* and use the same process. The *there* may be the new marriage, a new family, expanded business, a new home, increased income, or improved health and fitness.

This book is simply a guide to get you from *here* to *there*. I hope to inspire you to have a bigger *there*. The *there* that you think of today will be small compared to the *there* that you'll think of 10 years from now, if you apply what you learn daily to develop yourself. By applying the principles and action process in this book, you'll get *there*, and beyond.

MOTIVES AND MOTIVATIONS

YOU will need a lot of drive and energy to get from *here* to *there*. Most of that must come from within—from *intrinsic* motivation that comes from well-defined values and motives.

We need to understand why we act the way we do; otherwise, we won't know why we keep getting in our own way, or how to get out of our way when it counts.

Some time ago, during the apartheid era in South Africa, I was troubled by the violence and conflict in that country and wanted to make a difference in the thinking of a critical mass of people, including many leaders, both black and white.

I knew that I wasn't going to do much good in South Africa by sitting in Seattle. I had to take some action. But that action—in addition to being difficult and expensive—would largely be unwanted, unappreciated, and misunderstood. I knew that others would challenge the vision and question my motives.

The odds were stacked against me, even inside my own company. I had a few courageous people around me, willing to help make that vision happen, but many others in my own company told me: "Don't go; it will cost us millions of dollars."

As you may recall, at the time, several states would not do business with you if you did business with South Africa. So some people in my company told me, "You'll cost us our careers; you'll cost us our money; you'll cost us our future."

I said, "Then you'd better get another job, because I'm going. It's the right thing to do."

Sure, it cost us a few dollars. We lost some contracts because of it, but we weren't going there to make money. We were going there to improve the environment, to give people hope, and to provide them with life-changing tools. I trusted that if we went in with the right motives, we would eventually gain, even if we incurred significant near-term losses.

Make Sure Your Motives Are Right

Why do you want to be, do, or have what you want? Why do you want to get *there*? How unselfish are your motives?

I want you to get to the point in maturity where you do this unselfishly, where you give with no ulterior motive at all, where you are primarily interested in helping people around you because that's the greatest sense of reward that you can find.

You make it happen simply because it's the right thing to do, not to impress anyone, not because you want something from it. Your intent is unselfish. You're motivated by love and justice.

You can get yourself to that point. Sometimes I'm there, and other times I'm not. It isn't like once you're there, you're there forever. But when you get to that point, you'll find a great sense of fulfillment and purpose in your life. Coming up with your own "*why*" will give you courage to act. Perhaps it isn't an act of courage—it's just the right thing to do.

Acts of courage can come at all ages and stages of life; often little kids can show acts of moral courage because their motives are relatively pure and they have such great faith in the unseen.

Making sure your reasons or motives are right will help you develop your courage and give you the power of purpose to get from where you are, *here*, to *there*. But you've got to determine the *why*.

I want you to act with the right heart and the right spirit of intent. You'll want to, too, when you find out why. You'll want to because it will give you more strength, more depth, more satisfaction. It does you no good to gain wealth or to accumulate power if inside you know you're covering up a lie, if inside you're not proud of yourself.

I want you to be proud of yourself. I want you to feel that you are a great person and that you live a great life. I want you to feel happy with yourself. My purpose is to get you to achieve what you want to achieve, and to be proud of yourself in doing it. And I don't want anything for it. I don't want the acclaim or the applause. The only reason I would use the acclaim or applause or allow myself to be admired, is so I could take on another project or problem in the community. Otherwise, I don't want it.

Recently I returned home from a trip to Australia. I was bone-tired, but I was scheduled to fly out that same evening to London.

Now, if I looked at flying to London at midnight, losing a night's sleep, teaching, and getting on an airplane and flying home as, "I have to go to London," would I do a good job?

No, and so I think, "I don't have to go; I choose to go. I see the benefits of going." I must talk tough to myself, or I start whimpering and crying and feeling like a victim: "Ain't it awful."

I tell myself, "Well, then, don't go."

"But, I want to go. I can benefit people and create business."

"Okay, then, shut up and go. You want to, choose to."

That is how I try to talk to myself. But then one of my associates asked me that day, "Lou, why are you flying to London when you just returned from Australia? Is it the money?"

"No," I said, "I choose to work not for money, but for a mission—for what we can do to improve the quality of life for people and organizations."

"Don't give me that crap," said my friend. "We all work for money."

"Yes, we must all make some money to meet our needs and to satisfy some wants, but making money isn't all that I want."

"But why work so hard when you don't have to?"

"I want to," I said. "I choose to work with people where they are and help them get where they want to go. That's my mission."

I explained that that's why I work with militant atheists, hardened agnostics, disillusioned leaders, and convicted criminals. When I first talk to people who have spent 20 years inside a prison, I don't talk to them about ideals. I ask them, "How would you like to get out and stay out? How would you like to live without somebody chasing you? How would you like to fall in love?"

I try to get them to fall deeply in love with somebody or some cause—and then they have a reason to stay out. And once they have a reason to stay out, their choices are different. Then they say, "Well, what else could I do?" And I say, "Why don't you try this, why don't you try that." Before long these people are doing spectacular things and turning their lives around.

Identify Your Value System

Your value system gives you a reason *why* you work, *why* you are married, *why* you have children, *why* you sacrifice for them. Knowing your values gives you a framework for making choices and setting goals. You know that it isn't enough to just exist. You want a certain quality of life, not only for yourself but also for the people you care about. You want to create happiness-producing environments and events.

To identify your ideals or values, try the following.

1. Imagine taking your heart out of your body and into your hands. You can suspend your life with your heart in your hands for two minutes. Now, with your heart in your hands, ask yourself, "What do I want most in my life?" Your response might be, "I want to have my heart back. I want to live." So, put it back in. And then ask, "Now, what quality and quantity of life do I want?" You have the choice, the freedom, to choose to some degree the quality, and in some cases, the quantity of your life.

2. Imagine (or experience) some life-threatening event. Such events cause you to reassess your values. When your life is on the line, you tend to assess: "What is most important to me?" Life, yes. But what quality of life do I want?" If you're in ill physical or mental health, you don't have much of a choice. So if you value being well, you will adopt a wellness lifestyle. You will value mental, emotional, social, and spiritual health as much as physical health. You will create an internal and external mental climate that you want to live in. So, that would be the social life you want, the family life you want, the community life you want.

3. Experience some pain. Pain is the real reason why most people and organizations seek change. If you're living a life of pain, misery, stress, or illness, ask yourself, "What is the root cause of this pain? What can I do to relieve the pain?" You may realize that you value safety, free from the fear of being harmed or injured. Pain tends to focus us on our core values, like freedom and liberty and justice—those things that make up quality of life for you, for your children and grandchildren, and for the people around you.

4. Ask what makes you really happy. One characteristic of a mature human being is finding happiness in giving without selfish motivation. Until you reach that point, you're going to be scrambling, especially the older you get. Ask, "What do I need to be happy?" If you stop to think about it, you might realize that you don't need many material things—clothes, cars, houses. Those likely won't be on the top of your priority list. What do you think you need to be happy? Design the quality and quantity of creature comforts you want, the environment that you want, the relationships you want.

Learn to be happy along the way. If you're happy only when you get what you want, then you can only be happy when you achieve your desired end results. You hate the rest of the process. You don't want to start things because you don't want the hassle.

If you learn to enjoy the process—the building of the team, the family, or the company—you will want to start more things. If you love the process as much as you love the end result, you start and finish many more important things; and, you're a happier, more fulfilled human being along the way.

As a young high school teacher and coach, I got caught in the trap of hating football practice and the slow learning process. About the only time I was happy was when we'd win a game. I was like an empty bottle walking around with a funnel sticking out of its mouth. I was just hoping people would fill me up. I could be happy when somebody gave me a present, applauded me, recognized me, or thought I was a wonderful person. Unless I got my fill first, I couldn't be a very giving person. Once I got my fill, I could splash out a few drops on other people.

But over time, I started to realize that if the only way to be happy was to have somebody recognize, applaud, or praise me, then I couldn't be happy very often.

Suppose you could be happy by giving somebody a gift that you knew they really wanted. Suppose you had a special gift that you knew a child, spouse, or friend would love to receive, and you just gave them this gift. Imagine that you are as happy for giving as they are for receiving the gift.

Once you know that your happiness can be the same whether you give or receive, you can become a happy person by being a more giving person who looks for ways and things to give to people in need. You don't need to give just money. You can give of your time, help, skill, knowledge, ability, talent, and encouragement. A mother gives a wonderful gift when she gives her patience and her love to her children; in fact, that gift may surpass anything she might give to a community, school, business, or political organization.

When I was a high school teacher, I met a student named Bruce who had a cleft palate and was partially spastic. Many people at school avoided being around him. All I did was greet him every day as he would pass by me, ask him how he was doing, and occasionally talk to him. This went on for a couple of years. The day before he graduated, Bruce gave me a card with a note in it. He said, "Thank you, Mr. Tice, for saying hello to me every day at school."

That card meant so very much to me. Because at that time, I still thought that the *big time* in life meant winning the state championship. My concerns were— "How can I get my picture in the paper? What can I do to impress you? How can I make it big in this world?" But *bigness* was right in front of me. All I needed to do was to be a giving person. I didn't need to give money. I just needed to give a bit of my time, my compassion, myself, to Bruce.

5. Ask the tough questions. Take a hard look at what you value most. You need to ask yourself, "What do I value most in this life?" "What would I fight for?" "What would I die for?" Is it freedom, liberty, justice? Loved ones? Creature comforts? Mental and physical health? Sort out your values. When you get down the six or seven things that are most important to you in this life, you know what to hang your goals on.

For example, because I believe in eternal life, my spiritual life is more important than my physical life. My family comes second. Then I think my life's work is third. My health may be fourth. My community environment may come in fifth.

It's not an easy task to sort out your priorities. It takes some time. If things are tough at work, it's hard not to have it tough at home, too, because they're interrelated. If your work goes down, it may affect the economy of your family and lifestyle.

All Things are Not to be Valued Equally

If you don't know what you value most, you tend to value everything about the same—and that means you have a disaster every hour. How do people who value everything equally act when their car gets dented? They just fall apart! How do they act when they break a shoelace? They go into a fit! How do they act when their house is a mess? They think the world is coming to an end. How do they act when their business doesn't go right? They go crazy. Why? Because they're caught up in a system of values where everything is equal.

Years ago, I knew a man who was an athletic director of a university in the Midwest. He was ready to commit suicide because somebody dumped the 16-pound shot in the school swimming pool. That was it! That was suicidal for him. Stupid, you say, but not to him. See, everything was on equal plane and of equal value.

I told him, "You couldn't be more upset if somebody had just raped your daughter."

If everything is of equal value, then every disaster is of equal consequence and equal pressure. You may be with somebody who says, "How did your day go?" "Terrible!" "How come?" "Oh, it's raining outside." "Well, who cares?"

You need to sort out your values, so you can concentrate your time and energy on worthwhile goals. Every person should ask, "What is number one, number two, number three, number four, in order of preference?" If you truly value your children or spouse or the people around you most, your house could burn down and you wouldn't blow up, as long as nobody was hurt.

One time Diane and I returned from a trip to Australia, and we went out to dinner that evening with one of our daughters. We were sitting around the table talking when our daughter Bonnie said, "I need to give you some bad news. While you were gone, your horse, *Just a Pebble*, broke its leg in a race and had to be destroyed on the track."

Even though the horse represented a loss of many thousands of dollars, my first question to her was, "Was Jens hurt?" He was the jockey riding the horse.

Sure, the money was important, the horse was important, but far more important to me was the person riding the horse. And I didn't have to think about what mattered most to me at the table. Human life is much more important than the horse, or the money. But if I didn't understand that, I could have been very distraught at the restaurant.

It really helps me to have clear in my own mind what is important to me on a hierarchy of values. That way, I'm not thrown off by the little things.

I have learned, however, that the little things to me might be very big things to others—and that I need to respect their values.

Once Diane and I were racing two of our thoroughbred horses at Golden Gate, just outside of San Francisco, California. Again, one of our horses broke a leg and needed to be put down. This was a favorite horse of mine—one we had raised from a colt.

Our trainer, a young man who traveled with us and took our horses all over the nation at the time, was with us. And when they gave the horse a lethal injection, he started to cry.

That night we were having dinner, the three of us, and we started talking about the horse. And he started to cry again. And I said to him, "Wait a minute. How can you cry over a horse? You're eating a cow, you know."

I gave him lesson #77 in ethics and values and told him what was most important in the hierarchy of values, but it didn't seem to do any good. He was more disconsolate than ever.

Later that evening, Diane and I were talking, and she said, "You know, you've become very insensitive. I think that you're losing your sense of values."

Her statement hit me hard. And she said, "You didn't show much empathy for him. His whole life is tied up in racing. It isn't just losing the horse that hurt him, but your treatment of him. You lost your compassion, your sensitivity for the person and what his life is all about. You're starting to treat him not as a person, but like a possession. It's as if he's inhuman to you, as if he's just a thing to work with your horses to cause them to win. He has a right to be upset; this is his life."

All of a sudden I came to the realization, "Yes, I had started using people around me as if they were merely means to an end of what I wanted to possess." I don't cry very often but I started to cry right then. And I said to Diane, "I don't want to be that way. That isn't really me. I don't even know how I got that way."

I learned an important lesson: If you don't carefully sort out your values, and find out what is important, then gradually, without even knowing it, you lose what is really important. You lose touch with your core values, the things that are essential to you. I wouldn't treat people that way intentionally. But I sure did by accident or by neglect.

The Good Life

If you have everything on a level plane, you are very distraught when you lose your job, lose a client, lose a sale. Such things devastate the dickens out of you. Why? Because your uppermost values are not uppermost in your life.

When your uppermost values are consistent with permanent principles, natural laws, perhaps even eternal values, then all around you can change—you can even lose most of what you have— and you'll remain strong and centered. Now, the losses might bother you for a time, but they won't beat you.

Each one of us who chooses to be centered and strong needs to identify our own hierarchy of values. Sort out for yourself what the essentials are, why you are on earth, what is important to you, and what your life is worth. I encourage you to use affirmations and set goals to bring more of those things that are important to you abundantly into your life. If you don't have a hierarchy of values, if you don't have priorities already in your mind, you don't know how to make your choices or how to control reactions. You don't know what to get upset about. You don't know what a big deal is.

I admit that I have been like that. But now, I can sleep right through things that once upset me to no end. What changed? I know what I value and I have prioritized my goals.

Some values are more important than other values. Some things are more important than other things for you to do. When you know what those things are—why you exist, what's important to you—you'll have the courage to stop doing things of little importance at the expense of your family and your business associates.

One reason why you may have trouble sorting out your personal values is because our societal values are so distorted. For example, look at the money we pay to professional athletes and entertainers. It's out of proportion to their contribution.

People ask me, "But Lou, aren't you excited to work with professional coaches and athletes?" Are you kidding? Some of them make me sick. Why get so excited about sports when there are so many other important things in life?

I know where I want to spend my time. I know where I want to put my money. I know where I want to put my life's energy. I don't know if you do, but until you get it sorted out, you could be wasting your time and talents. You could be going after things—more and more things. How much is enough? What are you really after?

When you reach the point that you spend your life's energy doing your life's work, you can live without feeling that *quiet desperation* that Henry David Thoreau talks about. You won't even care if you die, because what you're doing is great. You're not thinking "I've got to live. I've got to do this and that." You're not pressured. If you go, you go.

Are you living the life you want to live, consistent with your deepest values? If so, you're living *the good life,* and you're highly motivated from within.

For Show or for Real?

When we do things, we can do them for show or for real. Some people go to church for show; others go to church to worship. Some people give to charity for show because it's good for business; others give for a generous or selfless reason, because it's the right thing to do.

If you go and give for show, it doesn't do you any good. It doesn't do me any good to impress you if I'm not impressed with me. I might fool you. You might think I'm a good person, but how can I live with me if I know I'm a jerk?

If I do things for my community to make people think I'm wonderful, but inside I know my motive is to gain popularity or power, or to be seen and thought of as generous, my giving is hollow. You need to do the right thing for the right reason because you have to live with you. What good does it do to impress a million people if you aren't impressed with you?

Your spirit of intent needs to be aligned with real love, real justice, real purpose, real truth. If you choose to be selfish, manipulative, dishonest, and deceptive, you've got to mask your spirit of intent. You might fool me at first, assuming you practice the public relations game of how to win friends and how to present a good face, but inside you know you're duplicitous. And over time you find it very difficult to mask your intent.

When your spirit is genuine and when you are interested in helping others, you can have weaknesses and people will still support you. If you're genuine, authentic and a good person, people will follow you anywhere.

Real leaders are guided more by internal than external regulation.

By contrast, many people I work with in prisons have no internal idea of right or wrong. They've been raised in environments where right and wrong are very confusing to them. What's wrong is getting caught. It isn't wrong to steal. So, in that situation, we need police forces and armies and sheriffs' departments and judicial systems to take care of people who don't even have the sense of right or wrong or ethics. Of course, there are many others who know the difference between right and wrong, but they choose the wrong, because it's the expedient thing or the shortcut to what they want.

False leaders may dress well and come off with a great presentation, but they are basically con artists. People look at them and say, "There's a fine-looking person" or "Gee whiz, wasn't that wonderful what that person did?" But it's very possible he didn't play by the rules, but instead used inside information to gain an advantage.

Goals achieved when you don't play by the rules are very hollow.

When you have a code by which you live, your own principles and your values that are based upon justice, fairness, and so on, you don't need a proctor for taking a test to ensure that you don't cheat. You don't cheat because it's wrong, not because you're afraid of getting caught, arrested, embarrassed, or punished. You don't steal because you don't steal. It's not the right thing to do.

Brokerage firms are getting a lot of national attention because many people are becoming very wealthy due to insider trading. But the governing principle in ethics is this: *An evil means never justifies a good end, no matter how good the end might be.*

In your dealings with people, do you ever have an ulterior motive or a hidden meaning? One of our adopted kids, Joe, would talk a mile a minute in the car. He'd drive us nuts. And about 20 minutes into a monologue, he'd mention that he stole this or broke that and forgot to tell us. We always needed to listen to his intent, not just his words.

It's not easy to work around people who hide their spirit of intent because you're always trying to find the underlying cause, the underlying reason or motive.

It's important to align your intent with truth and justice and love. Then you won't send mixed messages to your customers and your spouse, to your friends and your business associates. You may wonder why sometimes you're not getting your point across. You may wonder why sometimes people aren't buying what you're selling or why you're not getting the reaction that you want. And it could be that you're sending them a mixed message because your intent is manipulative or selfish—and maybe they are getting the message. You want them to get a different message, but they are reading your real intent. You think you mask it well because you are good with charm and words. But many people read your intent—they *get the vibes* or they *don't feel right* about the deal or the relationship. They sense that "something's wrong here." And they opt not to do business with you or to be around you.

I know that great things occur, miraculous things occur, way beyond what seems logical when we align our spirit, our true intent, with real love and real justice and honesty, and work for the good of other people.

Wake Up and Fly Right

Once I employed a pilot to fly our aircraft. He was a very nice person, but we had some differences of opinion. Once I needed to be flown someplace, and he said, "No, I'm taking the day off to do something with my family." I said, "Well, your family's important, but so is your job and income. Flying me where I need to go is the way you make your living to support your family."

Rather than argue with him, I let him go. Now, this man and his family lived in the same small community where we have our ranch. Their family lived close to us, and they were good friends. But his wife was furious with me when she learned that I made him make a decision to fly or find another job. And so, there wasn't much good said about me for a while.

Some time later, Diane and I were at the ranch, and we saw my former pilot's wife driving up in her car. She had a couple of her children with her in the car. I didn't want to spend any time talking to her about this situation, so I chose to creatively avoid it. I said, "Diane, you go ahead and say hello and see what she wants. I've got a phone call I need to make."

I went into my office and pretended to make a phone call. But my intent was to avoid being around her. She was a bother to me right now because she was upset with me. And with her was a five-year-old Filipino boy she was trying to adopt, even though he had some serious behavior problems.

In fact, the boy came right into my office and started pulling on my leg, grabbing my pants and trying to drag me out to see his mother. I couldn't kick the kid away, so I decided to go out and get it over with. That was my attitude, my spirit of intent. "Just be pleasant, and soon it'll be over with."

I entered the room with a false smile on my face. To my surprise, she didn't bring up the incident with her husband, but instead she said they were heading to Seattle to finalize the adoption of this boy. And I said, "Oh, that's wonderful."

While she and Diane talked, I started thinking about the adoption of our own children. My heart softened, and I said, "The adoption ceremony is very significant. I hope that it will be a wonderful occasion. To help celebrate it, we would love to have you bring your family over for a luncheon or something to make it a very special day for your boy and your family."

She said, "Well, our other three children aren't coming. They're going to stay in school; they didn't want to come."

Knowing how hard this boy was to live with and thinking how her natural children might feel about this adoption, I said, "Well, you go and tell your kids that the judge said the adoption won't be official unless they're there."

I don't know why I took charge. I suppose that I had changed my spirit to one of love, treating her with dignity and respect and justice. And then I said, "If you want, we could have a limousine pick them up, and you can fly over to Seattle in our airplane. I know a Filipino priest who would be happy to make this the most special day ever for this boy. He'll never forget it, and he'll know he belongs to your family."

Now, she broke down and started to cry. She said through her tears, "When I came here today, I was very bitter toward you. But I know you're right about this adoption ceremony. You know, as a teenager, I was very bitter toward my own father. I rebelled and became a hippie. And I didn't care about ceremonies. I didn't care about Christmas. I didn't care about birthdays. But I know what you mean now."

She said, "When we got him, I went out in the yard and planted a tree in his honor. It was a simple ceremony, but so important."

I said, "Yes, and you have to make this adoption so important that he knows he's part of your family, and, more importantly, so that your other children know that he's part of the family."

Well, we did have a wonderful day with all the important things involved. But if I had stayed on the phone with my selfish intent that event would have never occurred, at least not in that way.

When you work in harmony with justice and love, the spirit of good intent can work through you. But it's hard to work through you when your intent is selfish, bitter, resentful. If you align your spirit with the way things are supposed to be, then you aren't the one who does those things—you simply become an instrument.

In retrospect, I can see that the special adoption day was meant to be for this Filipino boy, and that I was supposed to have made it happen. But I almost missed the chance.

And so, in our dealings with people, at work and at home, we need to continually check our spirit of intent.

One time I asked one of my sons-in-law, "Who do you look to for a model or mentor?"

He named a person I knew, and I said, "Why him?"

"Oh," he said, "the guy is wonderful. He's so entertaining."

I said, "But this person is a showman. His life is shallow. He's working just to make a living, and he's entertaining because he wants people to applaud him."

I further said, "You don't need to sacrifice that joy in living, but you need to examine your motive. What if your purpose for working was to give so much of what you have to cause the life of other people to improve greatly? Suppose that was 75 percent of your intent, and 15 percent was to make a good living, and 10 percent was to feel good yourself."

I can guarantee you this: If you focus with 75 percent of your intent on doing good for others, you will make more money and you will feel better about yourself. If you focus on making money and feeling good first, you won't do much good for other people.

Why are you doing what you do? What is your real intent in dealing with the people in your life? If your intent is selfish, self-serving, dishonest, or shallow, it's up to you to change your intent using your own self-talk, and then go into the relationship or whatever you're doing with a new sense of purpose.

I guarantee that you will get back an absolutely surprising result: 2 + 2 no longer becomes 4; it becomes 16. With synergy, you can make a quantum leap forward, way beyond just the normal human relationship.

If you can get your spirit of intent to be one of generosity or giving or caring for another, you won't need to continually push away the rewards that come to you. If you're a giving human being, at the end of your life, you can say, "What a quality life!" In fact you'll hear people say, "There's a quality person. This is a quality company."

What does quality mean? What is the source? I submit that it's this selfless spirit of intent. In athletics, for example, one selfish, immature player can diminish the other talent on the team and destroy the team spirit.

So if you care about quality of product, quality of service, and quality of life, then take a good look at your spirit of intent and try to focus on being and doing for the right reasons.

It sounds so easy, but it can be so difficult. Once I was at Seattle University looking some things up at the library. I was preparing for a seminar I was scheduled to give in two hours across Puget Sound. To get there on time, I had to catch a ferry that was scheduled to leave in 20 minutes across town. If I missed it, I would need to drive four hours to get there.

So, I hopped into my sports car and sped away, only to find the traffic backed up. Now I was in a panic as I only had a few minutes to catch the ferry. I pulled over to look ahead and see what was blocking traffic.

I saw that an old Chinese gentleman was trying to cross the busy street. He'd start out, get frightened, turn back, chicken out, come back, start again, turn around, chicken out, come back. Goodness gracious.

So I pulled the hand brake on my car, got out, and approached this guy. I said, "Let me help you across the street." And I took him by the hand and walked with him across the street. He then said to me, "Thank you so much for helping me. I'll remember your kindness forever."

He made me feel like such a bum because I wasn't helping him across the street to be kind. I just wanted to catch the ferry. But he, and perhaps others who observed my action, not knowing my intent, came to the wrong conclusion: "Isn't he a wonderful person for helping the old man across the street?"

By the way, I did just catch the ferry. But I would have felt better about myself if, in getting from *here* to *there*, I had done the good deed for the right reason.

chapter 3

THE *WANT TO* VS.
HAVE TO ATTITUDE

BEYOND motive, we need to make sure our attitude is right. If your attitude is a *have to*, you resist. You can't drive yourself toward it. Motive and motivation are connected. So, you've got to shift from a negative *have to* to a constructive *want to* to release your creativity and passion.

When I was a high school football coach, before I switched my mind set, I would bitch and complain along with the other coaches, "We have to rely on these damn kids." Nothing creates more pressure than living in a *have to* environment. "It's out of our control. Why did we do this to ourselves?" And in a game, I would look across the field and see that the other coach was just as sick.

I remember the moment when I changed my attitude—and it changed my life forever. I was driving to the stadium, and I stopped at a light, right next to a tavern. I can still see it in my mind, and this has been almost 30 years. I said to myself, "You don't have to go to the game. Why don't you just stop the car, get out, and go get drunk in the tavern? Don't go. You don't have to go."

But then I said to myself, "What do you mean *you don't have to go?* What do you mean *don't go?* From the time you were nine years old you wanted to be a coach. You don't *have* to go, you *want* to go. And if somebody tried to take it away from you, you'd fight to keep it. So, shut your mouth and go. You choose to go. You want to go." Honestly, I've never been under such pressure since that day.

You create your own pressure by putting your task, your goals, your family, your life on a *have to* basis. Once you release the pressure, you become very effective. You allow yourself to flow. Otherwise, you engage in negative creativity to avoid the *have to* situation.

We develop attitudes about every aspect of our existence—our clothes, our cars, our politics, our friends, our careers, our ethics—all the norms of our daily life. We've had some attitudes so long that they become part of our automatic pilot system. If we want to change direction, we'll want to change some attitudes.

An attitude is an emotional predisposition to a situation or stimulus. Aeronautically, the *attitude* of an airplane is judged by the angle of the wings in relation to a fixed point on the horizon—in other words, the direction in which the plane is leaning. An attitude is the direction in which you lean. If you lean toward something, you have a positive attitude toward it. If you lean away, you have a negative attitude.

Even if you can see (visualize) the outcome or have good intentions (right motive), you can't just use the "just do it" approach. It doesn't work—unless you *want to* do it.

Constructive or Restrictive Motivation

Motivation is the incentive or drive that fuels and propels us forward. We can be motivated externally by the words or actions of others, or we can motivate ourselves internally by using our own smart talk. Depending on our self-talk, we are either constructively or restrictively motivated. Constructive motivation is on an "I *want to*, I *choose to*, I *like to*" basis. Restrictive motivation is on an "I *have to* or else" basis.

Examine your own internal motivation by asking yourself: "Am I my own person?" "Am I living the way I live because I choose to, or because I'm afraid to live any other way?" "Do I move optionally, creatively, freely flowing through life, or do I feel restricted, afraid, uptight?" "Do I assume personal accountability for my own actions, or do I think someone else is responsible?"

One way to answer these questions is to notice how you feel when you set out to achieve your goals. Constructive motivation causes you to feel energetic and creative about solving the problem. Under the restrictive form of motivation, you don't do things for the pleasure of enjoying the end result; you do them because you're afraid of the consequences. The differences between constructive and restrictive motivation can mean the difference between joyful achievement and unhappy failure.

Constructive motivation means visualizing what you *want* in life. You talk to yourself about why you'd *like* the new job, why you *want* the new salary, why you'd *enjoy* the new skill, the new adventure. You're more likely to act on a *want-to, choose-to, like-to* basis. You'll do things because you see their *benefits*. Constructively motivated people constantly imprint positive imagery into their subconscious—*solutions* to problems, *resolutions* to conflicts, *satisfying end results*. When you're constructively motivated, you look forward to the end results with feelings of pleasure, joy, fulfillment: "If I run for the position and win, how much good can I do for my community?" Constructive motivation creates a positive expectancy of joy and success.

If you want to see constructive motivation at work, try chaperoning an overnight co-ed teenage party sometime. About 2 a.m., try keeping the sexes apart. They've been visualizing the pleasure and profitability of being together for weeks, so they start sneaking through the windows, the vents, even cracks in the walls, just to be with each other. They walk through doors without *opening* them. Why? Because we get very inventive and creative when we *want to* do something. We feel as though nothing can stop us. When our willpower and our subconscious creativity *team up*, we are absolutely unbeatable.

Wouldn't it be ridiculous to tell your 16-year-old: "All right, I'll be gone for a week. Here are the keys to the car, and here are all my gas station credit cards. When I get back, I want to see 1,000 miles on that car. I'm not taking *no* for an answer." To prevent kids from driving that car, we would not only need to leave town with the keys, we would need to take the *distributor cap*, too. I'm talking from experience.

Restrictive motivation creates the opposite—fear of failure, rejection, and punishment. Instead of seeing the benefits, you see the awful consequence: "What if I ask her out, and she says no? I'll be humiliated." "What if I apply for that job, and they turn me down? I'll feel sick." "What if I don't make the sale? I'll be fired."

Even when I work with professional athletes, I don't use the competition for the purpose of motivation. Competition and comparison have a downside. We can get frozen by comparison. Steve Young, twice the MVP of the NFL, long lived in the shadow of Joe Montana; and in the eyes of the fans, he could never be as good as or as great as Joe. But in 1994, when he had another exceptional year, leading the San Francisco 49ers to the Super Bowl victory, he threw off the ghost of Joe Montana and became the team leader. He had to learn not to compare himself with Joe—but to be his best self and compete with only himself.

How you feel about a comparison depends on how you perceive the other person. If the person is close to you and doing well, you tend to want to distance yourself from that person, because it hurts every time you compare yourself and come up short. And so you say, "I don't care to compete." This is why the children of people who are very successful tend to want to move away. They feel frozen by comparison or by the fear of comparison.

Restrictive thinking is dwelling on the problem until you crash right into it. If you dwell on what you *don't* want to happen, you unconsciously help bring it about. When you picture *awful consequences*, your knees buckle, you sweat profusely, your stomach churns, you feel uptight.

Sadly, many of us were raised on restrictive motivation. Our parents, teachers, coaches, and spiritual mentors found it an effective way to get us to toe the line. So they instilled fear-based thinking in us that repeatedly set up "I can't" situations: "I can't go there." "I can't buy that." "I can't do that." As a result, we didn't allow ourselves to apply for the job, ask for the date, run for the seat on the Board. Instead of looking forward to the benefits, we feared the consequences.

Fear motivates us to do things for the wrong reasons. When we're fear-motivated, we don't embrace the adventure of life; instead, we weakly accept its burdens. Many of us absorbed a lot of fear-based motivation. We learned to be good, not so much because we *enjoyed* being good or *chose* to be good, but because we were told, "Either be good or you'll go to hell." We've trained ourselves to be good, not because it's personally beneficial, but because we're constantly trying to outrun the flames of hell.

When I went to my junior high school dances, the girls stood on one side of the gym and the boys on the other. We looked across at all these girls we wanted to dance with, but we knew if we walked over and asked, they'd probably say no. We dwelled on the fear of rejection, instead of the joy of success. And whenever we *did* go across, we stepped out of our comfort zones. We'd ask the girl to dance, and nothing would come out. "Uh, er." Sure enough, the girl would say, "No!" and we'd walk away thinking, "I *knew* she'd say no." To cover our embarrassment, we'd say to our friends, "She was ugly anyway. Who wants to dance? Let's go have some *real* fun."

That's how restrictive motivation prevents us from doing things we want to do. Some of us run our whole lives that way.

But we can know when we're being restrictively motivated with fear images if we understand the two most common forms of restrictive motivation: *coercive* and *inhibitive*.

Coercive Motivation. Coercive motivation is when you tell yourself "I have to or else." Your self-talk is, "I *have to* behave *or else* I have to pay the price." And when someone else tries to coerce you, they're saying, "Do it *or else* something awful will happen to you. And let me paint the picture of hell for you." It's like, "Shape up or ship out!"

or "It's my way or else." Those are classic coercive demands designed to restrict your behavior and keep you in line.

Examine all the *"I have to or else"* motivations in your life: "I *have to* do my work *or else* I won't get paid." "I *have to* go to the show *or else* my friend will be mad." "I *have to* clean the house *or else* the guests will think I'm a slob." "I *have to* increase my sales *or else* my boss will fire me." You know what happens when you tell yourself, *"I have to"*? The same thing as when you're physically pushed.

When someone tries to push you, you automatically resist by pushing back. It's a reflex action. Similarly, whenever you feel you *have to* do something, you feel you're being *pushed* into it, and, subconsciously, you push right back. You tell yourself, "I *have to* do this. I have no choice. But if I had my way, I wouldn't do it." Your subconscious chimes in, "Oh, but you *can* have your way. Let me show you how to get out of it or how to screw it up." And your subconscious works very hard to get you to push back through procrastination, slovenly work, and creative avoidance.

If you're a business owner or manager, are you interested in productivity? Do you use coercion to try to shove people into better performance? Do you know you're not only *not* eliciting better performance, you're setting your people up for *worse* performance? They slow down. They resist. They screw it up. If you keep pushing, they unconsciously push back. *Anyone* with high self-esteem will push back. They get infinitely creative finding ways to do *less* and to do it *poorly*. You can push them right into absenteeism, into tardiness, into illness, into carelessness, and into sabotage. You can push them so hard with *have to or else* motivation they'll slow to a standstill just to get you to shut up. It'll drive you absolutely nuts—and maybe out of business.

Parents do the same thing to their kids. I used to tell my kids, "Get out there and rake those leaves. I'm not going to tell you again. Do it, or else!" It would take them 45 minutes to get started. *Procrastination.* I'd get aggravated and yell, "What's taking so long?" They'd say, "We can't find the rake." And they weren't lying. In reaction to being pushed, they unconsciously built blind spots to the rake so they wouldn't *have to* do the work. I'd go out and immediately find the rake, and I'd say, "Now get to work. And do it right!" They'd take five swipes at the leaves and fall down, exhausted. *Slovenly work.* Then they'd check behind them to see if the *or else* factor was still there, and they'd say loud enough for me to hear, "Boy, I'm tired." Now, how can you possibly get tired searching for a rake? *Creative avoidance.* If you *have to* find it, you get creative at avoidance.

What happens when you demand that the kids wash the dishes after a big dinner? It's the last thing they want to do, but you figure, "It's my house.

As long as they're living under my roof, they'll play by my rules." That's how some parents motivate their kids to be cooperative at home. It's coercion, and it doesn't work very well. "Do the dishes, or else you're grounded for a month. And do them right!" The kids will say, "I thought you wanted me to do my homework." *Procrastination.* They didn't even *think* about homework until you said, "Wash the dishes." They'll do the dishes, but they'll take an hour to do a ten-minute job. "I was just watching the birds outside." *Creative avoidance.* And they won't do *all* the dishes, they'll leave crusty globs of food on the edges. *Slovenly work.* And they'll break two of your best china plates, and hide the frying pan you cooked the fish in by dumping it on the closet shelf above your cashmere coat—which, two days later, smells like dead trout. They're *pushing back.* Isn't that a wonderful way to work together? Everybody loses—but nobody knows why.

You get the same negative response when you push *yourself.* Some habitual smokers tell themselves, "You *have to* stop smoking!" Then they creatively, unconsciously get into a pressure situation, or cause someone to get mad at them, or disappoint someone they respect, just so they have an excuse to smoke again. When you push yourself, even if it's for your own good, your creative subconscious tries to stall, delay, and get you out of it. When you feel you *have to* grow, *have to* change, *have to* learn, *have to* make more money, your conscious willpower is at odds with your creative subconscious, and your creative subconscious will win every time.

If we feel we *have to* do something *or else,* we get very creative to get out of it. That's why you can't coerce people into doing their best at something they *don't* want to do. You can't coerce *yourself* into it, either. In areas where you can't get yourself to do things—lose weight, stop smoking, quit drinking, earn more money—I guarantee you, for the most part you're trying to coerce yourself into it. You tell yourself, "I *have to, or else.*"

Don't force yourself to change. Don't grow until you want to, because you won't do it anyway. All your goals must be on a *want to, choose to, like to* basis. It must be your idea; you must envision the value of achieving the goal, or it will be like trying to run with somebody holding onto your pockets—pushing and pulling at the same time, unconsciously sabotaging your own success.

Eliminate, as best as you can, all the *have to's* in your life. Banish "have to" from your self-talk. Don't allow yourself to think, "I *have to* get up in the morning." "I *have to* eat." "I *have to* go to work." Because it's not true. There's only one *have to* in life: You have to die. Everything else is a matter of free choice, to the degree that you want to exercise it. Sometimes the choices aren't great, but they *are* choices.

Want to Accountability

You can't build a quality life on a *have to* basis because you won't be willing to accept the consequence and be accountable. You become accountable only when you say, "I *choose* to. It's my idea. I'm good because I *choose* to be good. I work because I *choose* to work. I obey or disobey the law because I *choose* to."

One time I got stopped by Seattle's finest. I turned on a wrong street coming down First Avenue and turned left underneath the Spokane Street viaduct, and missed the light.

The sign said, "No left turn," but I turned left anyway, because I could only get on the freeway that way. A red light flashed right behind me, and I said, "Where did he come from?"

He walked up and said, "Didn't you see me?"

I thought to myself, "Are you kidding? If I had seen you I wouldn't have turned that way."

I said to him, "You know, I didn't see you. But that's all right. I turned on purpose. I mean, it was my fault. I did it on purpose. I wanted to turn this way. I didn't see it would cause any harm."

The guy just shook his head, as if to say, "This is unusual, for a guy to say he did it on purpose or admit it." And then he told me, "Just don't do it again." I think I stunned him by assuming accountability for having made the choice.

Another time, I was driving down a hill and ran a red light. It was snowing and I couldn't have stopped, so I went right through it. In the car with me were two friends, one from Canada and one from Hawaii. I said, "I can't see any cars coming, and so I'm going to run the light because I've got to get up that hill in front of us." Soon there appeared a flashing red light behind me.

"Where did he come from?" I asked aloud, as I rolled the window down. When the officer walked up, one friend in the car was saying, "Tell him you're from Hawaii, and you don't know how to drive in the snow." And my other friend said, "Tell him you are from Canada, and you didn't know the law."

But I rolled down the window and said, "I did it on purpose."

The officer just shook his head and said, "Don't do it again." He walked back to his car.

Accepting the accountability for your behavior will often pay great dividends, because people don't expect it. So, switch your life from a *have to* to a *want to*.

Once I worked with Kip Keino, a distance runner from Kenya who wanted to compete in the Montreal Olympics, and he wanted to know if he could do something psychologically to beat the excruciating pain that he always experienced during the last lap, the last quarter mile of the race.

I asked him, "What do you think about when you get to that point in the race?"

He said, "When I get to that point, I think, 'Man, I still have to run another quarter mile.' "

By thinking in terms of *have to*, he was coercing himself and thus creating more pain for himself.

So I said, "Well, I've got the solution, but you might not like it."

He said, "Tell me, please. What is it?"

"When you get to that point, when you know you *have to* run the last quarter mile, simply stop. Stop running. Stop right there and sit down on the inside curb of the track."

Kip said, "That's stupid. If I sit down, I will lose the race."

I said, "That's true, but at least your lungs will stop burning."

He said, "What do you think I run for?"

I said, "I haven't got the slightest idea. Look at me. Do you think I run? I can't stand the pain myself."

He said, "I run because if I win the Olympics in Montreal, I'll win a cow. They'll give me a cow. And in my country that will make me rich." He told me, "My family sacrificed to send me to the university in the United States. Now, I want to win the gold medal for my family and my country." Remember that his country pulled out of the Montreal Olympic games.

I said, "Why don't you just shut your mouth and run then? You don't have to run. You choose to run. You told me why you want to run. It's your idea. Really, you don't have to run. You don't have to finish the race. You could stop at any time."

He said, "I want to run and win."

I said, "Then focus on that. Put your training on a *want to, choose to, love to* basis."

I tell the same thing to college football players who get all uptight and start thinking, "I have to stop this guy from running on this side," or "I have to knock the pass down."

I say, "No, you don't. You can let them score. You don't *have to*, but you *want to* play."

One player I worked with was Johnnie Johnson, a three-time All-American out of Texas who became the highest-paid defensive back to ever be drafted into the NFL. From the time he was a sophomore in college, Johnnie always thought in terms of want to. "Throw it this way. I want you to. Give me the chance. Every time I intercept a pass, it's a $10,000 signing bonus." Instead of thinking, "If they throw it my way and I blow the coverage, we might lose the game and I'll be blamed for it," he thought, "Give it to me, give it to me, give it to me."

Most losers conduct their lives on a *have to* basis. They give up the accountability for everything they do. Whenever you tell yourself "I have to," you're not only giving up personal accountability, you're also tearing down your self-esteem. "I *have to*" means "I am not my own person. Someone else is controlling me." In *have to* situations, you're constantly telling yourself, "I'll do it. But if I had my way, I'd rather be doing something else." That means, "I'm being forced to do this against my will." It's like telling your spouse, "I *have to* stay late at work. The boss is making me finish my report." That means, "*They* are making me do it." Who are *"they"*? When you allow *"they"* to be in control, you lose self-respect. "I have no power over my own life." Instead, you must tell yourself, "I'm not going home yet. I *choose to* stay and finish my report so that, when I leave, my mind will be free."

Stop lying to yourself. You don't *have to* do anything. You don't *have to* change your kids' diapers. Leave them on; they'll eventually fall off by themselves. You don't *have to* turn on the heat in winter. You can wear heavy coats around the house, and you can buy new pipes when the old ones freeze.

You don't even *have to* pay your taxes. "Of course, I do," you say, "or they'll throw me in jail." "Possibly. Or you could go on welfare." "I don't want to go on welfare." "Then leave the country and work overseas." "I can't uproot my whole life like that."

You can do whatever you want in life—as long as you're prepared to accept the consequences. Your kids might say, "I have to study. If I don't study, the teacher will flunk me. I don't have a choice." Tell them, "Yes, you do have a choice. You can choose *not* to study. Maybe you can scrape by on what you already know or maybe you'll flunk. They're not great choices, but they *are* choices." The point is: Let's look at what's best for us and, instead of telling ourselves, " I *have to*," let's say, "I *choose to, I want to,* I *get to."* That way, *we* call the shots.

Throw away all the "have to" situations, and watch the tremendous surge of power that comes over you. You'll have greater energy, greater joy, a better marriage, a better family, a better career, a better life. You will radiate self-esteem and confidence from within, and you will attack life like the little kid looking forward to opening birthday gifts: "I can hardly wait!" Realize that you will want to be tough in this motivation business because life is tough stuff. Maybe you'd like to believe there's a magic formula to help you make choices. But visualization and affirmations aren't magic. The only magic formula is inside of you; it's called personal accountability. So take charge of your own future—not because you *have to,* but because you *want to.*

Inhibitive Motivation. The second restrictive motivation is called *inhibitive,* which means discouraging, restraining, prohibitive. Like coercive motivation, inhibitive motivation is fueled by fear. Where the trigger words for coercive motivation are "I *have to,*" the trigger words for inhibitive motivation are "I *can't.*" So the thrust of inhibitive self-talk is, "I can't misbehave or else something awful will happen."

Inhibitive motivation is restrictive because it blocks option-thinking and choice. In athletics, a coach will train the team in certain techniques, and if the players fail to execute those techniques, the coach will impose punishment—"200 push-ups and then run laps till you puke!" As a result, those players learn, "I *can't* misbehave, *or else* I'll feel terrible." The military sometimes uses restrictive training tactics: "March this way." "Carry your weapon that way." "Say 'Yes Sir,' or else you'll pay the penalty." So what do you learn? "I *can't* do things any other way *or else* I'll be punished."

For many of us, the command "*You can't*" is so powerful that sometimes we don't even question *why not?* We just experience an overwhelming flood of fear, and we obey.

First we *perceive* the situation through our senses. Then we *associate*: "Have I experienced anything like it before?" Then we *evaluate*: "What is this leading me toward?" If we're motivated by fear, the pattern of fear from our childhood, our religious training, our athletic training, our military training, is recorded as "I *can't*"—and we get that sudden flood of fear. And we conclude, "Nothing good!" Finally, we *decide*, "You *can't* change. Stay in line. Don't make waves."

If employees are motivated by fear, the manager may say one day, "Okay, now I want you to try something new." They'll say, "Sorry, we *can't!*" Do you have people like that in your family, on your team, in your company? They're scared to death to try anything new, perhaps because they were inhibited or punished physically and psychologically so often in the past that they know it hurts too much to learn something new. So they think, "I *can't* make a mistake!"

When you have people on a team or in a company, for example, who have been groomed through inhibitive fear to be afraid of making mistakes, they'll fight change in the company. They'll think, "Don't try to mess with my responsibilities. Don't try to make a change. It'll *hurt* too much."

They're responding to the fear of the new task. So things remain the same. Even if the change would be advantageous, their resistance rushes up in a flood of fear: "That's not in my job description! It's out of my area! I don't do that!" That motivation breeds inhibition to options, change, and growth. And so you get stagnation and rigidity.

You and I must recognize that it's all right to make mistakes. You don't *want* to make them, you don't *choose to* make them, you don't *like to* make them—but when you make a mistake, take responsibility for it and tell yourself, "That's not like me. I'll correct it next time."

Freely Choose to Do It

When it appears to you that you have no choice in the matter, that you're being coerced into something against your own will, either from the outside or from the inside, you think, "I have no choice in the matter. I *have to, or else* something awful will happen to me."

When you feel that you *have to*, you slow down. You engage in avoidant behavior and procrastination. You get involved in activity that has nothing to do with your objective or goal. You may still accomplish the goal, but with minimal quality or results. You do it just good enough to get by, never striving for excellence.

You won't be at your best or achieve the goals that you're capable of achieving, until you switch from a coercive to a constructive attitude and eliminate the *or-else* factors in your life. Whenever you look at your goals or aspirations on a *have-to-or-else* basis, your chance of achieving them is slight.

When you feel that you *have to*, you may think that you need more discipline to achieve the goal. You say, "I've got to get tougher with myself." But the more you force, the more you unconsciously avoid the appropriate behavior.

If you've ever worked in an environment where people *have to* go to work, you know how they are—they're exhausted, they complain, they do minimal work, and you don't want to be standing in the doorway at quitting time because you'll get run over as they leave the site.

Have you ever tried to teach or learn in a school where people feel that they have to be there? I have, and I can tell you that they are not learning organizations. As a teacher, I would tell my students: "You don't have to go to school, and you certainly don't have to learn. You have other options. But if you want to learn, I'm here to help. I'm not here to entertain you but to educate you. I'll try to make education attractive, even entertaining, but unless you want it and use it, we're both wasting our time."

If we pay a price for our education, we will value it. For example, I once brought in Dr. Bill Beaners from Princeton Theological Seminary. I paid him $5,000—and this was 25 years ago—

for the day, plus expenses—to teach me about nonverbal communication. Imagine: for one day, just Diane and I, in our house. He thought he was coming to do a big seminar. Do you know how many notes I took? Volumes. Do you think I applied what he said? Sure, I didn't want to look stupid for spending that much money.

Learning has a lot to do with accountability. When students have no accountability, they may say, "Okay, teacher, just try to teach me. Go ahead. I dare you."

High-performance people accept the consequences of their choices. They are responsible and accountable. If they choose not to learn, they choose not to grow. But at least they are willing to accept the consequences. And that's much better than saying, "I have to."

Turn the *have-to* into a *want-to*. For many years, I would complain to myself, "This is a *have to*." I'd make a *have to* out of everything. And I would just tough it out. Finally, I realized, "That's not true. You don't have to do this." And the day I shifted my attitude from a *have to* to a *want to, choose to, like it, love it, it's my idea,* it stimulated the drive and energy that put me on an aggressive growth path.

Put your life mission on a *want to* basis. Put your goals on a *want to* basis. Put this year's campaign on a *want to* basis. If they become a *have to*, sit down and have a good talk with yourself. Either stop what you're doing, or make the shift. As you apply this lesson, you'll see boundless energy in yourself.

That's the way I teach. That's the way I live. That's the way I work. That's the way I run our company. And if I don't *want to* go someplace, quite frankly, I don't go. I don't do much that I don't want to do.

Think of a strong *want to* reason. You won't *want to* get up early in the morning, unless and until you have a strong want, like a new baby. Then you'll be up any time of the day or night.

A friend once told me that his teenage son stopped working with him and started working at a ski resort, even though he had to get up at 5:00 in the morning. "And he's up," said my astonished friend. "I'm amazed. I could not have gotten him up at 5:00 in the morning to help me—not with a forklift."

You can't coerce people into doing what they don't want to do. But you can help them to want to do it. It's stupid to try to coerce people into anything. So find out what your people *want to* do, and why. And then work more on developing the want. If you just make a decision to do it, you may be committed rationally but not emotionally. If I just make a rational decision to do it, I'll go in halfway, half-hearted. "Why don't you write a book?" "Well, okay." "Why don't you go?" "All right, I'll go." It isn't quite a "have to," but it's not much of a "want to" either.

Stop the witchcraft. You may work with people who have the attitude "there's nothing I can do about it." They feel helpless or hopeless. They don't see that the thing that needs to be done about a problem is something that they could do. They believe that other people or situations control their lives. They don't believe they can cause anything to happen themselves, and so they rely on some form of voodoo, witchcraft, superstitions, and signs.

Even when they try to make an *attitude adjustment*, they do it with booze, drugs, or peer pressure. They try to override their subconscious fear in a very ineffective way. "Well, if I have a few drinks, I can do that." Or, "If I get high, I could do great things." That's a poor way of getting yourself through the challenge. One time, maybe a second time, and soon it becomes a habit. Before long, there you are—stuck.

I know a bright young lady from Croatia who wants to be a model but who now works in a restaurant and lives in the United States. I once asked her, "What would you like to do with your future?"

"I'd like to go to Paris to be a model," she said. She also said that she wanted to graduate from an American university.

"Then why don't you?" I asked.

"I'm waiting for a sign," she said. "Usually I get a sign."

I said, "What do you mean by *a sign*?"

"Oh," she said, "a sign like the stars, or something outside of me. Something outside of me will make the choice."

You've got to be careful you don't allow yourself to become superstitious. Some athletes and coaches get so superstitious.

One coach I know had this one pair of *lucky* pants that he would wear to every ballgame. Now he was going to the playoffs, but the day before the big game, the cleaners lost his pants. None of his assistants would tell him. They were frightened to death to tell him that his special pants, his game pants, were lost.

So one assistant went out and bought another pair that looked like them and had them tailored to the right size. Nobody ever told the coach about it, because they figured he would be very upset if he didn't have his *special* pants on for the game.

Imagine how many people manipulate their lives with superstition, believing that the power lies outside themselves. What they're saying is "I don't have the power. The power is outside of me, not inside me. I can't change the environment or circumstances in which I am living."

Yes, you can, if you align your attitudes and goals.

Align your attitudes with your goals. Attitudes are subconscious emotional responses that surface once we set a goal, and these attitudes affect our behavior, direction, creativity, and motivation.

Attitudes aren't positive or negative until you set a goal. Once you set a goal, you must ask yourself, "Does my present attitude lead me *toward* accomplishment of the goal, or *away* from it?" You might not be aware of your attitude, but subconsciously you may be saying, "I can't bring myself to do it." So what happens? Instead of changing the attitude, you give up on the goal: "I guess I'm not cut out for this job." "I guess I don't deserve that car." "I guess I'm not tall enough to play on this team. That's just the way it is." No—that's the way *you* are. All you need to do is change your attitude.

Take a moment to visualize your residence. You have an attitude about how you run your home. If you're an orderly person, your attitude might be, "I like my house neat and clean." Suppose your brother is staying with you for a week, and his attitude is, "I like my house messy." How would you feel if you came home one night and found your brother's belongings scattered everywhere? You'd feel uptight, irritated. Your self-talk might be, "This isn't the way I live." You would have a problem.

Suppose as a college student you have the attitude: "I can't stand left-handed people"—and, upon reporting to campus for your room assignment, you discover, to your horror, that your roommate is left-handed. You have a problem. Especially if *he* can't stand *right-handed* people. Attitudes solidify over centuries of conflict between Arabs and Jews; black and white South Africans, Irish Catholics and Irish Protestants; Sandinistas and Contras. Each side has an attitude about the other that limits interaction and prohibits positive change.

Some of our outmoded attitudes prevent us, and others whom we influence, from making positive changes. In the 1950s, most Americans shared the attitude that "A woman's place is in the home." Most women today—single and married—are in the workforce. Until 1947, blacks were not accepted in major league baseball. Then Jackie Robinson broke the *color barrier* and integrated the game. Today, that old, restrictive racial policy is unacceptable. Times change and values change. So attitudes must change along with them.

Years ago, after Diane and I quit teaching school and decided to go into business for ourselves, we were getting ready to fly to Denver to work with some people at the University of Colorado. When I walked into our house, Diane was scrubbing the kitchen floor. I said, "Aren't you going? We've got a plane to catch in a half-hour."

She said, "I'll be ready as soon as I finish this."

I said, "Diane, why are you scrubbing the kitchen floor?"

She said, "Well, I don't feel like a mother unless I scrub the floor."

How do you argue with that? You don't. But you may not get to Denver, either. At the time, we had changed our lives dramatically—but scrubbing the kitchen floor could have prevented us from *enjoying* our new lifestyle. Sometimes you've got to give up an old attitude about what it means to be a mother.

"Well," she said, "If I don't get this done, I won't feel right about going."

I said, "Why not hire somebody this time to do it for you?"

She said, "No, I wouldn't feel comfortable with that." To Diane, at that time, scrubbing the floor was a mother's obligation. But that attitude was holding up our lives.

So how do you apply this to *your* life? Well, if you have this knowledge, you'll recognize that you may be lugging around a lot of outmoded attitudes that keep you from reaching your goals. And once you learn how to change old, negative attitudes, you will see that you don't have to give up your goals. You can pursue them aggressively, with great anticipation.

Creative avoidance. You might ask, "How will I know if I have a negative attitude?" Just observe yourself in action. If you have a positive attitude about something, you seek it out and try to possess it—whether it's music, career, love, money, art, food, adventure. If you have a negative attitude, you unconsciously lean away; you try to duck it. How do you know if your children have a negative attitude about school? If they do, they'll break out, psychosomatically, in spots and a fever, to creatively avoid getting out of bed. When we perceive or anticipate an uncomfortable situation, we get creative to avoid it.

How do we acquire our attitudes about success; about money; about travel; about the death penalty; about selling; about war; about love? When we ask ourselves, the answer often is, "I don't know."

For example, I have a good friend who runs a hair salon. Years ago, I had the attitude that running a hair salon was a strange business for a man. At that time, my friend was helping me conduct seminars for convicts as they were released into our custody. While I worked on their *inside* image, he worked on their *outside* image—acquainting them with the latest clothing and hairstyles.

One day I was teaching this seminar to some people who were being paroled. It was lunchtime, and since I hadn't talked to my friend for a while, I suggested that we cross the street to the campus cafeteria and have lunch together. He agreed. So after I finished teaching, we walked outside. It was winter, and he was wearing a stylish coat, which was fine. But he also had a *purse* slung over his shoulder.

Well, I do not walk with men who carry purses. That was my attitude. But I didn't realize it until we started across the street. What went through my mind *then* was, "I'm crossing the street with my ex-friend and his purse." Subconsciously, I'd already created my avoidance. When we entered the cafeteria, I stopped to talk to the first person I met—a guy I didn't even *know*. I turned back to my friend and said, "Go ahead and get in line. I'll be right with you." I acted as if I had met an old friend. My creative subconscious was taking over; I wasn't *consciously* aware that I was avoiding my friend—and his purse.

If I didn't know better, I might have fixed the blame on my friend and quit the friendship. But he didn't have the problem; I did. It was *my attitude*, not *his purse*.

The solution was to simply realize that fashions change, ideas change, and so do people. By changing my attitude, the problem was solved and our friendship preserved.

Your subconscious works the same way. It could be causing you to creatively avoid a friend—new jobs, restaurants, neighborhoods, new experiences. Unless we closely monitor ourselves, we don't recognize a negative attitude until the damage is done.

By changing our attitudes, we allow ourselves to achieve what we're capable of achieving. It isn't just a matter of thinking better of yourself, dwelling on positive thoughts and visualizing end results. We also have to work at changing old, inappropriate attitudes and habits that prevent us from reaching our potential.

How to Change Negative Attitudes

As you pursue a vision with your present attitudes, you may experience negative emotion. This negative emotion will stimulate avoidant behavior. You have stored emotional responses to the situation that you've experienced in the past.

Remember: An attitude is the direction in which you're leaning. An attitude is positive if you lean toward and seek to possess the good that you perceive in it. An attitude is negative when you anticipate a negative outcome—such as pain, displeasure, embarrassment, ridicule, punishment, or hurt. Your subconscious stimulates negative creativity to get you to move away from what would be uncomfortable in that setting or environment. Positive attitudes generate creativity to seek the outcome; negative attitudes stimulate creativity to avoid the outcome.

Once you declare the goal, do your present attitudes cause you to seek the goal in a positive, creative, venturous way? Or, do you start the journey but soon find yourself engaged in activities or events that have nothing to do with the goal?

If so, don't give up on your goal—just change your attitude.

How do you change your negative attitudes?

1. Discover what attitudes you need to change. When you set a goal, you don't know what your attitude will be; so monitor your attitudes until you achieve the goal. And this isn't a grit-your-teeth override; it's just a matter of setting the goal deeply in your subconscious.

You don't know *what* attitudes you need to change, and you may not know how either. That's why you first need to discover your negative attitudes.

In today's world, you will discover your attitudes as you encounter *boundaryless organizations* and multicultural developments. Your attitudes toward men and women at work, your attitudes toward minorities, your attitudes toward religion, your attitudes toward different cultures and languages, your attitudes toward the wealthy and the poor, your attitudes toward the unemployed—all these attitudes will surface as you encounter different people and situations.

You might say, "This is what I want to do, but now our company is merging. I'm working with different people who are a different color and speak a different language." Watch what your self-talk is like, and watch your avoidant behavior. Watch how negative attitudes limit your potential, and the potential of the team.

As I work with people in Northern Ireland, I encourage them to change attitudes that are not conducive to peace and economic prosperity. They've got some negative attitudes. These surface when they learn the religion of another person, just as surely as running into a man who carries a purse.

I once looked at a book of pictures of the integrated school in Derry and asked my host, "How do you know who's Catholic or Protestant? It's hard looking at the pictures because they all look alike."

"Oh," he said, "we find out immediately by asking, 'What school did you go to?' If you went to a different school, I immediately have a negative attitude toward you; in fact, it comes out as hatred. I don't know that I hate you until I find out what school you attended."

We all have certain prejudices that we were raised with, and sometimes we don't even know what they are. When did you get your attitude about masculinity and femininity? You probably don't even know when you acquired the attitude—you just assimilated the prejudices and fears of the culture. You don't even know you have them until you're assigned to go to India or to open a business in Hong Kong. Now, you may get sick, just so you don't have to go. In global markets and boundaryless companies, you must try to get past these limiting attitudes.

2. Keep a reflective thinking journal. Are you engaged in activities that lead you aggressively and positively toward the outcome that you want? Or, do you have difficulty getting yourself to do things that would lead you to the goal? Do you have difficulty making the phone call, meeting the person, studying for the test?

In your journal, keep track of how you act. Watch your behavior, watch your action. Observe the activities of people around you. Is their activity moving them progressively toward the outcome? Or, do they say they want to be an all-American, but they won't lift weights, won't go to practice, won't learn the plays? Become a student of human behavior, especially your own. Note, for example, that you might say that you want to be a successful salesperson. Why, then, do you go home early, not come to meetings, and not follow up?

3. See the consequences of avoidant behavior. Much of what you find yourself doing as you pursue your goals is avoiding doing what you really want because you have a negative attitude about it. You can waste a lot of time and energy engaged in avoidant activity and behavior. So be honest with yourself. Ask yourself, "Is this serendipitous behavior letting me flow, or is it getting me out of doing something I don't want to do?"

If you see somebody at work you don't want to be around, watch how you go around so you don't have to go past them. You find ways to avoid them. You engage in avoidant activity when you perceive a negative situation or an embarrassing negative outcome. And you don't consciously do this. Your subconscious seeks to protect you from the pain. You become inventive and creative at getting yourself out of things you don't want to do.

4. Create the Big Want. You need to spend more time on creating the Big Want. Even though you may want to do something, like be successful in raising your children, you won't spend much time with your kids unless you create the Big Want. Or, you may wish to succeed in real estate, but you discover that you don't like asking people to buy or asking for listings. You don't even know you have a negative attitude; it just jumps out at you when you set a goal. And when you can't get yourself to do the things that are essential to achieve the goal, you give up on the goal. You say, "I'm just not born to be a good salesperson." "I'm not cut out for this business."

In your life, you assimilate many attitudes about what can or can't be done. You've assimilated many attitudes that you don't even know you have. And they don't surface until you're faced with a situation.

Once you're faced with a situation, your attitudes come out. And you won't change your attitude to release yourself from your avoidant behavior unless you have a Big Want.

5. Use your genius to stimulate positive creativity. You become very inventive and creative when you want someone or something. When you see a person of the opposite sex that you would like to be with, you become very creative. "Oh, I didn't know you walked home this way." Sure you didn't. You get so inventive and so creative to be in the company of that person.

If you want to go to a football game but you have many things to do that day, watch how you get creative to get the things done to go.

Years ago Diane and I decided to build a log cabin at our ranch. We'd never built a house before, let alone a log cabin, but as soon as we decided, we heard about people who built log cabins. They were everywhere, from St. Louis to Seattle. And we started to see magazines and other material on log cabins. Before long, we were experts on log cabins. So you set the goal, you learn, and then you express your creativity.

One time I was walking with a friend who is a wonderful photographer along a path leading from a conference center to a restaurant at a resort. All of a sudden, he stopped and said, "Hold it. Stop a moment. The light and the moisture are just right." And he went over and he took a picture of a single blackberry blossom. I didn't even see the blackberry blossom, but he saw one where the moisture and light were perfect for a photograph. Now, we were in the middle of a conversation; he wasn't looking for this, but as soon as we came upon the creative opportunity, he took it.

6. Use the affirmation process to make adjustments. Once I recognize my negative attitudes, I write out a positive description of the emotion that I want controlling my automatic behavior.

For example, remember when you were a child learning how to ride a bicycle. You see in your path a rock, an obstacle. You don't want to hit the obstacle, but you keep looking at the rock. And so, what happens? Even though you don't want to hit it, you steer your bicycle into it.

Later, when you get good on your bike, when you see the obstacle, you are physiologically coordinated to look where you want to go. You look your way around the problem. You look your way around the rock. And you just flow around it.

When you start writing down your goals or changing your attitude, when you run up against the rock (a negative attitude), you ask, "Do I want it?" And you let yourself describe it. "Well, how do I want it? If this is what I don't want, how do I want it?" It's as simple as that. And then you write the description down. "If this is my problem, what would it look like when I don't have the problem?" And you describe it as though you already are there and while you're describing it, you write it down. What you write down becomes your affirmation. You're describing to yourself the positive response, the positive emotion, that you want to be an automatic part of your subconscious process.

It takes time and repeated affirmation to change an attitude, but once you change it, boom, you let yourself go.

Cutting the grass. When we moved into our home 20 years ago, I had a negative attitude about cutting the grass. When Diane showed me the home, all I could see were the three acres of grass around it, and so I said, "We can't get this house."

"Why?" she asked. "Is it because you don't think we can afford it? Is it because you don't like the looks of it?"

"No, it's because of the grass. Three acres of grass. I hate cutting the grass." That was my attitude.

She then said, "Well, if we buy it, you wouldn't need to cut it. You could get a gardener."

"Good grief, can you imagine what my coaching friends would think of me with a gardener? I wouldn't have a friend left." See, I also had an attitude about gardeners. My solution was to give up on the goal. We couldn't have the house because of an attitude about cutting the grass or having a gardener.

But Diane said, "Well, why don't you change your attitude?" Which one do you think I changed? Yeah, I got the house, with the grass and the gardener.

See how you must change an attitude to release yourself, to allow yourself to do something or to have something. Not wanting to cut the grass almost kept us out of that house. I keep that picture in my mind when I set goals. You need a picture for reference. "Here's another grass-cutting deal," I say to myself. "So I better change my attitude, or give up on the goal."

Drunk drivers. Maybe you've been stuck with monumental personal and corporate problems for a long time, and the negative attitude you have stimulates punitive, negative creativity.

Jeff Jared, a good friend of ours, once visited us at the ranch. He's from New South Wales, where he's Commissioner of Police and Public Safety. We were talking about the attitudes of law enforcement that need to change. For example, one problem in Sydney, New South Wales (population of five million people) is the deaths on the highway from drunk drivers.

Now what is your attitude about drunk drivers? You want to lock them up, catch them, punish them, put them in jail. If nothing else, give them a ride home. That's the way they were trying to solve the problem. They had over 1,500 drunk drivers a year who were killed on the highways.

Nothing was working. So the people who were faced with that problem needed to change their attitude. The attitude became "How do we get the drunks home safely, without hurting themselves or hurting anybody else?" It was as simple as that.

When they changed their attitude toward the problem and toward the drunk driver, they came up with the idea that they would build highways for drunks. The goal was to get them home safely. So they asked themselves, "How do we build highways for drunks? What does a highway for drunks look like? How do you get them on it when they are drunk?"

They decided to modify existing highways by taking out the dangerous turns, putting up larger dividers, adding bumps along the sides to jar drivers when they hit them, and making all the light poles and signposts out of collapsible metal that would fold when hit. They got very creative with "How do we get them home safely?" And they reduced deaths from 1,500 to 650 in one year.

As you change your attitude, you stimulate creativity in a constructive way. An attitude shift will stimulate creativity. So now when you're stuck with problems about inner city, about peace, about corrections, about whatever, ask yourself, "How do I build a highway for drunks?" Once you understand the story, you will shift your attitude. Shift your attitude, and watch how your creativity changes. Shift your attitude, and you will find solutions.

Dealing with a person who has a bad attitude. The way another person behaves toward you should not affect how you feel. You have the control over how you feel. You don't let other people determine how you feel today, how you're going to act, how you're going to behave. You don't allow them to alter your internal idea of how you are, who you are, and how you act.

Now, if they have power to make policy or rules or law, then you may need to leave the environment. You can't be entrapped by it. In some situations, avoidance may be necessary for survival. Avoid the activity where it's negative. Just make sure that you're not capitulating, that you're not giving up on the problem. Our self-esteem is nothing but the favorable and unfavorable attitudes we develop about ourselves. Your attitude toward yourself affects your self-esteem. When you have a very positive attitude about yourself, it elevates your self-esteem. You project your attitude about yourself to the people around you through body language, behavior, and verbal communication. And they treat you according to your own attitude about yourself.

DIANE'S STORY

Part II: We Have a Fight on Our Hands

LOU: At the hospital, I waited for Diane to come out of the anesthetic. When she did, I held her hand and said, "Diane, I'm going to tell you the truth. The operation was a success, but the cancer has broken loose in your system. We have a hell of a fight on our hands." She didn't flinch. She looked me straight in the eyes and said, "Okay. Let's get started. What's the first step?"

The next day, people called from all over the world—the U.S., Australia, England, Africa, Japan—to share their concern and prayers for Diane's welfare. We were both overwhelmed by the genuine love that poured in. I remember Diane saying, "It's very powerful. You can almost feel their energy." I told myself, "I will find ways to multiply this energy, so Diane can feel it every day."

I thought about my friend Gene who, some years earlier, applied many of the principles we teach to help keep his son, Terry, reasonably healthy through a long, tragic ordeal with leukemia. Terry eventually succumbed to the disease, but I remembered the day-to-day positive benefits from Gene's careful regulation of Terry's environment. So I talked to Gene about how we might constructively apply some of those things to Diane's situation.

I wanted to create an emotional climate of normalcy, wellness, and hope around Diane at all times. We started by decorating the room brightly with familiar photos and fresh flowers and many of Diane's familiar personal items. We surrounded her with humorous people; we showed a lot of comedy films in her room, even though after a chemotherapy treatment it was tough for her to laugh; we kidded and joked and played lots of games. In other words, we created a light, relaxed, upbeat atmosphere. Diane and I both understood the power of humor and joy to promote physical and mental health, so it was a natural approach for us anyway.

DIANE: When people I knew came to visit me, they brought their prayers and such strong spiritual, positive energy into my room. I could physically feel it inside me. I drew on it during my whole recuperation. But it's important to know that you don't have to take our curriculum to become a positive and constructive person. What made the difference wasn't that the people who came to see me had been through, or understood, our program. It was that they naturally exemplified the concepts we teach. It was just the kind of people they were; they were naturally positive and constructive, and they gave me spiritual support.

Actually, there's a lot of constructive information in the negative, too, because you can evaluate and assimilate *all* the information in current reality and make more measured judgments. So it's a mistake to think that this curriculum is Pollyannish, and everybody is always smiling. It's not that way. It's just that, in stressful situations, a positive atmosphere of lightness and humor and upbeat conversation helps carry the stress from your body so you can strengthen your immune system. With that kind of energy and strength, even in the face of the worst, you're always able to look for the best. And if the worst is all there is, you still know you can learn something from it. Lou and everyone else around me during that period weren't creating a Pollyanna world of "Don't look at the truth, Diane." In fact, they were helping me *find* the truth.

LOU: We also realized that doctors, interns, orderlies, and nurses had their own personal and professional beliefs and their own sources of truth. I remembered how the hospital personnel had projected their limiting, negative realities into young Terry's mind, and how Gene tried to battle that. Doctors have blind spots. They're sometimes so narrowly focused on their own methods that they don't readily see other options. When they hear information contrary to what they believe, they tend to rationalize it as "an exception to the rule."

They don't mean to be that way. They just believe in their own reality—like I sometimes do in my business, like all of us do—and they aren't aware that they're communicating it. ***Remember: Human beings act in accordance with the truth as they believe it.*** And we unconsciously project our *truth* through facial expressions, body language, manner, tone of voice. Now, we know that doctors and nurses see patients die every day. That becomes a powerful negative reality: "It doesn't matter what we do. They still die." So we had to be prepared for these people coming into Diane's room, projecting their histories of patients who didn't make it, and regarding Diane as just another statistic.

I regard doctors and nurses as highly skilled, very necessary, even precious—but, ultimately, as just human beings. Quite frankly, many become detached in their statistical reality—like the doctor who broke the news to Diane over the phone. They can easily develop blind spots of the greatest magnitude. But my conviction was this: In life-and-death situations, scotomas and negative *truths* are absolutely unacceptable. So I decided to take extreme measures to counteract the negative realities of all the *experts* who would be telling Diane *the truth.*

Since we aren't sure what we control in this world, I decided to take control of darn near everything. First, we needed to overpower the negative affirmations of the experts. We needed to overpower their "doom and gloom" realities. So we began by stressing the idea that, even though others had died from this type of cancer, it wouldn't necessarily happen to Diane. And I made sure that either myself or someone else in our family—particularly our daughters Bonnie, Nancy, and Mary, and my sister Carol—or a close personal friend would take turns being with Diane during all her waking hours. That way, when doctors, nurses, or interns said anything contrary to the goal of success, we would immediately say in front of them, "That isn't necessarily true" or "We don't believe that stuff." Sometimes, the doctor would discuss postoperative treatments with Diane: "You've *got* to do this" and "This is the way it *must* be done." And we would say, "We aren't so sure about that." We wanted Diane to become her *own* authority.

Lock on to the end result that you *want* in your life, regardless of the present reality and present circumstances. When you've got information that casts doubt, you must be strong in your own mind to know that your subconscious draws you to the images you focus on. So, sometimes you may need to deny current reality, deny what your peers and the experts and the people you respect insist is *the truth*, and hold the image of what you *want* in the future. High-performance people have the tenacity and resiliency to face the "gloom and doom" and "Ain't it awful?" attitudes and not be overwhelmed, or let it destroy their hope.

From the beginning, Diane was extremely positive and focused on the end result of getting well. Diane is a naturally positive person. All the time she was ill, she never talked in terms of death or giving up. She always regarded her illness as a temporary setback: "What are my plans for tomorrow?" We know that her positive, future-oriented attitude made a difference. And that's what we worked to support.

DIANE: I never despaired. When I was a child in school and I got a grade of 92 percent in spelling, I never thought of it as an 8 percent failure. I considered it a 92 percent success. It always irritated me when they wrote on my papers "Minus 8 percent." I immediately translated it back into the positive. I still do that.

When I was preparing for the surgery, I researched statistics on the cure rates for my form of cancer, and it was something like 90 percent failure and 10 percent success. I always visualized myself in the 10 percent. If it was only 1 percent, I would still see myself there. I read somewhere that thousands of people have cancer but don't know it, and they survive to a ripe old age. I also discovered there's no cancer known that someone hasn't overcome. Actually, more people recover from cancer than ever die from it. That's the kind of information I dwelled on. I always saw myself in the *success* category. I thought, "Well, if only one person can beat this, I will certainly be that person." It never entered my mind that it could be any other way.

I was convinced I would get better, but I didn't ignore the possibility of death. I knew I couldn't entirely control what happened inside my body, and that it was possible I could end up in the 90 percent category. I just never *imagined* myself there. Occasionally, funny little thoughts would seep in—but not in a morbid, defeated sense. Like one time when I wasn't feeling well, I was talking to Lou and I said, completely out of the blue, "Well, that grandfather clock you gave me, I think Glen should have it." It was such a strange remark out of nowhere that we both started laughing.

I never visualized myself dying, so I didn't plan for that eventuality. I knew we had a well-organized will, and that our estate planning was already taken care of. The only contingency I considered came out in a funny conversation I had with a close friend. I said, "In case anyone might wonder what my opinion would be on this, here it is. I think our son Glen should have my grandfather clock because he loves clocks and has enjoyed taking my watches apart to see how they work. And I know there are women out there who would love to get involved with Lou." I even had a list of names and I started pointing to them, one at a time: "Now, this one is definitely out. This one is out, too. But this one would certainly be okay." We had a great time with it. That was the extent of me talking about "Well, what will happen if I'm not here?"

Continued on page 107.

STEP 2:
Engage in Constructive Self-Talk

THIS step allows us to put mind over matter, as our creative subconscious helps us see options and see potential.

When I was young, I thought I was dumb, in part because of the way I was treated and conditioned by parents and teachers. So I concluded: "I don't have the aptitude." Millions of people have felt that way about themselves.

Then I found that others got the ideas, the right answers—not because they were smarter, but because they were conditioned to see differently. I discovered that when I was bounced up against information that I was not prepared to see, I didn't see it.

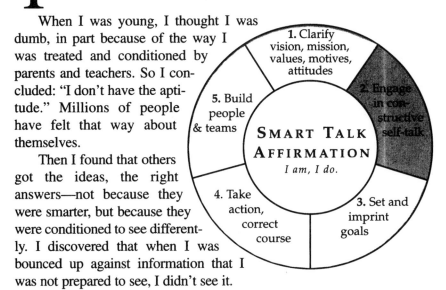

1. Clarify vision, mission, values, motives, attitudes

2. Engage in constructive self-talk

5. Build people & teams

SMART TALK AFFIRMATION
I am, I do.

4. Take action, correct course

3. Set and imprint goals

I started to think, "Wow, you mean that all I've got to do is to be more self-aware of my conditioning, and I will begin to see things— look at that, look at that, look at that." That's the way I now go after life.

If you don't have that knowledge, then you don't let yourself set the aspiration because you don't know how. You can't see how. If you're stuck on a problem, you conclude either that there's no answer or that you're not smart enough to get it.

Chapter 4 explains what makes up our thinking process, which consists of conscious thought, our subconscious, and our creative subconscious. Once you can consciously control your thought process, you will be able to change the way you think—which will change how you act. Controlling your thought process will help you make better decisions, and follow through with them.

Chapter 5 deals with overcoming our blind spots. We tend to *lock on* to certain ideas, and *lock out* any other options. High-performance people are able to see new options, and break through old barriers that were blocking their growth. Rather than limiting your beliefs, you begin to look *past* them, just as Columbus overcame the belief that the world was flat.

Chapter 6 shows how our self-image is created through our self-talk. We become what we think, and if we focus on what we *don't* want, that is what we will get. The *who-saids* in our lives also affect us. By learning to have superstar self-talk and by assimilating past accomplishments into your thoughts, you will become better every day.

There is a direct relationship between the quality of the knowledge and information you hold in your mind and the way your life goes. If your life isn't going well out there, the problem may be in your mind. Change the inside, and the outside changes.

c h a p t e r   4

THE CREATIVE THOUGHT PROCESS

Y OUR thought processes control your effectiveness and performance. Understanding the thought process empowers you, because you see it as a way to create your future rather than waiting for some outside force or inspiration to change you.

The Thinking Process

There are three parts to the thinking process: *the conscious, the subconscious,* and *the creative subconscious.* By understanding these functions, you can learn why you think and act as you do.

1. Conscious thought. In the conscious process, there are five basic functions: *perception, assimilation, association, evaluation, and decision.*

• *Perception.* Through your senses, you perceive your feelings, thoughts, and emotions, as well as the external world. Your senses tell you, "This is the way the world is." Perception takes place even before your birth. You start gathering information about the world in the womb. That's when you first perceived movement, balance, and sound. And you add other senses after birth. You pick up added information about the way the world is. You call this information *the truth.* You also call it *reality.* But it's not really reality, as reality might be; it's *your* version of reality. That information is part of a subconscious encyclopedia about you that you're continually updating.

• *Assimilation.* You assimilate good and bad models, correct and incorrect information. As you grow up, you record and store all the information gathered through your senses in a sort of data bank: your first words as a baby, the books you read, every fight you had, every time you cried, people you met, places you went, secrets told you, the joy of every triumph, the pain of every loss. You store what you perceive and assimilate it in your brain. All the information you've been exposed to from birth—the radio and television programs, the conversations, the school, the playground, the books you've read, magazines, stories—all of that information is stored in the neurons of your brain, never to be lost, never to be forgotten. There are various ways of retrieving it to recall things you wouldn't even know you had stored in your memory.

• *Association*. Once you perceive and assimilate something, you associate it with anything similar stored in your "data bank" by asking, "Have I experienced anything like this before?" If you've had a similar experience, the event will make sense to you. Association is bouncing this perception off the reality that you have stored on the subconscious level. You ask, "Have I seen anything like this before?"

• *Evaluation*. After associating what you perceive, you evaluate it against previous information in your "data bank" by asking, "What is this probably leading me toward?" You assess the probabilities. "Is it leading me toward happiness, pleasure, and fun, or is it leading me toward stress, discomfort, and pain?" In other words, "Will this be good or bad for me?" We judge probabilities based on the experiences we've had. And then we make evaluations. "What is this leading me to?"

You and I could view the same event and have very different evaluations. For example, when two critics review a movie, one might say, "It's an original film with real people full of real passion. I give it four stars." The other might say, "Original? Oh, c'mon! It was one long cliché. 'Real people full of real passion?' More like stick figures full of *baloney*! I give it half a star. Save your money." They saw the same film, but recorded different versions of the *truth*.

• *Decision*. You decide on a course of action based on your immediate needs and goals. You may react by taking action; you may let someone else make the decision; you may choose to ignore or repress the matter entirely. Our choices are often based not on what could be, but what once was. Many decisions you make are based not on what is happening to you *presently*, but rather on what has happened to you in the *past*.

For example, suppose a 10-year-old boy gets up in front of the classroom for his first Show and Tell. As he starts telling his story, he is very serious. But everybody cracks up laughing. So he gets flustered, forgets what he wants to say, and hurries back to his seat. His friend leans over and says to him, "Dummy! Your *fly* is unzipped!" The boy's emotional response to this event—his feeling of humiliation—is recorded in his *data bank* as a strongly negative experience.

Now, suppose that 25 years pass. At age 35, he has an opportunity to speak to a local Boys Club. He thinks, "Have I experienced anything like this before?" He evaluates, "What is this leading me toward? Nothing good!" So he makes the decision: "I'm too busy to give the talk." He makes this decision, at 35, very likely because his pants were unzipped when he was 10.

2. The subconscious mind. Your subconscious mind is like a high-fidelity sensory tape recorder that captures and stores your version of *reality*. It stores all of your experiences—what you think, say, sense, feel, and imagine about yourself, along with your emotional attitudes and reactions to your experiences.

Your subconscious is like a blank canvas at conception. With every life experience, you dab a little paint on the canvas. You paint your own picture of *the truth* about yourself—the *real* you. Every artist paints his or her own version. Like fingerprints, no two are alike. Once you dab on attitudes and opinions about yourself and the world—no matter how detrimental they are—you're stuck with them, until you decide *consciously* to repaint the picture.

The subconscious also handles learned functions of living, like tying your shoelaces, walking, driving, playing sports, adding, and subtracting. These activities originate on the conscious level. But through repeated brush strokes, a picture emerges on your subconscious canvas, incorporating them as habits. You perform them with a free-flowing ease because you no longer have to consciously think about them.

Tying your shoelaces, walking, and knowing how to add and subtract are positive habits. They allow you to function efficiently. But some subconscious habits can become barriers to growth. They can become obsolete—like an old, ribbon typewriter in the computer age. They still do the job, but they lock out change. Because they're so *comfortable,* they can keep people from venturing into new situations such as accepting a new job, adjusting to a new environment, or risking a new relationship.

3. The creative subconscious. The creative subconscious enforces your behavior. It maintains your present version of reality by causing you to act like the person you believe yourself to be. It maintains order and sanity by maintaining the inner picture of the truth that you've come to accept as "just like me." Once you get an idea about who you are, you don't need to get up every morning and remember how you are. As long as that self-image is imprinted into your belief system, you will automatically behave like you. That's not so bad because it keeps you from being different every day in every situation. There's something inside you that allows you to consistently be you.

Suppose you've convinced yourself that you always get lost when you drive to unfamiliar places. You don't have to wake up every morning and remind yourself, "Don't forget to get lost today." Your creative subconscious will take care of it automatically. Maybe you feel you have a mental block when it comes to remembering people's names. You won't need to remind yourself to forget: Your creative subconscious will take care of that for you. "Oh, I'm forgetful." Okay. Don't worry. You don't need to remember to be forgetful. Your subconscious will make you forget even though you have the potential to remember. "Oh, I'm lazy." You don't have to remember to be lazy; your subconscious will get you to act lazy. "Oh, I've got a terrible temper." Well, you don't need to remember to blow up. Your subconscious will allow you to blow up in situations that you deem appropriate.

Remember: Your creative subconscious always maintains your presently dominant self-image. It maintains your present idea of how good you are, how successful, how athletic, how smart, how loving. It isn't concerned with what you *used* to be, what you *want* to be, or what you have the *potential* to be. It maintains whatever you decide is *good enough* for you right now.

Your creative subconscious is so powerful in maintaining your present self-image, it can influence how other people act toward you. We know, for example, that body language and tone of voice are tied to self-image. In communicating to others what you believe, words carry only minimal validity; tone of voice carries a bit more; body language carries the most validity. So you can negate what you say with your body language and tone of voice.

If you think of yourself as shy, and you're invited to a cocktail party where you don't know anyone, your creative subconscious will invent ways to keep people away. You might stand in a corner, arms folded, feet crossed, eyes averted. Your body language will scream, "I'm shy. Leave me alone." If people get too close, you'll escape—away from the crowd. Afterwards, when you're home alone, you'll reaffirm, "See, I *am* shy."

If you want to be a leader, but believe yourself to be a follower, you will automatically act like you believe yourself to be when a crisis occurs. If you feel out of place, tension constricts your vocal chords so your voice changes. That's why, when someone gets up in front of a group of people and says in a squeaky, timid voice, "I'm looking forward to this," you sense they're lying.

To your creative subconscious, maintaining your present idea of *reality,* your idea of how things are supposed to be, is more important than wealth, happiness, success, even health. You maintain your sanity by making things on the outside match what you believe inside. Then you won't seem crazy to yourself for believing what you believe.

For example, suppose that you're 30 pounds overweight, but you suddenly decide to look better and feel healthier by losing some weight. So you skip breakfast and lunch. But your creative subconscious knows you don't see yourself as thin. So it goes to work, not to make you look thinner and feel healthier, but rather to maintain your dominant self-image. So, when you skip breakfast and lunch, it *corrects for the mistake* by getting you to eat *two helpings of dinner*. Your creative subconscious says, "Well, you didn't eat enough earlier in the day." You say, "Enough for what? I want to *lose weight!*" It says, "You don't believe that. It's not like you. You believe you're 30 pounds overweight. If you get thin, you'll feel *crazy*."

If you lose weight, your external picture (your body) will no longer match your internal picture of being 30 pounds overweight. So your creative subconscious sets off its sanity alarm: "Hey! Don't try to be thin! That's not *you!* Get back to being you." And so you eat two helpings of dinner.

The creative subconscious won't quit pressuring you until the two pictures match again. So, after dinner, it works even harder to correct for the mistake: "Hey! Get hungry again!" Finally, at about 10 p.m., you feel starved. You say, "I've gotta have a piece of cake—but no frosting." That's your conscious mind talking. Your creative subconscious says, "Oh no. We need all the frosting we can get. And some ice cream!" So you go back in, and you not only eat one piece—with all the frosting—but you end up eating *the whole cake* with some ice cream on the side. You wake up the next morning and say, "Why'd I eat the whole cake? It doesn't make sense!"

No, it doesn't make sense *consciously*, but your creative subconscious knew you couldn't stay 30 pounds overweight if you didn't eat the whole cake. So it automatically maintains your present picture of you—until you change that picture.

What would happen if you knew you didn't deserve a good marriage, but your spouse was always gracious, warm, loving, and kind, and the marriage was going well? Your creative subconscious would correct for the mistake by causing you to do dumb things to mess up your marriage. And your spouse would say, "What did you do that for?" And you'd say, "I don't know. Doesn't make much sense, does it?" It made sense to your creative subconscious, because it made you act like the person you believed yourself to be. Not what you *wanted* to be, not what you *could* be. Maintaining sanity was more important than a happy marriage.

I suppose that's why the rich get richer, and the poor keep getting poorer. Imagine a gambler who wins about $300,000, but in a few weeks he's broke again. He gives money away, throws it away, gambles it away, drinks it away. Could his self-image have been, "I'm poor. I don't deserve all this money. It's a mistake for me to be rich"? Do you suppose his creative subconscious corrected for the mistake?

Have you ever observed rich people who *know* they should be rich, and then they suddenly go broke? They will correct for the mistake and come right back to being rich again.

The term "poverty consciousness" applies to more than simply money. It applies to an attitude about life in general. People know, subconsciously, whether they're supposed to be rich or poor with regard to life's bounty—relationships, friendships, family, spirit, career, love. If you know you're supposed to be rich in life but things go wrong, you correct for the *mistake.* But if you believe you're supposed to be poor in life, and you have a chance to get a raise, go into business for yourself, or have a better house in a nicer neighborhood, your creative subconscious will sabotage your chances for success to "get you back where you belong."

Again, we behave not according to the real truth, but *the truth* as we believe it. When you do dumb things, it doesn't make much sense *consciously.* But subconsciously it makes perfect sense. Because your creative subconscious keeps you from coming unglued. It keeps you from being one thing today and something else tomorrow. It maintains consistency in your behavior—whether it's to your benefit or not. That stability is necessary. But it also makes it tough for you to change—unless you know how to alter your inner picture of what you deserve.

If you have the idea that the world is against you, you go out and unconsciously do things to get the world against you. It isn't genes, it isn't coincidence, and it sure isn't luck. Change you, and the world will change around you. When you learn how to change your picture, your belief, your self-image, and bring it closer to your real potential, you will automatically behave like that until you change the picture again.

Examine your beliefs about yourself by asking, "What do I believe about my physical, intellectual, social, spiritual, and financial potential?" "Who have I allowed to see *the truth* for me?" "What negative wizards have I listened to?" "Do I tell myself, 'Oh, it's impossible to change. You can't teach an old dog new tricks?'" "Do I believe, 'I was born this way. It's just my nature?'" "What do I expect of me—as a parent, spouse, friend, professional?" "What's good enough for me?"

Remember: *If you change the way you think, you change the way you act.* If you change the way you think about yourself, people will respond differently to you. You aren't born *lucky*. You make your own breaks based on *the truth* that you believe about yourself. You make your own *reality*. If you don't change your negative self-image, people will behave toward you the way you see yourself—and you'll believe you were born that way.

Making Decisions, Solving Problems

Our decisions aren't any more accurate than the information on which they're based. Do you know anyone who has gone through a traumatic breakup in a relationship? A few years later, they have a chance to get involved with someone else, but they associate, *"Have I experienced anything like this before?"* They evaluate, *"What is this leading me toward? Nothing good!"* Then they decide, "No thanks. I don't want any part of it." Their decision is not based on feelings for the *new* person, but rather on the trauma caused by the old relationship.

For instance, some women I've met in state penitentiaries can't figure out why their relationships always fall apart. They can't seem to keep their marriage or family together. Many of them were abused as children, and so they assimilate bad models. Even if they get into a good relationship, they perceive the new relationship in terms of the old. They self-sabotage, and foul it up. They don't just have bad luck and keep running into the wrong guy. They seek the wrong guy. And when they go to work, they mess up on the job. They can't get along with the manager. What is their impression of people in authority? If they were beaten or pushed around, their perception of anybody in authority is negative. So, they think it's all the boss's fault. They've just had a series of bad luck. If you go through a disappointing marriage and get a divorce with a lot of emotional upheaval, you store that negative emotion in your image of reality. And so when you later get involved with a wonderful person, you perceive this new relationship in terms of the old, and you decide not to get involved.

Many of us make our future choices based upon the emotional, erroneous information from a painful past. We limit our future growth and choices and goals because of what has happened, not what can happen. To the degree we put misinformation into our minds, we can't expect the right answers to come out.

Since many decisions about your future are based on what happened in the past, you need to modify and update *the truth* recorded in your subconscious *data bank* to improve your chances for future success. As you change your internal picture using goal-setting, affirmations, visualization, and imprinting, you will make decisions that are more appropriate to the person you are today.

Richard Gregory, an expert from the United Kingdom on how the mind works, once told me, "Intelligence is the art of correct guesswork. Anything we do to improve our guesswork will make us more intelligent." This process of growing and getting better is all about improving our guesswork—guesswork of which route to take, which person to marry, what schools to attend, who to invest with, what plays to call. Intelligence is the art of guessing correctly.

The art of guessing correctly is an ongoing process. If I go to the racetrack, which horse am I going to bet on? Or if I get into the race-horse business, which horse do I buy? Which trainer do I use? Intelligence is just the art of guessing correctly. What school do I put my five-year-old child in? Who is the best person to give her piano lessons? A bad choice may keep the child from ever developing her talent. So you want the right information.

The quality of information you have stored about how the world works affects the validity of the choices you make. Your creative subconscious causes you to act and behave like the person you know yourself to be. It's constantly at work making your personality and behavior congruent to the image of how you're to be.

Unfortunately, we likely have a lot of *misinformation* stored on the subconscious level. We're all full of misinformation about business, about markets, about relationships. Old information may have served us well while we were stuck in some comfort zone, but it is not okay now. For example, as long as I was a high school teacher and coach, I could function adequately with the knowledge I had, but when I left that protected world, I struggled to run a business. I would listen to friends and advisors, but frankly they were feeding me a lot of garbage because they too were very limited in knowledge and experience. Some information I got from people when I first went into business helped me reach the $5,000 a month level. But to get to the $500,000 level, I had to stop operating on misinformation and change some old beliefs and habits.

We often act on the basis of partial truths, half-truths, or untruths. We may accept information as *the truth*, even though we don't know it's true for sure. If you feed misinformation into a computer, you can't expect the right answer to come out. The same with the quality of your decisions. They won't be any more accurate than the information on which you base them.

Suppose that you once invested and lost. Now here comes another opportunity to invest. Are you making the choice on the future investment or the past investment? Are you making an emotional choice not to invest this time because of the memory of last time?

Quality of Knowledge and Information

There is a direct relationship between the quality of the knowledge and information you hold in your mind and the way your life goes. If your life isn't going well out there, the problem is probably in your mind. Change the inside, and the outside changes. But most people keep waiting for the outside to change.

Knowing you have the right information is tricky. So-called experts give you the *good information*, and yet if you examine it you might say, "I don't know. This doesn't seem right to me."

In today's world, we have lost knowledge amid a sea of information; and lost wisdom in the knowledge explosion.

When you were six years old, the parent in the home, the teacher in school, or the big kids on the playground or in the neighborhood were the experts. You listened to *the truth* they shared, perhaps because you knew no better source.

When you're new in an organization, you don't know who to listen to. You just step in and search for *the truth*. You ask, "How do things work in this business? Who do you report to? What happens?" You might hear *the truth* from someone who has only been there for six weeks or from some disgruntled person who plans to quit in 20 days. And once you lock on to *the truth* in your mind, you become blind to other ideas. Once you get an opinion stuck in your mind, you selectively perceive and gather information based upon your starting premise.

Who do you listen to? Who do your children listen to? Where do you get your information? Where do you find *the truth*? Who is world-class in knowledge? How can you benchmark them?

This is an ongoing process of gathering and correcting the right information. When I started my video-based training business, I knew nothing about making and marketing videos, but I kept learning. I tried to get the best information I could get. When I discovered something better, I changed and improved.

To release your potential, you need to correct the misinformation that you have stored about life and business. How do you know where your misinformation is? ***Ask wise and experienced people, do some reflective thinking, and keep a journal.*** There are musts if you're going to grow. You have 50,000 thoughts going through your mind every day. You need to capture your best thinking, reflect on your decisions and actions, and then make affirmations to correct misinformation by reading, studying, going to the library, making a phone call, asking questions, and listening to your inner wisdom.

Trusting Yourself

Often we think we've got to override the whole system, but I learned a long time ago to program properly the right skills, the right information, and then relax. You want to consciously prepare and let your subconscious take action. You're at your creative best when you flow.

Trust how smart you are, trust your genius, trust you'll come up with the answer, trust you'll be inventive. Relax and trust. You are so much smarter on the subconscious level than you are on the conscious level.

I'm at my superstar best when I just let it flow. Sometimes when I teach, I don't have the slightest idea of what I'm going to say or what I've said. I only know the end result I want. I visualize the end result and let it flow. I may study hard ahead of time to put knowledge and information in my mind, but then I visualize the end result and let it flow.

Once in Chicago, I was scheduled to be a keynote speaker at the "Million Dollar Club" convention. There were thousands of people in the audience, and the lights were flashing, music was playing, and one motivational speaker after another preceded me on the program. The Club officials asked me to arrive a day early to go through rehearsal. But I showed up 15 minutes before I was scheduled to speak. They were frantic. They told me what to do, and asked, "Where's your speech? You were supposed to have it here." I said, "I haven't thought of it yet." They were stunned.

I did this on purpose. I knew what I was doing. I had studied and prepared in my own way, and I wanted to walk on the stage deliberately not knowing what I'd talk about.

I got a standing ovation, but I made my speech up as I went along. I wasn't even sure what I'd said until I watched the video.

You'll be at your best when you work hard to prepare well and then let it go. This is a free-flowing process. I'm not talking about duplicating something you've already done successfully. I'm talking about stretching, throwing yourself out into the unknown. Knowing how to use the creative subconscious will help you see how you can set goals, take charge of your future, self-regulate, create opportunity, solve problems, and make better decisions.

chapter 5

OVERCOMING BLIND SPOTS

ARE you hearing all the answers—or just the ones you want to hear? Are you seeing all the possibilities—or just the ones you've been conditioned to see?

I would submit that you don't see what is, you see what you've been conditioned to see. For example, read this sentence one time. As you read, count the number of letter F's that you see in the sentence.

FINISHED FILES ARE THE RESULT OF YEARS OF SCIENTIFIC STUDY COMBINED WITH THE EXPERIENCE OF MANY YEARS.

How many *F*'s did you see? There are six *F*'s in that sentence. If you don't believe it, look carefully again. Why don't you see them all the first time?

For years you've been reading English phonetically. The *F* in "of" is pronounced *OV*, not *OF*. And once your mind is conditioned *OV*, you build a blind spot to the *F* in the word "of." Trying hard doesn't do it. In fact, the better reader you are, the more likely you will miss it. You're so caught up in the phonics that you block out the *F*'s. But a graphic designer, multi-linguist, sight reader, or proofreader might easily pick them up.

Seeing the Hole in the Rug

Once I came home from a trip and saw that Diane had company seated in our living room right in front of the fireplace. I decided to join them. As I was drinking a glass of wine with the company, I noticed that while I was gone, somebody burned a big hole in our carpet. Diane did not even mention it when I talked to her on the phone. And she was now just drinking wine with the company, as if nothing had happened.

81

I got upset. But not wanting to make a fool of myself in front of the company, I whispered to Diane, "Can we talk in the hall for a minute?"

Once out of earshot, I asked, "What in the hell happened to our rug?"

She said, "Didn't I tell you when you called?"

Now what difference would that have made? Even if she had told me about the hole, what could I have done about it on the airplane? Nothing, except imagine the hole in my mind and be prepared for the shock.

Diane then explained how it happened. "Bob Olson, who used to work for us, was cleaning the fireplace. He put the ashes from the night before into a plastic bucket. He then moved the bucket off the hearth onto the rug to sweep the hearth. But the hot cinders from the night before burned a hole in the bucket...and in our rug."

Before I could respond, she continued, "I called the man at the rug repair store, and he promised that he'd fix it tomorrow."

Now why would she say that? So I could see a resolution to the problem. But I wasn't falling for that, and she knew it. So she went right out into the hall, brought in a small oriental rug, and put it over the hole in the carpet. How come? No feedback, no problem.

If you don't see the hole in the rug, you tend to forget there's a problem. In fact, after a week you get used to the oriental rug and become blind to the hole. That's called a scotoma.

Scotomas influence perception. Look at this illustration.

"My wife and my mother-in-law." First published in *Puck*, 1915.

Is this an old woman or a young lady? The answer is yes. There is both an old woman and a young lady there. But if you only see the one, you build a scotoma to the other. If you lock on to the old woman, you lock out the young lady. When you lock on to the young lady, you lock out the old woman.

Can you see both? It's tough because you have difficulty holding two conflicting thoughts or "pictures" in your mind at the same time. If you see the old lady first, you think, "Got it. It's the old lady." And that becomes your belief; it becomes "the truth." If somebody says, "No, it's a *young* lady," you say, "You're crazy. I know what I see."

Sometimes we lock on to tradition. "It's the way we've always done it. If there were another way, we'd see it, wouldn't we?" The answer is no. Sometimes we make snap judgments by locking on too quickly and closing our minds to other options.

The Pygmalion Principle

In your mind, if you get a picture of how you want something to turn out, if you hold that picture in your mind, the way you behave toward the people in the situation will often illicit the behavior you expect of them. This is known as the Pygmalion principle.

The person named Pygmalion exists only in Greek mythology. Pygmalion was such a good sculptor that one time he sculpted the statue of a lady with such beauty and likeness that the guy fell in love with the statue and wanted to marry it. So, along came the goddess of love, took an arrow, shot it into the heart of the statue and transformed the statue into a real woman.

The Pygmalion principle is this: When we treat other people in ways that are consistent with the image we hold of them, they tend to behave and become like the image.

Remember the movie *My Fair Lady* based on the Pygmalion principle? Remember Eliza Doolittle and Professor Higgins? Professor Higgins thought he was such a good manager, coach, and teacher that he could take the lowliest flower girl off the streets of London, and, by improving her speech and manners and appearance, pass her off as royalty just to win the bet. So he did. And he won his bet. But when Eliza was talking to her friend, she said, "I will always be a flower girl to Professor Higgins, because he'll always see me as a flower girl. But I will always be a lady to you because you always see me and treat me like a lady."

Professor Higgins never let go of his perception of Eliza at the entry level. Don't you do that sometimes to the people around you? You hold an image of what they were, and you don't allow them to change and progress. You may also do that to yourself. You know every mistake you've ever made. You know all your messes, your fears, and your short-comings. You know what went wrong and you carry that with you in this historical self-image, and you don't allow yourself to rise above it.

Are you constantly blinding yourself to aspects of the truth that don't match what you believe? For example, do you ever look for something, and tell yourself you lost it? As soon as you say, "I lost it," your subconscious becomes blind to the object. Your subconscious is more concerned with proving that you aren't crazy for believing what you believe than with discovering the truth. So, if you tell yourself that you've lost your keys, what would make you look crazy? *Finding them!* Your subconscious says, "Oh, you lost your keys?" and so it builds a blind spot to your keys. The keys can be six inches away, but you won't see them. Then somebody will come along and say, "Here they are. You're looking right at them!" And you will then say, "Who *moved* them? They weren't there a minute ago."

Our image of present reality is only a partial picture. Our physical sens-es are limited. For example, we can only see between red and violet. Even when there's light beyond the red-violet spectrum, without augmenting our vision with special glasses or scopes, we might deny it existed. If we want to see details of the planets, we need a telescope; if we want to see inside the human body, we need an X-ray; if we want to look into a living cell, we need a microscope. So, what else are we missing about reality?

We hear low-pitch sound at about 50 vibrations per second and high-pitch at about 19,500. Did you ever blow a dog whistle? You hear no sound come out, and yet the dog responds because dogs hear at about 24,000 vibrations per second—well beyond our range. Bats hear at 80,000, and some porpoises at an even higher rate. There are sounds in our environment we don't even know about.

Our sense of smell is also very limited compared to animals who rely on it for protection and to find food. A world record holder for the sense of smell is the male silkworm moth, who can detect the odor of the female moth more than a mile away. And that female moth emits only .001 of a milligram of the odor-producing chemical!

Our senses are limited in detecting the outside reality in which we live our lives. We still haven't discovered all there is to be discovered, and we can't perceive all there is to perceive. So we can't go by what is *appar-ent*. What is apparent may be only what we've allowed ourselves to see.

Lock On, Lock Out

We tend to think that we know the truth when we see it, but we can look right at something and not see it. We tend to lock on to conventional and conditioned ways of thinking, which lock out options that would be open to us through possibility thinking—seeing beyond convention or conditioning and focusing on what we want in life.

Possibility thinkers constantly search for options and new ways to get things done. If one way doesn't work, they try another—until they win.

Ask yourself, "Do I lock on more to the problem than the solution? Would I *see* the solution if it was right in front of me? Or have I built a blind spot that says, 'It can't be done?' "

When talking about blind spots, I use the word *scotoma,* which is Greek for blindness. When someone complains, "I don't get it" or "It doesn't make sense to me," he or she has a scotoma. Scotoma is when your senses lock out the environment. It's not just visual, it can affect *all* the senses. You can be in a conversation and not hear what the other person says; you can be having fun at a party and not smell the smoke from a fire outside; you might not taste something you normally hate in your food; you could be boxing, and not feel the punch that breaks your nose.

Scotomas cause us to see what we expect to see, hear what we expect to hear, think what we expect to think. "They can't win—they never do." "She won't go out with me—she never does." "We can't sell to that company—we never have." This blocking out of optional truths around us is common. When you lock on to an opinion, belief, or attitude, you build scotomas to anything that doesn't verify what you believe. You become a prisoner to preconceived ways of seeing things and habitual ways of doing things.

Scotomas block change, flexibility, and creativity because they make us gather information selectively. When you see the old lady, you blind yourself to the young.

Scotomas cause friendships to dissolve, marriages to fail, nations to go to war. Each side thinks, "What's the matter with you? Are you blind?" Frankly, the answer is yes. *Everybody* has blind spots.

Once you understand scotomas, you will begin to see many more options and opportunities in your life. You will apply this to the way you look at your business, your children, your spouse, your clients, your friends, your career, and yourself.

When we lock on, we lock out. What have you locked on to about your life? Have you locked on that "I can't win," "This won't sell," "She's no good," "He's all right," "That won't work," "This will work"? Be aware that you manipulate your very senses by these conclusions. You blind yourself to options, even when you're immersed in them.

Have you ever been around people who lock on forever? They don't see any other option. "This is how I live. There *is* no other way." "I've been in this relationship forever. There *is* no other relationship." "It's tradition in this company. My grandfather did it this way, my father did it this way, and I do it this way. There *is* no other way." For them, there is no other way. Why? Because when they lock on that this is the *only* way, they build a scotoma to options, no matter what you say or do or show them. They sincerely believe, "I know the truth when I see it."

Seeing New Options

When I was coach at Kennedy High School, I had my players for four years, so I thought I knew them very well. I would lock on to my opinion of their capability. That made me dumb and blind. I was so locked on to what I thought was *the truth* about everybody else, that I could never see my players clearly. My self-esteem was so low that it had blocked me from listening to the kids on my team. "What would people think if I asked the *players* what to do? After all, *I* was supposed to know it all." I knew I didn't know it all, but my low self-esteem made me too embarrassed to ask for help.

You may be the same way. When you see a new option for the first time, you'll be very embarrassed. You'll say to yourself, "Why didn't I see that before?"

Often we don't know we have a blind spot. We continue our daily routines—raising a family, running a business, doing our jobs—in a state of semi-myopia. We don't see all the optional truths around us. Scotomas not only prevent us from finding the solution, they also block us from seeing the problem. "It's right in front of your nose!" "No, it isn't. Where?" "Over *there!*" "Well, it wasn't there before. Who *moved* it?"

Did you ever argue with your children or spouse, and say, "It's so obvious! How can you deny it? You're just being stubborn and belligerent!" You see the young lady, and they only see the old. They think you're crazy, and you think they're nuts!

But scotomas can be highly constructive. The lock-on process—building your own scotomas to outside distractions—helps you focus intently on the challenge at hand. You lock on to achieve a goal: to make more money, create a successful marriage, make a speech or throw a football under pressure.

However, this very ability to concentrate single-mindedly on an objective can become your weakness. Because you *are* so strong and opinionated and because you need that very strength to win, you may be blind to the other options. Along with distractions, you may also be locking out a better way.

We look at successful people, and often we say, "They're lucky.

Things break well for them." *Are* they lucky? Or do they just see more than you see? Do they see *differently?* A different point of view can suddenly open up so much more.

What sets high-performance people apart is that they have fewer scotomas than other people. They are intensely focused on their goals, yet they remain skeptical and analytical. They recognize that they don't see the whole truth, so they take creative risks in search of *more* truth. As the quantity of truth that they see increases, so do the lucky *breaks* in their lives. That has little to do with coincidence, intelligence, or luck—it has to do with the way that they think.

When you apply these principles, you will gain more open-mindedness, flexibility, option thinking—"What can I be? What can I do? What don't I see? How can I see it?" *Now* if I don't know something—or if I think I have a scotoma to it—I say, *"Please show me."*

As you learn to use these skills, your life will *break* better for you. Every time you look around, you'll see an option you never saw before: "I'll be darned. Look at that. There's another one."

Scotoma Busting

We must keep an open mind and hold the belief: ***The answers are there. I just don't see them yet. But I will see them soon.*** And we must believe that about ourselves and others.

If I lock on that you don't have what it takes, it'll be difficult for you to succeed. I will build a scotoma to anything you do that would make me look crazy for believing what I believe. You could struggle to improve, but if I believe that you were born without it, I won't see you making the grade.

You may have to become a *Scotoma Buster* for yourself and others by learning how to see what you may not presently see; how to make life easier for yourself and your children. You've got to learn to resist negative conditioning. You've got to keep reminding yourself: *"The answers are there. I just don't see them yet. But I will see them soon."* You've got to *un*condition yourself in areas where you're working too hard to make things happen. With that approach, you'll be off on a great treasure hunt: "I'll find out how. I'll find solutions along the way."

Ask yourself the big questions: "What have I locked on to about me? What attitudes, beliefs, truths?" Once you label yourself, you build scotomas to other things you can be. There are options and alternatives, if you're open-minded and flexible.

The only difference between average and high-performance people—those who constantly seem to get the *breaks*—is that *they see more* because *they think differently.*

As you change the way you *think*, you change the way you *are*. Progress starts in the mind, where *thoughts accumulate to build beliefs*. If you accumulate false or partially true beliefs about your capabilities and potential, then that's how you'll behave.

How would you behave if you believed "It is easier for a camel to slip through the eye of a needle than it is for a rich man to get to heaven?" If you had the opportunity to be rich—but you also wanted to go to heaven someday—your subconscious would cause you to push away riches with both hands. It's not just money. If you believe, for example, that because of a mistake you made in the past, you don't deserve happiness, then every time happiness approaches you'll shove it away with both hands. And you'll wonder why your life isn't going so well.

Years ago, I worked with some ex-convicts. One man, Emmett, had just gotten out of prison after being in for a long time. He was about 60, and he'd been a drunk and a burglar. After I taught Emmett, he decided, "I'll go legitimate." He chose the upholstery business—reupholstering furniture. He'd never been in business before, but he'd learned that skill in prison.

He had a problem, though. He needed a sewing machine that cost hundreds of dollars, but all Emmett had was $56. Right away, he figured "I can't do it." I said, "How do you know that?" He said, "Well, Don told me." Don was a prisoner inside Walla Walla who'd been locked up for 13 years. He was the tough guy who ran the prison, and he knew it all. So the information that Emmett got from Don was that ex-convicts can't get credit. To Emmett, that was "the truth."

I said, "Why don't you try it?" Finally, he did. And somehow he got a sewing machine on credit. He came back to one of our follow-up sessions and told me his success story. He said, "I went in and put my $56 down, and the guy *gave* me a sewing machine on credit!" Emmett then added, "The guy didn't even ask me if I was a convict!" He got his sewing machine because he kept his old attitude from sabotaging his goal.

How to See a — Study this difficult puzzle by concentrating on the objects in black.

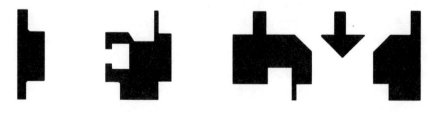

The easiest one to identify is an arrow. The next easiest one is a comb with some teeth broken away from the top and bottom. Got the comb? Can you also see the silhouette of an Indian brave's head with a feather on top? How about a log cabin with a chimney? The toughest is the letter "F." Can you see that? How about the letter "L"? The letter "Y"? Can you see the word "FLY" in there?

Language influences your perception, your beliefs, your behavior. You've got to contest what people tell you. Because if they say, "It'll take you five years to get that job" or "The word 'FLY' is the toughest to see"—and you *believe* them—your subconscious will say, "Sure enough" and you'll act like your belief.

So—can you see the word "FLY"? Not yet? Does this help?

It should jump right out at you. You were looking right at it, you just didn't see it. One reason is because *the letters in the first illustration are in white with black spacing*—and most of us have built a scotoma to that. Blind spots are the result of how we've been *conditioned* to see the world. For years, you were conditioned to read black lettering with white spacing. When you look at white lettering with black spacing, you can't see the letters.

Another reason you had trouble seeing "FLY" was that I focused you on the objects in black, not the letters in white. I said, "There's a comb, there's an arrow, there's a brave's head." Then you saw what you *expected* to see—a comb, an arrow, a brave's head. And you missed the only thing that really *is* there: the word "FLY."

A third reason you had a problem was that I said it would be very difficult to see the word "FLY." If you accepted that, your subconscious said, "Fine. I'll *make* it difficult." You told yourself, "This will be hard," and then that's what you expected. So, sure enough, it *was* hard.

Who blocked you from seeing "FLY"? *You* did. You might say, "Something's wrong with me. I didn't get it. I must be stupid." No. It's just that your conditioning wouldn't let you see.

This happens all the time. If you're not careful, you will constantly imprint a false opinion of yourself into your subconscious: "I'm not good enough. I can't do it. I don't have what it takes." But it has nothing to do with intelligence or aptitude. It has to do with conditioning.

When I first found the word "FLY," I was on an airplane, and I read it in a magazine—on the *children's* page. I had to look up the solution in the back. I was so disgusted with myself, I tore the page out. When I got home, Diane was in the living room. I hurried in, held the page up and said, "Diane, tell me what you see here." I couldn't wait to surprise her.

Right away she said, "FLY." Darn, that made me mad. I didn't tell her I had to look it up. I said, "How did you see that so quickly?" She said, "In art classes, we were taught to look at spacing first, and then lettering." So her conditioning made the word "FLY" practically jump right out at her, while all I saw were arrows and combs with missing teeth.

That's going to be true of some of your future associates, employers, supervisors, coaches, and teachers. They're going to know it says "FLY." They won't be brighter than you; their conditioning will just match the situation. When Diane found the word "FLY" so quickly, I could have felt stupid. I could have said, "I don't have it!" and quit. But I knew better.

The main reason we don't see the word "FLY" is because *we don't see only with our eyes. We see with our mind as well.* That's also why we can't find new business or new resources. We only perceive light with our eyes, and then our brain interprets the light based upon how we've been conditioned to interpret the light. If what we're *looking at* doesn't match what we've been *conditioned* to see, we won't see it at all.

So your senses leave out the word "FLY" for the same reason they leave out information that could help you achieve your goals. You could be looking right at a new job, new customers, finances. But if your past conditioning doesn't match what you're looking at, you'll conclude "There's no way. It's not there." "I looked everywhere and there's no money." "I looked a hundred times and there is no 'FLY.' "

Throughout your life, you'll meet many people who will tell you why you aren't ready yet, and what you have to do to get ready. If you believe them, you'll be seeing combs with broken teeth when you should be seeing "FLY." If you're not careful, scotomas can sabotage your success without your knowing it.

How will you ever see what you're conditioned *not* to see? You possess a remarkable device that can help you see whatever you want to see. You can program it an unlimited number of times to help you find whatever you want. Once you learn how to use it properly, it'll be like money in the bank.

Barriers That Block Growth

When you determine to become much more than you presently are, you encounter barriers to block your growth. Often, the barriers are not the circumstances *outside* you. They're the way you think *inside*—the way you view yourself and the rest of the world. Your belief system can prevent you from using your potential. Sensory barriers can block you from the real truth, sealing in your old beliefs and blocking out the new. That's why doing more and improving the quality of your life won't be a matter of working harder but of *thinking differently*.

We think and act not in accordance with the real truth, but the truth as we believe it. Our self-image causes us to behave exactly as we believe ourself to be—whether it's good for us or not. *If we change the way we think, we change the way we act.*

Nine Dots. To understand what holds you back, try this puzzle. Using a pencil, try to connect the nine dots with just four straight lines—without lifting your pencil from the paper or retracing any of the lines.

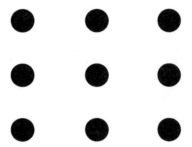

Can you do it? Looks simple, doesn't it? It isn't. If you can't find the solution, don't feel embarrassed. The person who gave me this puzzle gave me a few *weeks* to figure it out—and I couldn't do it. Extra time doesn't help. Neither does trying harder. Why is it so difficult? *Because of how we think.*

What holds most of us back is that we try to solve the problem by working within the confines of the nine dots. To solve it, we have to venture *outside* the dots.

Now, you might argue, "You didn't *say* we could cross the lines." That's right. But I didn't say you *couldn't*. You did. Or you might claim, "You didn't *say* we could go outside the dots." But I didn't say you *couldn't*. You did. You gave yourself limitations that weren't there. We all do that: "I can't quit my job; I don't know anything else," "Oh, I'm too old," "I'm too young," "I'm not the right color," "I'm not the right sex," "I'm too tall," "I'm too short," or "There's no way."

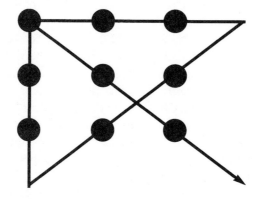

This limited thinking blocks you the same way as when you trapped yourself inside the nine dots: "Oh, I *can't* cross the lines. I *can't* go outside the dots." You constantly block yourself by the way you think—about your business, your future career, your finances, your capabilities. Your limiting thoughts recur all the time. You could be driving with your spouse, who might suggest, "Let's visit the Taylors." And you might say, "We can't. They're probably not home." A friend might say, "Why don't you try for that job?" and you say, "They wouldn't hire me anyway. I don't have what they want." Or a business associate suggests, "Let's call this client" and you say, "No. They'd never buy our product."

We limit ourselves by the way that we think. We must learn to think outside of our limitations.

Flat-World Thinking

At the time of Columbus, many people believed the world was flat. Knowing the world was flat, they'd sail out only so far because they *knew* that disaster was just ahead. Then they'd lose their courage, turn around, and come back. But to them, coming back wasn't losing courage. They thought, "If we sail any farther, whoops, off the edge we go."

So here comes Columbus with these crazy notions of an earth without edges! People thought, "Why's this nut allowed to walk the streets like we *sane* folk?" So his problem wasn't just what *he* believed, his problem was also, "How do I get *someone else* to believe it, so I can get financing to prove it?" It's the same in your company or your family. "I know this approach will work. How can I convince the others it will work?"

If I'm Columbus and I come into your bank for a loan and I lay the blueprints in front of you, what do you say? "Boy, those are very big ships. What on this flat earth will you use them for?" And I say, "I'm sorry you asked that. I've heard speculation that the earth is round. I want to sail out there and prove it." You look at me like I'm crazy, and you say, "Not with *our* money."

Now, for me to win, I can't just walk away, thinking, "That's stupid." I have to recognize that people have their own beliefs, and they aren't being deliberately obstinate. They just don't see—and they think I'm nuts. So, for me to win, I've got to assume accountability to help them see.

Do you know the loser's motto? It's not "If at first you don't succeed, try, try again." It's, "If at first you don't succeed, *fix the blame fast*. It isn't *me!* It's these people I have to work with. *I* know the world's round. Why don't *they* know it?" Because you weren't good enough to show them.

Now, once Columbus got the money, he had another problem: getting a crew. You think you have problems leading your family or your company? Columbus had to convince a crew to sail with him off the edge of their flat earth!

You and I face the same challenge today. Everybody has flat worlds inside them. For example, you may know that your kids have potential, that they're bright, but the problem is, "How do I get my *kids* to see what they can do?" That's what you must overcome. To do that, you must be willing to accept that the earth might be round. And you must be ready to sail out there to see for yourself. If you change your level of expectation and belief, you can change your performance. The belief makes it so.

Remember: Before Columbus believed strongly enough that the earth was round, the earth in effect *was* flat, wasn't it? Yet, where is that flat earth today?

Reflect on the beliefs that are presently controlling your behavior on the job, with your family, in your relationships. To change the way you act, you need to change the way you think. You need to become an option-thinker, a creative thinker, a possibility-thinker. You need to open up your own flat-world thinking. You must ask yourself, "What attitudes, what habits, what skills, what beliefs have I locked on to that are no longer relevant?" Eventually, to grow and change, you must overcome your flat-world "truths."

When you encounter a nine-dots situation in your life, instead of saying, "It can't be done," ask, "What if I cross the lines? What if I go outside the dots?" Like Columbus, you can become an explorer of all the "what if's." That's the route to success.

c h a p t e r   6

POSITIVE SELF-TALK AND SELF-IMAGE

O NE time, one of my girls wanted to try out for cheerleader at school, but at the last minute she opted not to try out. I thought that she would have been a very good cheerleader, so I asked her, "Why did you quit? You can't get into a pattern where you fold and don't follow through on something you want."

Then she got mad at me and said, "Well, I didn't want to try and fail. You never fail. You always win at everything. You're always successful."

Her answer startled me because I didn't think she thought that about me. I started thinking, "She doesn't see all the times when I fail, all the places where I lose, all the things that don't go right. She only sees the success of our business or our life."

I said to her, "All you see are the things that are successful. You don't see that I start 10 things and lose at six or seven of them. You only see the three or four things that go right. And so now you say, 'I've got to be perfect. My parents are perfect. People around me are perfect. They never screw up.' But that's not true."

What happens to your self-talk, self-esteem, and goal-setting ability if you think others are perfect and you're flawed? You don't start things. You don't go after goals that are worthy of you. If you get that feeling or belief that you can't make a mistake or that everybody is always successful, you won't let yourself do things that you're capable of doing, or you set your goals so close to the end of your nose that they're easily attainable. You never stretch to be what you're capable of being.

You need confidence or reassurance that you can attain the vision and reach the goal even when you don't have the slightest idea how you're going to get there at the outset.

Low self-esteem won't let you set your goal too far out. If you set a stretch goal, you then think, "I'll never get there being me, and so I've got to override the system."

Imagine yourself fishing off the stern of a boat that's heading north. You're not catching any fish, so you decide to change the boat's direction. You grab the steering wheel and turn the boat to the east. Then you let go of the wheel and head back to the stern. As you do, the boat starts swinging back to the north on its own because you forgot to adjust the automatic pilot system. You only tried to override it.

You can *temporarily* act brave if you're scared; you can *temporarily* act outgoing if you're shy; you can *temporarily* act calm if you're mad. You can override your automatic pilot system anytime. But if you don't change the picture of who you are, the moment you let go of the steering wheel, the automatic pilot will kick in and draw you back again. You'll feel the strain and regress.

There's a better way. You can learn to turn the boat to the east without ever touching the steering wheel. How? Just change the automatic pilot system, and the boat will automatically go east.

The automatic pilot, of course, is your self-image. It determines the direction you lean—east or north, positive or negative.

Smart Talk Gets You There

How do you change your self-image? *By controlling and changing your self-talk.* Constructive self-talk is what I call *Smart Talk*.

Self-talk is the continual dialogue you have with yourself. It is also the raw material from which you manufacture your own self-image: "Oh, I'm clumsy," "I'm graceful," "It's easy for me," "It's hard for me."

Your subconscious believes what you tell yourself, and then makes sure you act according to your belief. Language has power over behavior. If you control your self-talk, you can use your subconscious to help you achieve your goals.

When you observe an event in the external world—in your community, your family, your marriage, your career—you don't record the actual event. You *interpret* it with your own self-talk. You tell yourself what you think is happening: "She was angry, but she didn't mean what she said. I know what she *really* meant." If you know that the world you perceive through your senses is only your *version* of the world, then you realize you can change it anytime you choose. You can't change the event, but you can change your interpretation of the event by controlling your self-talk.

Remember: You move toward, and become like, that which you think about. Your present thoughts determine your future. Whatever you repeatedly tell yourself with your own self-talk determines your beliefs and self-image, which affect your behavior. Unless you change your stored beliefs by changing your self-talk, you won't alter your behavior. Your future will look a lot like your past.

Suppose your boss fires you, and you tell yourself, "I'm worthless without this job. I don't want to live." You may choose to kill yourself, directly or indirectly. Who's responsible for your behavior—your boss or you?

Now change the scenario. After being fired, instead of telling yourself, "I'm worthless. I don't want to live," you think, "I wasn't growing there anyway. Now I can find a much better job." And you look for another job.

Who's responsible for your behavior—your boss or you? You are responsible. Because it isn't the event—the firing—that causes your behavior. It's the way you choose to *interpret* the event. "I'm worthless" is your self-talk version of what happened to you. "I don't want to live" is your self-talk *truth*." Instantly, that most obedient slave, your creative subconscious, says, "Okay, whatever you want"—even if it means self-destruction.

Thoughts accumulate to build beliefs. Have you ever made a mistake and asked yourself, "What's the matter with me, anyway?" Each time you and I allow ourselves to dwell on negative self-talk (dumb talk), we add weight to our negative beliefs about ourselves. If you had a friend who talked to you the way you talk to yourself sometimes, would you keep that friend very long?

Be very selective about what you tell yourself. You can talk yourself into or out of, toward or away from, anything. Attitudes are neither right nor wrong, good nor bad—except in relation to something you *value*. Yesterday's old pictures, accumulated through self-talk, may make you lean away from something that is of great value and benefit to you today—or toward something of great harm.

If I only had one thing to teach my grandchildren, I would teach them how *reality* is built. Reality isn't built just once—it's always being built. You think it was just done when we were children? Sure, in the first five years that reality is strongly formed. But it isn't over. Our subconscious image of reality is built by the way that we think and talk, especially by the way we talk to ourselves in words, images, and emotions.

Self-talk is the conversation that you carry on in your own mind. Every thought is assimilated in your brain, and every thought accumulates to build beliefs. "So what?" you ask. You self-regulate at your belief level, not your potential level. You build your own beliefs with your own thoughts—beliefs about business, about wealth, about relationships, about your potential, about whether you're a morning person or a night person, a smart person or a dumb person. You do that by how you speak to yourself.

Events don't need to keep occurring for you to build a belief. You can relive one occurrence thousands of times in your mind. All you have to do is replay the image. Every time you remind yourself about an event with your self-talk, you visualize it as though it's happening again. Usually, one thought doesn't make a solid *take* on the subconscious level. There *are* exceptions, such as one-time affirmations from authority figures, marriage vows, graduation ceremonies, prayers, and sacred oaths or covenants. But, for the most part, it takes repetition. The event itself does not have to recur because when you *think* about something vividly, your subconscious believes that it's actually happening.

Any time you imagine something vividly and you feel the related emotions, it makes a solid imprint and becomes *reality*. Every time you remember it, you reinforce the image. *Remember: You move toward and become that which you think about. Your present thoughts determine your future. Smart Talk will mean a better future.*

Self-Image Formed by Self-Talk

Your *self-image* is your subconscious opinion of you—based upon the countless beliefs and attitudes you've recorded in your *data bank.* It's your inner *picture* of who you are and what you expect of yourself. "I'm outgoing," "I'm shy," "I'm a fast learner," "I don't like books," "I have rhythm," "I can't dance," "I'm popular," "I'm a loner." Your *picture* is a composite of everything you've learned.

You build your own self-image by what you sanction of what is said about you. A self-image is the standard by which you self-regulate. You build this standard with your every thought, and you self-regulate around it. Every time you perceive yourself beneath it, you correct up. If you perceive yourself above it, you correct back.

The key to releasing your wonderful potential and achieving your goals is how you talk to yourself and to the people around you.

When we belittle another person, we ask them to *be little*. When we devalue another person, we ask them to be less than they are. I belittle others more when my self-esteem, my feeling of worth, is down. I then use biting words to make people littler than I am; in effect, I say, "Be littler than I am, so that I can look bigger."

Rather than tell ourselves and others "Be little," we ought to say, "Be big—big in esteem, big in value, big in worth." And yet we use words to belittle, to make our associates, children, spouses, parents, feel smaller than we are—not in physical stature but in attitude, confidence, courage.

Belittling means, "I want you to be of less significance so that I am of more significance." Instead of going about it the right way—making myself more significant by improving my character attributes, knowledge, and skills—I try to make people around me less significant by devaluing them.

What does devalue mean? How do you make a person of less value? You say, "Oh, she's not so hot; I know this about her. I don't know why you think he's so powerful. I will show you that he has less power than you think."

How tragic it is to belittle ourselves and others when we could be building feelings of esteem, worth and value. Children, and other so-called *little people* in your life, especially need you to build their esteem.

How might you build a good self-image in a child? Suppose a three-year-old boy is learning how to draw. He colors a picture, thinks he has done something well, and so he seeks the approval of an authority, a five-year-old sister who has her art displayed on the refrigerator. So, he runs up to his sister and says, "Look, look what I did."

The sister says, "What is it? Stupid, you didn't even color inside the lines."

Now the boy accepts and gives sanction to her appraisal. "Sister says I'm dumb and stupid and can't draw." As this self-talk goes on in his mind, he puts a great big, negative weight on his attitudinal balance scale, which causes him to lean in a negative direction with the belief "I can't draw because sister says so."

He draws another picture, and this time he shows it to an older brother and says, "Look what I did."

Now brother doesn't want to be bothered, and so he says, "Get out of here, stupid. You can't draw."

If the boy gives sanction to his brother's appraisal, his thoughts accumulate to build the belief: "I'm stupid and can't draw."

Suppose that now he spends all day painting the best picture of his life. He shows it to his mom and says, "Look what I did."

She wrinkles her nose and says, "My goodness. What have you done? That's awful."

Now, what is that kid thinking? "Boy, I can't draw. And that's the truth."

Now, when he goes to kindergarten, the teacher says, "All right, class, we've got a wonderful surprise today. We're going to pass out the crayons, and we're all going to draw."

That boy thinks, "No, I'm not. The last time I drew, I felt like I got my feelings hurt. I can't draw."

You act, not in accordance with your potential, but in accordance with the truth as you see it. When you treat people negatively, when you devalue and belittle them, you damage their self-image of reality if they sanction it. And they will sanction it if you have credibility with them as a leader, parent, spouse, or sibling.

You have beliefs and expectations about every aspect of your life—what kind of person you are morally, socially, spiritually, intellectually. So, in a sense, you don't have just one self-image, you have thousands.

For example, you have a belief about what kind of leader you are—and within that belief, you may have self-images. You may think, "I'm a leader on my softball team and as a teacher at school, but I'm *not* a leader in my community or church." You also have an opinion about what kind of athlete you are. You may say, "I'm great at tennis, golf, and bowling, but I'm a lousy swimmer." You've recorded a self-image for every skill or experience, real or imagined. Each one is built with a belief, and these beliefs control your life.

Remember: We think and act not in accordance with the real truth, but the truth as we believe it. If you build your self-image on negative beliefs, those beliefs are recorded in your mind as "Just like me," and that's how you behave. If you don't change your beliefs, you can't change your self-image—and you will continue to act as you believe yourself to be.

At some point, you may wonder, "How did I get these beliefs?" You acquired them through your own self-talk—the conversations you have with yourself in your own mind. Thoughts make up those silent conversations, and *thoughts accumulate to build beliefs*. We think in *words*, which trigger *pictures*, which bring about *emotions*. Your thoughts and emotions are recorded in your brain as *the truth*. Then you start reinforcing *the truth* with your "Just like me" behavior. So your self-talk is the foundation of your self-image.

Focusing on What You *Don't* Want

Often, what you fear most comes upon you because when your self-talk imprints in your mind—when you give it sanction—it controls your behaviors. If you dwell on something you *don't* want to happen, you will subconsciously move toward it.

Do you know any accident-prone people? What do you suppose they think about? *Having accidents*! The insurance industry knows that most accidents are caused by accident-prone people who are looking for each other. When you *know* you're accident-prone, you create an accident.

To the degree that you focus on what you don't want, you are drawn in that direction. You can sit around with others and talk about what's wrong in life, but your negative, destructive talk will only keep you away from what you want. The positive way to think is, "What will it look like when we *don't* have the problem? What will things look like when they're *fixed*?"

What you focus on is what you get. For example, once you learn the skills of driving a car, driving becomes an unconscious habit. You simply picture where you *want* the car to go, and you automatically turn the steering wheel in that direction. You don't have to consciously think, "Turn left, turn right, foot on the brake, foot on the gas." You automatically adjust according to the image you hold in your mind of where you want to go. So how do accidents occur? They occur when you start picturing what you don't want to happen.

Imagine yourself teaching a teenager to drive. The kid's driving down the road, crowding the center line, and you visualize a head-on collision any minute. So you say, "Watch out for the oncoming cars." Where does the kid look? At the oncoming cars! Automatically, his subconscious tells him, "Aim for those cars!" When the kid drifts over the center line, you get upset and say, "Get over on the curb!" Those words trigger another picture, and the kid drives right onto the curb! You get mad and say, "Watch out for that parked car!" Smack! Right into the parked car. You then fix the blame fast: "It's this problem *kid*! Why won't he *listen* to me?" Well, that's just it: He *did* listen.

What you visualize most vividly is what you get, whether it's good for you or not. For example, if you golf and have a hook or slice that always puts you in the sand or water, what do you tend to think about when you're playing? You reaffirm that you've got this terrible slice. And that produces the perfect slice—just like steering your bike or driving your car. Once your self-talk says "I always slice the ball," your body will automatically recreate your inner picture on the outside so the two pictures match. Not what you *want*, but what you *think about*.

You say, "No, not me." But when you approach the tee on that most treacherous hole, if you really visualize your ball landing on the green, why are you taking out your bad ball? See, the difficulty is in controlling your self-talk. If you know there's a water hazard and you tell yourself, "I don't want to slice the ball into the water," even though you may think you're doing the opposite, your subconscious draws you toward your most dominant picture. The "don't want to" doesn't create a picture. "Water" is the picture, so water is where you're drawn.

But then, as you're walking down the fairway, you say to yourself "There I go again. That's just like me." So you not only slice the ball once when you hit it, but you do it again every time you think about it: "I must have sliced a hundred times if I've sliced once. In fact, I've always had this slice." By the time the game is over, you've mentally *hit* about 500 slices! You're better than you give yourself credit for: you've been slicing so often, you're an *expert* at it!

So, with your self-talk, you're setting yourself up for *failure*. Some people continually set themselves up by anticipating what will go wrong in their marriage, what will go wrong in their company, what will go wrong with their health. Worrying is negative goal-setting. It focuses you on what you *don't* want—so that's exactly what you get.

Business leaders—consider the way you lead your people. Parents—think about how you guide your children. Coaches—how do you run your teams? Spiritual leaders—how are you counseling your people? Are you giving them images of what you *don't* want them to do? Are you leading them into the parked car?

Sanctioning Beliefs

You need to *sanction your own beliefs* and build belief through self-talk. No one else can build a belief within you unless you sanction it. I could tell you that you're the most delightful, wonderful person I've met. But you might think, "What's he up to? What's he want?" You can deny or reject my statement, thinking, "No. I don't believe him."

Who's an authority in your world? Remember when you were nine? The authorities were the kids who were 12. When you're vulnerable in school and you want the grade, you try to please the teacher. "Please tell me coach, could I make the team?" So you're very vulnerable; you need the approval of people you see as authorities. But these people may have ulterior motives or low self-esteem.

Low self-esteem leaders and teachers are the most sarcastic, belittling people to be with. They're always trying to put you in your place, and your place is below them, so they can control you. And if you fall for it, you're caught in a low self-esteem marriage, and you'll never do anything right.

Whatever you choose to accept becomes part of your reality. Nobody can build a belief in you until you *sanction* it first. So be careful whom you listen to. You need not be a victim of what is said to you and around you. Only when you sanction it does it become a part of your image of reality. People can devalue you, call you stupid or incompetent, but you can say, "Who are you to tell me that? You aren't so bright yourself."

But how many people don't know this when they are in school? How many abused spouses haven't got the slightest idea that the husband is a jerk? When he tells her, "Who are you to think you can get a job? You can't even organize the house. Get down where you belong," why do you suppose she falls for that? Because she loves him, or cares for him, or thinks he's an authority.

When children are raised by parents who are negative, sarcastic, and belittling, the kids suffer from poor self-images. I've raised adopted kids, some of whom had self-images so low they could enter a room without even opening the door. They could slide right under it. They know they're of no value, and they behave like it.

On the other hand, when children are raised with very affirming beliefs about themselves, they tend to have high self-esteem and expectations. For example, some of our adopted kids were raised when Diane and I were school teachers, during the vow of poverty. But our daughter, Nancy, came along a couple of years after we started our business and started staying at nice resorts. We constantly affirmed Nancy, and her self-esteem skyrocketed. Once when Nancy was about six years old, we flew to Phoenix and took all the kids. As our other kids were at baggage claim looking for their bags, Nancy was looking for a porter! She didn't think she needed to carry her own bags.

Another time, we went to a beautiful resort in Canada, where we had stayed many times before. We usually had a suite so we could entertain. Nancy was about nine then, and she had invited some friends along. I arrived and checked in early, but our suite wasn't ready, so they put me temporarily in a nice cabin. When Diane and the kids arrived, they received the keys to put their things away. When Nancy got to the cabin, she said, "Dad, we've got the wrong room. They've made a mistake. I would never stay in a place like this." The room was okay for me, but not for Nancy. She knew that she was something special, and she behaved like it.

You build your own self-image with your own thoughts, but when you're little you don't know who to listen to. So it just happens to be the circumstance, the lot you happen to be dropped into, or the environment in which you're raised. And so here you are creating a self-image, and you just think it's you, and so off you go for the rest of your life if you don't change it by behaving like the person you know yourself to be.

Suppose a 10-year-old goes out for football. He gets hit and his nose starts to bleed, so he comes to the sidelines to rest. But his coach says, "You little wimp! Get back out there! We don't want any cowards here."

Now, even that won't make an imprint until the kid starts thinking, *"I don't have what it takes."* That night, the kid can't sleep for thinking about what happened at practice; he reviews it 100 times in his mind. The next morning, he wakes up thinking about it, still feeling the same way. So, within 24 hours, that one event could have happened 200 times in his mind. That's enough to make a deep imprint in his self-image.

Language alone is an empty vehicle. It has to carry the spirit of intent. Even then, you must sanction it before it records as *the truth*. The power is in the *receiver*, not the words or the sender of the words. The power is in you. So the real truth is that you're not the victim of your teacher, your coach, your spouse, your brother, sister, mom, or dad. When you sanction somebody else as an "expert," you become a victim of *you*. As you talk to yourself in your mind, you build your self-image, and you start to self-regulate around it.

Superstar Self-Talk

When I work with athletes, I teach them the power of their self-talk to direct their performance. For example, when I work with football players, I tell them that after they drop the ball, the worst thing they can do is return to the huddle affirming what they just did wrong: "I've got this problem. I'm dropping the ball." If that's the vivid picture they paint with their self-talk, the next time the situation arises, they'll re-create the problem. They'll keep dropping the ball, until they change the automatic pilot.

That's how slumps occur in sports and in life. As you keep affirm-ing the reality that you observe, you keep perpetuating it. What you tell yourself is what you picture, and what you picture is what you get: "I always strike out when it counts." "She makes me sick." "I never make the sale." "We always lose." "I can't get the job." "I've always been poor." It's a self-fulfilling prophecy; you can predict an outcome with your self-talk, and then you make it happen.

If you keep affirming past mistakes, you'll perpetuate them in the future. Instead, affirm what you *want* to achieve, what you *intend* to cre-ate. Replay in your mind only past *successes*, and tell yourself, "That's like me. Next time, I intend to do it again." Such thinking breeds greatness.

One of the real superstars of self-talk is Johnnie Johnson, whom I first met when he played football for the University of Texas. Before every game, he would affirm his abilities and visualize intercepting a pass or returning a punt for a touchdown. In the big Texas-Arkansas game, the punter was kicking the ball either away from him or high and short into a strong wind. But Johnson kept telling himself, "The kicker is going to miss one, so be ready. It only takes one." Finally in the fourth quarter of the tight ballgame, Johnny got his chance...and he returned the punt some 60 yards to set up the winning score.

You manage your self-image by managing your own self-talk. Control your self-talk, and you can change your self-image. Change your self-image, and you can change your life.

Eliminate from your own self-talk and your talk to others all destructive sarcasm—all the devaluation, all the belittling, teasing, demeaning, fault-finding. As you start thinking better of yourself and others, you trigger the images you want.

Take personal responsibility for your thoughts. *You* are responsible for your own health and happiness. Don't fix the blame for your difficulties on circumstances outside yourself, thinking "I have no control." By managing your self-talk, you can became more confident in your ability to create your future. You can begin to feel, "Now I can see the way tomorrow looks. In fact, I can make tomorrow look the way I *want!*"

To change your circumstances outside, you have to change inside first. You are immersed in two realities—internal and external. If you change one, you can change the other. Everyone would like to change their external circumstances, but few know how to do it. Some may think that making more money will bring about the change they want, or driving a particular car, or wearing certain clothes, or marrying the right person. They're wrong. The power doesn't reside in money, material goods, or other people. The power is inside. ***Remember: All meaningful and lasting change starts on the inside first and works its way out.***

But don't think, "Oh well, my image is built. I've fixed it." You've got to keep fixing it. This is a continuous improvement process. The information you sanction affects your perception of reality. Once you lock on, assimilate, or believe that *this is the way the world is*, you don't let yourself perceive other options or other information that does not match what you already believe. You're stuck. That's why groups get stuck. Nations get stuck. Religious groups become prejudiced. It causes bitterness, hostility, death, despair. They don't know they're doing it, they just think: "It's the truth; it's the way the world is."

Your self-image is so powerful that it controls not only what you presently are but also what you will be in the future. It controls how much of your potential you will use. We won't know how much potential we have, nor what we can achieve, until we remove our self-imposed limitations.

We may also need to stop listening to well-meaning people who tell us: "Be happy with what you have, dear. That's good enough for you. If you start expecting things you don't have, it will only make you sick. It's because I love you that I tell you this. If I didn't care, you'd go out and bite off things that are too big for you. I know you. You should be satisfied with stale bread, holes in your shoes, just like me. If you start wanting things on the other side, it will only make you unhappy. So, why don't you just be happy, and not dissatisfied. Be happy with your lot in life. That's good enough for you."

If you buy into such advice from parents, teachers, spouses, coaches or counselors who mean well, you will make sure that the size and scope of your goals—where you allow yourself to go—will be close to what you're already doing.

Fortunately, your self-image is not fixed. If you aren't satisfied with your life, if you aren't happy with how you think or feel or behave, you have an option. You can change your self-image. To be the happy, successful, high-performance person you're capable of being, you'll need to use Smart Talk regularly to boost your self-image and self-esteem.

During the next 24 hours, monitor your self-talk and try to eliminate all the put-downs, hostility, cynicism, devaluation, and belittling of yourself and others. Avoid negative affirmations, such as "What's the matter with me, anyway" or "How could I be so stupid?" Don't allow teasing or sarcasm, even in jest. The subconscious mind doesn't know a joke from a literal put-down. If you put yourself or somebody else down, you must immediately correct by silently affirming, "That's not like me." Then state what you'll do the next time the situation occurs.

This may be the quietest 24 hours you've ever spent in your life. What will you say? Well, positively affirm others. Positively affirm yourself. Tell yourself what you're doing right. Do this very quietly to yourself but out loud to others.

Score each positive put-up and negative put-down about yourself or someone else. After 24 hours, you'll be more aware of your self-talk cycle. Start using Smart Talk to release the inner you.

DIANE'S STORY

Part III: Ask Her About Her Future

LOU: Because so many people cared about Diane, we knew she would have a constant flow of visitors after surgery. Here again, each person's negative expectancy could be communicated through body language, manner, tone of voice. And the question most people would ask would be, "How do you feel?" If so, Diane would need to continually affirm how she felt. After so much repetition, she might get tired and inadvertently say one time, "I don't feel so well" or "I'm scared." We wanted to make sure that she wasn't set up for negative affirmations like that.

I placed family members outside Diane's room to greet people before they entered, and to discuss what they should talk about with her. I had meetings at our company about that. I told our people, "We won't leave anything to chance." I told them that I intended to orchestrate and structure Diane's environment so that it was always positive, hopeful, and future-oriented. At home, we had family conferences about how we could help Diane fight her illness. We said we wouldn't ignore the reality of the cancer, but that we considered it temporary. We visualized the way we *wanted* things to be, and the way things would look if Diane didn't have the problem. Pretty soon, everybody painted the same picture of the environment that we wanted to create around Diane.

While Diane had surgery, I posted a sign outside her hospital door that read:

> If you're here to see Diane,
> You're here to *give* her energy,
> Not to take her energy away.
> Don't ask her how she feels.
> Ask her about her grandchildren,
> About decorating our new lodge,
> About her upcoming trip to Australia.
> *Ask her about her future.*

This way, we controlled the input of information. I knew that the only people who saw Diane would be talking wellness, hope, and future.

After the surgery, Diane was faced with some very tough decisions about continued treatment: chemotherapy, radiation, how much of this, when to do that. I knew she needed to make those decisions herself. That was very difficult for me. But I understood that she alone should make these decisions because it was her life. Once she made them, she would assume accountability to make them work. I wanted her to feel, "It isn't up to the doctors. It isn't up to Lou. It isn't up to the treatments. It's up to *me*. I am responsible for my own wellness."

I realized that the best way I could help Diane was to provide her with the best medical information available. So I immediately relieved Betty Tisdale of her regular duties as my personal secretary and assigned her to direct a "Wellness Command Center" in our offices. Her new full-time objective was to coordinate a worldwide search for the most up-to-date research on successful treatments for Diane's type of cancer. Betty's husband is a physician, and she's an aggressive, *make things happen* type of person, so I knew she was the right one. I gave her priority access to all our people, who could drop everything they were doing if she needed them.

Betty contacted the most renowned doctors and health care professionals in the world who had success treating this kind of cancer; she called major cancer treatment and research centers for case studies and success ratios—San Diego, Washington, D.C., Idaho, Houston, New York, Montreal, Mexico, Greece, the Bahamas, West Germany, the Philippines, Japan—wherever she had a lead. We pursued every option—people working on projects for a Nobel Prize, faith-healers, immunology projects, metaphysics studies, nutrition and exercise, herbal care approaches, parapsychology, hypnotherapy, the Simonton visualization techniques, and best-selling books on cancer therapies.

I convened study groups of speed-readers who devoured relevant literature in magazines, periodicals, journals, pamphlets, and books so we could quickly pass along an abundance of information to Diane. One person would read something, summarize the main points and highlights in a report, and trade with someone else, who would read the same stuff and write a second report. That way, we always had a safeguard against being locked on to a particular treatment because of personal bias or a blind spot.

Then Betty checked the validity of all this information with the best physicians we knew, so that we didn't make hasty, emotional decisions about what to leave out and what to include. We condensed everything into study formats and presented them to Diane. She would study the materials and make her decisions: "Well, let's try this" or "Let's call this doctor and find out more about his method."

We agreed that she wouldn't follow the protocol of any one doctor. So we retained three doctors—which made at least two of them uncomfortable, because they wondered, "Why are you questioning my judgment? Why are you interfering?" Well, the reason was that we wanted to weigh opinions carefully to try to find the best one. We were searching for the *truth*, so we weren't concerned about bruising someone's ego. Now that takes high self-esteem, because Diane could easily have given up accountability to any one of the doctors: "Doctor, make me well. You know so much more than I do. I will go by your judgment." I think that most people do that. But she knew it was crucial for her to participate in her own recovery. Accountability is a central concept in what we teach: *Take accountability for your own life.* Become your own authority, your own expert, and make your own decisions about your future.

DIANE: I started on a quest to become an expert on what I was about to go through. I read all the research compiled for me, and I gathered materials myself, so I had a multitude of choices. I had one of the best surgeons. But I discovered that, in being the best, he had very narrow views on how this cancer should be treated. It was like macrophotography where you magnify your subject many times and become focused on small details. I would say he had that view. His total protocol was surgery, then maximum chemotherapy, then maximum radiation.

I started out questioning him, and I never let up. I learned later that one characteristic of typical cancer survivors is that they question things. Many doctors consider those kind of people *difficult* because they're always asking, "Why?" My surgeon said I would need chemotherapy once a month for six months, and I said, "Why six?" And after that, he said I'd need five-and-a-half weeks of radiation treatments. I said, "Why five-and-a-half?"

I finally learned that he was doing a study of ten cancer patients, and they were all on the same protocol. Seven had died already, and I was the eighth. Another woman was doing fairly well, and the doctor hadn't found the tenth person yet. I didn't know how long his study had been going on, but I was very irritated that just because he was doing a study, I was *assigned* six sessions of chemotherapy. I didn't want to be a guinea pig. So I said, "Well, I won't say 'yes' to six. I'll say 'yes' to one at a time and see how far I want to go."

I felt an obligation to my family to go ahead with chemotherapy. I had gathered and read enough statistical data on success percentages to know that it was very effective. In fact, I had the first chemotherapy treatment the night of the day I had the surgery. Of course, afterward there was a lot of discomfort and some throwing up. The challenge was to fight off those images and not allow myself to think, "I'm going to be sick again." So I just kept visualizing the chemicals destroying the cancer cells and removing them from my body, and telling myself, "You're getting stronger every day."

This is when everybody decorated my room, and people came to visit, and share humor and fun, along with research and upbeat ideas of what to do next. I actually found the process very interesting. I sketched a sort of wellness wheel to depict all the positive approaches taken by cancer patients who got well. And as I accumulated more information, I added options to the wheel.

Simply stated, I developed cancer because my immune system was stressed. I used these things A) to build up and support my immune system to fight the cancer; B) to recognize and change the basic building blocks in my life which may have contributed to the development of my cancer; and C) to alleviate the existing cancer.

Continued on page 167.

STEP 3:
Set and Imprint Goals

WITHOUT new visions and goals, we tend to recreate the old ones. So, last year looks like this year; and next year will look like this year. You say, "Things don't change much around here."

Genius and creativity come alive when you've got an inspiring vision in front of you. As you learn to set and imprint goals, as you put in a new picture of reality—a new vision, ideal, or target—you find a way to become more every day.

1. Clarify vision, mission, values, motives, attitudes

2. Engage in constructive self-talk

5. Build people & teams

SMART TALK AFFIRMATION
I am, I do.

4. Take action, correct course

3. Set and imprint goals

Chapter 7 deals with the teleological nature inside each of us. It is vital that we have targets; without that kind of focus, we wither and die. Without new goals, we can't help but recreate the old ones, which prevents growth. People who have no goals succumb rather easily to the ideas of other people, whether those ideas are good or bad.

Chapter 8 can help you become more goal-oriented. We orient toward goals according to what we visualize, the words we say both to ourselves and to others, and the emotional ties we have to our goals. High-performance people make the extraordinary appear ordinary. Goals should be big enough that you will need to grow into them.

Having big goals will help you open your eyes to resources you didn't know about before you started.

Chapter 9 is an important chapter on writing and affirming your goals. You will learn how to write stretch goals that trigger positive imagery and emotion and drive needed change.

Chapter 10 deals with imprinting new goals and changing old ones that no longer serve you. You will learn to read and imprint daily affirmations, while seeing yourself in the new situation and feeling the emotion.

The sky is the limit to one who understands the why and how of setting and imprinting goals.

c h a p t e r   7

WHY SET GOALS?

WHEN I was young, living with my mother in West Seattle, we didn't have much in the way of material possessions. For example, we had an old icebox, but no refrigerator. Everyone else in the neighborhood had refrigerators, and so it was embarrassing for me to have people come over to our house and see this old-fashioned icebox. I tried to talk Mother into buying a refrigerator, but she said, "We don't need one; we can better spend the money some other way."

One day my mother's sister learned she had polio. When she was released from the hospital, Mom went to take care of her sister for a while, leaving me at our home with my sister. My mom's sister had a nice home in the Queen Anne district. The home had an updated, modern kitchen with a refrigerator and all the latest appliances, and so Mom started using the refrigerator at her sister's house.

Mother could see other people having refrigerators, but now for the first time could see herself having a refrigerator. After she used her sister's refrigerator for a while, she started imagining one in her kitchen—not just once, but over and over again, until she changed her self-image and her environmental comfort zone. When she returned home, we still didn't have a refrigerator. But she set a goal to get one, without knowing how she would pay for it. She also started finding fault with the icebox. Now the "crummy, ugly, smelly, leaky, old" icebox just had to go. She started saying that with "the money we could save" on ice and spoiled food, we could afford a new refrigerator.

As she changed the picture of what was acceptable on the inside first, she become very dissatisfied with the old picture. By setting a goal, she started this improvement process. We all became very dissatisfied with the old icebox, and looked for ways to get a new refrigerator. We still didn't have the money to buy one, however. But Mom entered a contest and won a refrigerator!

Now, why set goals? If you create the vision, you invent the way. You might think that we would have gotten a refrigerator anyway. I don't think so. It wasn't luck. Mom wrote a poem and entered a poetry contest to win a beautiful new 8-cubic-foot refrigerator, the first one we ever had.

Six Reasons to Set Goals

You might ask, "Why are goals so important?" "Why set goals?" I see at least six good reasons.

1. *If we don't set any goals or ideals—if we don't have anything to keep us looking forward, with positive expectancy, to the future— we can waste away, self-destruct, or die.*

A few years ago in Vienna, I met Victor Frankl, author of the book *Man's Search for Meaning* and founder of LOGO psychology. He states: "It's essential for human beings to have an ideal or a goal; without a goal, you die or self-destruct."

He's right: if you don't have a goal, you die. It was proven in the Korean War. We lost more prisoners of war in Korea than in any war in American history. Why? Because the Chinese and the North Korean Communists destroyed the goal orientation of the prisoners through relentless mental torture: constantly painting a bleak future; rewarding prisoners for ratting on each other; providing "Dear John" letters, divorce subpoenas, bill collection notices; brainwashing with false versions of history. They thoroughly obliterated the prisoners' hopes of the future. They destroyed hope; the prisoners then had nothing to live for. These young men, ages 18 to 23, would crawl into a corner, pull blankets over their heads, and within 48 hours, they would die, from no physical cause. At first, this phenomenon was labeled *give-up-itis*. Later, it was identified as clostermorastis—a withdrawal behavior usually observed in children.

Observe people who are married for a long time and who are close companions. When one dies, the other one soon follows. Look at people who retire with no goal in front of them. On average, they die in 18 months, regardless of the age of retirement. You have a goal, or you die. Companies without goals also die.

When you give up on your goals, or have no goals at all, your whole system shuts down.

2. *We all need targets; otherwise, just like missiles without targets, we will fizzle out and self-destruct.* Goals allow us to orient and operate in relation to a target. Human beings are teleological in nature. We have the power or ability to seek out targets. Our subconscious gets us to move toward whatever goal or image is uppermost in our minds.

Our goals can be anything. For some, it might be the next episode of a favorite soap opera: "I can hardly wait for tomorrow's *General Hospital*," or it might be, "I can hardly wait for Friday." Or, "I can hardly wait to finish work and go out for a beer." Others look forward to building a new home, finding a solution to a vexing problem at work, or founding a new company.

Since we are teleological by nature, we are directed toward and shaped by our goals. When we function properly, we think in terms of purposes and goals. Our teleological thoughts and ways of perceiving are like the guidance system of a missile; they direct us toward our target. Our guidance system is our inner picture of how things are supposed to be: "I have a picture of the way I want my family to be." "I have a picture of the way I want my company to be." "I have a picture of where I'm going on my next vacation." "I have a picture of how much money I will earn this year."

Your guidance system keeps you on course as you work toward your goals. So don't join the Thank God It's Friday club. You need goals to change and grow. Do your goals cause you to linger in the past, float in the present, or leap into the future? Once you learn how to program this teleological mechanism, it can guide you anywhere you choose to go.

3. *If you don't deliberately give yourself a goal for survival, you recreate the one you've got.* Your tomorrows won't look much different than your todays or your yesteryears if you don't give yourself a new ideal, image, or goal to shoot for. All you will do is make the next week or next year, the next generation or the next situation, look amazingly like the last one. So, goal setting is an important part of causing growth and development in you.

Having goals is absolutely essential to your existence. *We move toward, and we become like, that which we think about.* So if you don't deliberately anticipate the way you want your life to be, the way you want your family to be, the way you want your career to be next week, next month, next year, then your subconscious will duplicate your presently dominant picture. You will end up repeating last year's goals again and again. That's what happens when people allow themselves to stay in a routine job, repeating the same tasks day after day. We commonly call that a *rut*. If you don't put in a new target or picture, you use the old picture of your neighborhood, of your home, of your income, of your family. The image for you is already constructed in the neuron cells of your brain. You've let this picture develop by assimilating what's in the environment, by growing up on one side of the tracks, by absorbing how people behave toward you.

4. If you don't set your own new goals, you adopt the agendas and suggestions other people have for you. You then get caught up in doing what the crowd does. You become too lazy or too afraid to think for yourself. "Let's drop that client." "Oh, that's a good idea." "Let's go to that new movie." "Oh, that's a good idea." "Why don't we sell our car?" "Oh, that's a good idea." See, *anything* is a good idea—and you move toward whatever anybody triggers in your mind. "My minister inspires me." "My coach gets me up for the game." "My parents guide me."

If you don't set a goal for yourself, you become very open to every suggestion. And it could be rap music, something that somebody mentions, or a complaint, gripe, "isn't this awful," "nothing to do." So you become very susceptible to the environment and to the suggestions and opinions of people around you. If you don't set the goal yourself, your subconscious knows it. And so you'll do what everybody's doing. You'll hang around, go have a beer. "Sure, that's a good idea. I've got nothing better to do."

5. By having goals and affirmations, you build resiliency to setbacks. When you have a positive expectancy of winning, you take every setback as temporary. For example, Rose Kennedy kept a family together in spite of many setbacks. She had a child that was born retarded, and she bounced back. She had a son and daughter killed during World War II, and she bounced back. She had a son who was the President assassinated, and she bounced back. And she had another son assassinated while campaigning for president, and she bounced back. She had a son scandalized, and she bounced right back. She had a husband die on her, and she bounced back. She had a grandson with a leg amputated, and she bounced back. She broke her hip, and you expect her to bounce right back.

I believe that her tremendous tenacity and resilience came from her vision and goal of what she wanted her family to be.

How many disappointments and setbacks can you take and not quit? Thomas Edison, the man who invented the filament for electric lights, had over 3,000 temporary setbacks—3,000 failures before he got it right. You'd think a guy would give up.

To build resiliency within a person or team, you must first create a positive expectancy of winning, and an attitude of taking all setbacks and pains as temporary. In athletics, I would tell my players, "As you keep putting out, the opponent will tire of hitting you; and the moment they hesitate, you'll run right over the top of them."

Once I set a worthwhile goal and commit myself deeply to that goal, I become tenacious. I have a positive expectancy of winning, and I take every setback as temporary. As an exercise, I would visualize myself running full speed through a dark forest at night, and striking a tree. I would sense the pain. And then I would get up and strike another tree; I would recoil, bounce back, and strike another one, until I worked my way through the woods. Such visualization in connection with goal setting builds resiliency.

Diane and I have a positive expectancy of our family being very happy, and we take every setback as temporary. Diane is extremely tough. She will not give up on a child. I know she makes this affirmation, and she has tremendous resiliency. For instance, soon after we adopted our son Joey at age six, he ran away, and the sheriff brought him home. Then things got worse. Every day was a crisis: he would break something or hurt somebody. By the time he was 13, the community could no longer handle him; he needed to go to a mental institution. Then, because they couldn't hold him and because he had attempted murder in there, he needed to go into protective custody for himself and for others. He spent over seven years incarcerated at one time.

Once he came home for Christmas when he was 14. Everything went well Christmas day, but the next night he got up and stole everybody's presents and left.

Now, I was ready to say, "the hell with it." But Diane would never give up, never give up on Joey being a happy, successful person. Her heroic efforts and her tenacity come from a deep-seated belief that by holding on with the end result in mind, and taking every disappointment as temporary, Joey will spend at least some time in his life as a happy and successful person who makes a contribution to society.

6. Another reason to set goals is to create cognitive dissonance and its positive byproducts—creative energy, motivation, drive, and direction. We are always striving for order in our minds. We gain order when our internal picture of *the way things are supposed to be* in our environment, our social life, our business life, and our home life matches the external picture we perceive through our senses. When we perceive disorder, our system creates energy to bring us back to *where we belong*. In other words, when the pictures don't match, we have a problem: "This doesn't taste right." "That doesn't look right." "This doesn't sound right." "Something doesn't feel right to me."

Sometimes, we resist change because we feel awkward, uptight, uncomfortable, even when the changes would be good for us. It's the difference that causes the negative tension in our system which drives us back to *where we belong*. But our creative subconscious has the ability to transform that same negative tension into the positive energy we need to solve problems, resolve conflicts, make changes, and accomplish our goals.

In 1957, the psychologist Leon Festinger termed this inner tension cognitive dissonance. "Cognitive" means idea, attitude, opinion, belief. In other words, your perception of *the truth.* "Dissonance" means discord, tension, disharmony. Cognitive dissonance is the fuel that propels us to solve problems, resolve conflicts, achieve goals. Festinger found that we experience cognitive dissonance—anger, irritation, stress—whenever we hold two conflicting ideas, attitudes, opinions, or beliefs in our mind at the same time. That's why, when you hold a strong belief about something and somebody challenges you with an opposing view, you get upset. The dissonance really stings.

When the pictures are out of line, that stimulates enough dissonance within us to resolve the conflict. Have you ever had the urge to straighten a painting hanging crookedly on the wall? That's a response to the dissonance: "That painting doesn't look the way it's supposed to look." Or you have an idea of how your living room should look. You come home and find that it's a mess. You think, "This upsets me!" Why? Because it doesn't look the way it's supposed to look. So now you become a manager: "Find the person who did this!" And when you find the culprit who messed up your picture, you say, "I won't live this way. Straighten up the mess!"

Then you walk into the kitchen—and it looks like a garbage pit! That ticks you off; it doesn't look the way it's supposed to look. Again, your subconscious provides the energy and drive to clean the mess, restore order, and get it back to the way it should be.

Broken Window. Many years ago, I came home from a trip and walked into the entry of our home where there are some leaded glass windows that go from the floor to the ceiling. Well, as I looked out to see Lake Washington, I noticed that one of our beautiful leaded glass windows was broken.

So I asked Diane, "Who broke the window?"

She said, "Danny Breen." (A man who used to work for us.) "As he was cleaning the windows, the ladder slipped and went through the window."

She said, "I called the guy at the glass repair shop, and he promised that he would fix it tomorrow."

Now, I started to relax because I could hear the resolution of the problem and see the picture coming together.

The next day I came home and walked into the house, and the window was still broken; in fact, the glass was still on the floor. I said, "I thought we were going to get the window fixed."

Diane said, "Me too. The guy called and said that he couldn't make it today, but he promised he would fix it tomorrow."

Well, the next day, I came home fully expecting to see the window repaired; however, it was still broken. But this time, it didn't bother me so much because I was now starting to get used to it; in fact, I was losing my motivation to fix it.

Your level of excellence is determined by the quality and quantity of what you get used to in life.

What's Good Enough for You?

Often you have the cognitive dissonance to straighten up a mess—but once order is restored, you tend to relax; you lose your creative energy and drive. Why don't you start repainting the kitchen? Why don't you put new doors on the cupboards? Why don't you install a new sink? "Because this is good enough for me."

You have a picture in your mind of the quantity and quality of excellence necessary for you. When the picture outside matches the picture inside, it shuts off your creative dissonance. Your motivation stops, and you can go to sleep.

Have you ever told your kids to wash the dishes? What do they do? They go in, start washing, and come back out. Then you go in and check: "Hey! What about the silverware?" And they say, "You didn't say to wash the silverware. You said to wash the dishes!" That's how your creative subconscious works when you try to solve problems or achieve goals. It does only what you tell it to do—but nothing more. That's why, once we achieve a goal—once we straighten up the mess so it's good enough for us—we *flatten out* emotionally and lose our motivation. The subconscious burns all the necessary fuel; there isn't any need for creative dissonance to do anything more.

How much power, drive, and energy can you get out of yourself to achieve a goal? Very little beyond the picture of excellence you hold in your mind.

Suppose you're a professional football coach and, at summer practice, you decide that the team goal for the coming season will be "to get to the Super Bowl." And let's say the team adopts that goal and gets to the Super Bowl. How do you think they'll do in the Super Bowl game if their opponent's goal is "to win the Super Bowl?" Who's likely to have more creative dissonance—more energy, drive and motivation—to win that game?

We lose our drive when we allow ourselves to get used to something. Some people get used to having no money in their savings account. They tell themselves, "I can't save money yet. There isn't enough to live on.

I'll save when I earn more money." So their subconscious causes them to earn only enough money for what they need right now.

Your subconscious does only what you tell it to do; it delivers what you expect of yourself—but no more. How much money do you give to charity? "Well, I don't give to charity. I can't afford it. Someday, when I'm rich, I'll give lot to charity." Will you? If you maintain the picture of "I can't afford it," you won't allow yourself to be rich. That would almost make you feel crazy. It's not part of the picture.

What Do You Get Used To?

Remember how my mother had become used to the old icebox and resisted getting a refrigerator? What have you allowed yourself to get used to? What's good enough for you?

For example, do you work hard to clean your house for company because "I don't want them to see me living in a mess like this?" You vacuum, dust, polish, sweep, scrub, repair, rearrange, and clean until your place sparkles. You clean it better than your own picture of how it should be! The question is: Why aren't you living in a house that nice all the time?

"Oh no," you say, "that's too nice for me. Don't expect me to keep it that clean all the time, only on special occasions."

And isn't it great when the company leaves? Now you can relax and go back to what you're used to. You can go back to being yourself. It takes work, struggle, and effort to achieve and maintain a level of excellence that's beyond your own picture of what's acceptable. You get your house unusually clean for special guests, but the moment the company leaves, you let things slide back to the way they're supposed to be: "There. That's more like me."

Have you ever moved into a new residence to find certain things aren't fixed the way you expected? You find closet doors stacked in the hall, and maybe a leak in the roof. At first, you're upset: "Boy that makes me mad. That should've been fixed last week." Later, you tell yourself, "Well, I'll fix it myself while I'm living here." But while you're living here, you keep looking at things as they are. Soon, without realizing it, you get used to it. A few days later, the dissonance is gone, and you're doing *easy time* with closet doors stacked in the hall and the leaky roof. You've lost the motivation and drive to straighten up the mess. You've adjusted your inside picture to match your environment.

We often fail to realize our potential because we allow ourselves to assimilate into your image of reality the way we are treated, our level of income, level of indebtedness, our quality of life.

Suppose you have a new car. Somebody bashes a dent in the fender. It upsets you because it doesn't look new, the way it's supposed to look. But, if you don't repair it for a month, and you keep looking at the dent, you probably won't do anything about it until you sell it or trade it in—because you will assimilate the dent into your image of reality and lose the motivation.

So the question, that you must constantly ask as you walk around your home, your office, your world, is "What have I gotten used to?" As you assimilate the details of what's wrong in your current environment into your image of reality, you lose the tremendous power you have for growth and change.

One of the flour mills in Seattle had a slogan, "The World's Finest Flour," on a big sign on their building. Over time the building fell into complete disrepair. The place looked like a dump, and yet the sign was still up.

So what did the owners do after a while? They painted out the words "world's finest" and just had their brand name and "flour." They didn't fix the problem; they just changed the standard.

You may do that, too. Most women, when they first get married, are used to being courted, not abused. They are like beautiful flowers. But if a woman puts up with verbal or physical abuse, soon she gets used to it, and takes it. In fact, over time if she's not abused, she'll do something to cause it. Abuse becomes so deeply assimilated into her image of reality that when it doesn't occur, she'll do something to cause it.

Decide What Standard You Want

Goal setting is deliberately deciding what you're going to get used to in the future—and then assimilating that decision, that standard, into your mind. Once you assimilate the new standard into your mind, then as you look around, you see all the things wrong with the present situation. They used to be all right. But as you visualize the new, you become very dissatisfied with the old. That's the process.

Here you are, comfortable in current reality; but then you have this vision up here, and you set a goal. You become dissatisfied with the standard of excellence that presently exists.

Current reality is the key to helping you realize your visions and achieve your goals. It's the combination of looking squarely at current reality and holding a vivid mental picture of your goal that stimulates the creative dissonance energy you need. Some people will set a vision der why they aren't getting there. They won't look at the real score of the game; they won't check the chart to see how their sales are really going; they won't step on the scale to see their real weight. "Don't tell me the truth. It stings too much."

Once we set a vision of how we'd like things to be, and we look squarely at the way they are, we're going to experience the string of negative feedback—the sense of incompletion or contradiction. That's why most people are reluctant to venture out of their comfort zone to change.

As you raise the level of your expectation and your standards of personal excellence, you become increasingly discontent with the status quo. What was good enough for you last year will no longer satisfy you today: "That's not the way things are supposed to be. Straighten up the mess!" But, if you allow dirty laundry to stay stacked in the hall and you let the roof leak, you'll tolerate it, get used to it, and lose the motivation to change it. In fact, very soon you won't see the mess anymore.

The goal comes first, and then you see. You open up your awareness to the information you need—to the *how*—simply by deciding what's important.

Of course, threats get through, too. One time I was flying from Seattle to our ranch in Twisp. All of a sudden, I woke up because the engine shut off. Silence can wake you up if it's a threat.

A friend of mine, a policeman in Detroit, told me about some tough bars he used to have trouble in all the time. There'd be arguments and brawls and people busting things up. My friend and his partner used to go in with shotguns, and they'd yell, "Police! Knock it off! Sit down and shut up!" Nobody paid attention.

One time, my friend and his partner went into this bar during a fight, and my friend loaded a shell into his shotgun. All of a sudden, total silence. The place froze. My friend couldn't figure it out. But from then on, he kept doing the same thing—and it worked every time. Finally, he figured it out. The *threat* got through. In the past, when he went in there and yelled, "Police! Knock it off!" no one heard. But the much less noticeable sound of a single shell being pumped into his shotgun, *everybody* heard. Threats get through.

Great athletes use this system to their advantage. Some players can't tell what is important, so they don't filter out the junk. That's one reason why a rookie quarterback will often be blind to receivers standing wide open in the end zone. He hasn't filtered out the distractions, so he sees *everything*; he's not focused only on what he *needs* to see.

An excellent quarterback knows exactly what to let through. Even though he's immersed in feedback from 80,000 people yelling all around him, when he drops back to pass, he focuses instantly. Like one of those automatic zoom lenses, his consciousness zooms in on his primary receiver in the end zone. Then, click, he spots his secondary receiver open on a curl. Click, out of the corner of his eye, he finds his halfback open in the flat. And while he's busy seeing his open receivers, he starts sensing the threats. Five yards to his left, he *feels* a 300-pound defensive lineman charging in, ready to rip his head off. He also sees two linebackers breaking free of their blocks.

He sees value and he sees threats; he builds scotomas to everything else. He doesn't see the crowd, the vendors, the cheerleaders, the officials, the players on the bench. There could be the players frothing at the mouth to kill him, but as long as they're being *blocked*, he doesn't need to see them. You could offer this guy a million dollars to describe the umpire standing three feet away, and he wouldn't win his money. He might be looking right at the umpire, but he won't see him. No *value*.

Peak performers are vision-oriented, goal-oriented, and end-result-oriented—even though they presently don't know where the information and resources they need are coming from. Mediocrity demands the evidence before building belief: "Show me. Where's it coming from? How will we do it?" High performance operates in the reverse: belief without evidence. Once you set a specific goal, you have the belief—the faith that you'll find what you need—and *then* the evidence starts shooting through. If you don't have faith in how you work, you don't see the evidence.

In summary, the main reason you set goals is to *transcend* your current reality. If you visualize the goal as if it's already been achieved, you will then find what you need to achieve it. Most people base their future only on what they know presently. If they can't figure out how they'll achieve a goal based on their present resources and skills, they'll say, "Well, we can't do it yet," and they'll back the goal up closer to their present reality: "We have to wait a few months before we go ahead."

The process of goal setting increases your awareness to information and resources in your environment that will help you achieve the desired outcome or goal.

So where do you want to grow? Wherever it is, you've got to make yourself discontent with the present by visualizing the new. How much money is good enough for you? What quantity and quality of product service is good enough for your company? What kind of relationship with your parents is good enough for you? How much abuse do you take in your marriage before you decide, "This just isn't good enough?" You have the ability to create and achieve almost anything.

c h a p t e r   8

BECOME GOAL ORIENTED

THERE are many ways to use your imagination correctly. One of the best ways is to become goal oriented. High-performance people set their own goals and find their own motivation and inspiration. Once you know what you want to achieve, you can learn to affirm, visualize, and imprint, and let your goal orientation guide you.

When Diane and I had nine children to feed at home, we had taken the vow of poverty, by mistake. Diane felt that she needed to stop working outside the home to take care of the kids, and I continued to teach and coach high school kids. Our cars were junkers. Every year we'd need to get a *new* car. We would say, "We've got to get a new car." But we weren't talking about a $10,000 car or even a $5,000 car. It was closer to a $500 car.

When we said, "We've got to get a new car," we meant a new junker. It wasn't like we thought of a new car and then adjusted back to a used car. The new car never even came into our minds.

We've purchased new cars since then, so the potential was there inside of us, but we didn't have the aspiration or goal.

You won't think expansively if you lack inner strength. You won't dream big enough for the real potential inside yourself. You face a constant need to improve yourself so that you dream bigger. You won't let yourself think about what you don't believe you can cause. If you lack self-esteem, you will limit your dreams. If you don't dream big enough early, you may wake up when you're 50 and say to yourself, "My gosh, I could have owned the trucking firm. I didn't need to be driving trucks all my life." But you figure it's too late now, so you resign yourself to what you have.

Three Dimensions of Goal Orientation

Goal orientation means using a teleological process to move toward and become what we think about. We think in images and in words; and the imagery and language we use trigger emotions. So it's three-dimensional: pictures, words, and feelings.

1. Pictures. How do you want things to look in the future? You must have the target, the new picture of what you want, so that your sensory system can hone in on the picture.

Goal setting is changing the imagery or environment *inside your mind*—your income level, inside your mind; your social status, inside your mind. All meaningful and lasting change starts on the inside, then works its way out. It starts first in your imagination. If you don't like where you are, imagine a different future. As you visualize the new, you become unhappy with the old. The more graphic and visual your goal, the stronger the initial imprint.

2. Words. If you are particular about your future, you will be careful what you think and talk about, both with yourself and others. Your choice of words determines whether it's Smart Talk or dumb talk.

• *Self-talk.* Dozens of thoughts go through your mind every hour. These thoughts are part of your self-talk. So, in a sense, you're setting goals all the time. You're deciding how things are by the way you choose to talk to yourself. You're setting the quality and quantity standards that will guide you in the future.

You constantly tell yourself how your world is as you talk to yourself. You interpret what you perceive and experience, and you create images in your mind, including your own self-image, with your thoughts. You create your own environment, limitations, and standards with your own thoughts and words.

The key to learning, growth, and achievement is to use your imagination and self-talk correctly to focus on near-term goals and future events. As you think about the new, you won't like some aspects about the ways things are.

If you dwell on the *good old days*, you may also become dissatisfied with the way things are—but that dissatisfaction doesn't lead to progress. It's a retreat into the past. Old folks who sit on the porch or in the park, rocking and talking about how good life used to be, become unhappy with the present generation. They want to go back, not forward.

To the degree you keep describing past problems and current troubles in your self-talk, you establish a negative reality. Your sensory feedback then confirms how bad things are, reducing motivation to move forward. You then become stuck in the current reality. Don't keep telling yourself how bad things are if you don't want them to be that way.

When we ask astronauts who went to the moon to speak to us, we always invite them to tell us what it was like on the moon. And so we trap these people in history. Similarly, a salesperson who wallows in the success of the last sale may miss several opportunities today. Likewise, we ask old athletes to talk endlessly about the game they won 10 years ago. Even athletes who just won a big game may think about it all week and lose the drive to prepare for their next game. When they get beat, we may hear, "They just couldn't get up for the game."

Rather than get trapped in history, you can learn to use history to help you grow. You can reflect on your past success briefly to spring into the future. You can think and talk about a desired future as if it's a done deal. This is the gutsy part of growth and goal setting. The words that you use in your self-talk trigger emotion. So your talk becomes the way you want things to be before they ever are.

At first, this *future* of yours may seem laughable. And so you may talk back to yourself: "Who are you to think that? It's stupid of you to even think that way."

But you may see other people being, doing, or having what you want, and soon you think, "I think I can do it." And then, "I know I can do it. And soon, you say, "I'm doing it."

When I first started my business, I said, "I will need to double my income." I think I was making about $1,300 a month at the time. It was hard for me to find a person who was making $2,600 a month. None of my friends were making that much money. At first, my self-talk was, "My gosh, that is absolutely ridiculous."

• *Public talk.* Not only was I laughing about my income goal, but if I discussed it with other people, they also laughed at it. And that was worse. People whom I respected when I was a football coach were laughing at me, and they were telling everybody what an idiot I was. "Who is this guy? He's not even a head coach of a college. He's not a professor of a university."

So I quit talking to them. I quit telling people about my vision of the future. I had to stop telling them because they kept giving me negative feedback. I was getting enough of it from myself; I didn't need it from other people.

You've got to be careful who you share your dream with. Some people don't want you to grow in the first place, and some don't want you to leave your current position. And so they'll say, "What do you want to do that for? We're having a good time here. Why don't you stay where you are?" So be very careful who you share your goals with. Your public talk must be as smart as your self-talk.

3. Feelings. We commonly underestimate the emotional component of goal setting. If we set goals and make decisions only on an intellectual level, we forfeit the strong passion of the emotional level. Our goals, particularly the tough goals, should trigger feelings of joy and fulfillment. particularly the tough goals. If you approach these solely on an intellectual level, you simply won't care enough. The purpose and the passion won't be there. So ask yourself, "Why do I want it?" And create the depth of purpose, the intensity of mission, and the power and passion of emotion.

To make your vision, ideal, goal, or future stronger in your mind than the reality that you're currently living with, you need to use the power of emotion. You probably spend too much time describing the *what* (creating the vision), and too little time telling yourself *why*. You need to find the *why* that drives you, because the *why* is the source of passion. When you're emotional or passionate about a goal, nothing holds you back. You get things done. But if you just make an intellectual decision, you don't care enough. Things go wrong because you don't set the goal with a strong vision, reason, and passion. So ask yourself, "What do I want? Why do I want it? What is the purpose behind it?"

You may want to change and know how to change, but you won't change much if you don't get emotion into your goals. If you don't want something with passion, it won't happen. To change the inner reality of how things are, you need to dream about the change, visualize it, think about it, talk about it, plan it, and dwell on it with emotion.

Eight Principles of Goal Orientation

The following eight principles will help you achieve a goal orientation in your life.

1. Prepare your mind before taking action. Preparing for personal change and growth is a process of familiarizing yourself *beforehand* with the new situation; familiarizing yourself *beforehand* with a new environment; familiarizing yourself *beforehand* with the new behavior. *Remember: All meaningful and lasting change starts on the inside first, and works its way out.* Change starts in the imagination, and *then* manifests itself externally.

If first you don't change your internal picture of who you are, you tend to revert to the familiar. For example, suppose that you consciously force yourself to lose weight without first changing your self-picture. If you still see yourself as 20 pounds overweight, your belief system will keep you there. You might *temporarily* lose weight, but when you let go of conscious control, you return automatically to your currently dominant picture, to the way things are *supposed to* be.

This is like cooking from a recipe. When you open a cookbook to a recipe, what do you see? The ingredients. But what do you see in your mind's eye? *The finished product*—a baked cake.

The recipe for change is to deliberately throw your system out of order. Create dissonance inside yourself so you will have the energy and drive to change your picture. Take your ideal and visualize it and affirm it as if it's already done in the first person, present tense.

Suppose you know you're usually in debt for only $500, and then bills suddenly come in to put you in debt for $5,000. You think, "I've got a problem. This is more debt than I'm used to." That prompts your creative energy and drive. You stop spending foolishly; start saving money; get an extra job; and do whatever it takes to get the two pictures to match.

If you use affirmation and visualization to upgrade "where you belong" *before* you go out of your comfort zone, you won't feel the tension when you actually get there. For example, to prepare your kids for kindergarten, you talk with them about it months in advance, not the day before. You get the kids to visualize the kindergarten environment so vividly, they feel as though they've already been there. Then you can't keep them home. If the child visualizes kindergarten in advance and affirms, "I'm going to have a great time," that child will comfortably adapt.

That's how you feel when you set goals properly: "I've *been* there. This goal is *mine*."

You can deliberately prepare to be a better father, mother, son, or daughter; deliberately prepare to be a more dynamic leader; deliberately prepare to have a free-flowing memory; deliberately prepare to become financially secure; deliberately prepare to do all the things you want to do.

Why prepare your mind first? Why not take immediate action? If you're an action-oriented person, as soon as you imagine a new future, you want to get to it right away. You immediately start coming up with *how to's*. "Well, we can do it this way." But when you take immediate action, you make three bad things happen: 1) you limit the emotional component; 2) you lock on to the first or second idea; 3) you eliminate the chance for others to be part of the creative team and buy in to the project—and these are people you may need to achieve the end result.

Also, if you take immediate action, you may find yourself in a new situation with an old self-image and mind-set. You'll be far out of your comfort zone. Even if you do the new behavior one time, you go right back to being your old self, back to your old comfort zone, because you haven't changed your internal idea of the way things are supposed to be.

2. Change your internal image of reality. Millions of dollars are spent on television commercials to produce imagery to get you so discontent with the old that you buy the new. In a car commercial, for example, the camera slides you behind the wheel so you can imagine vividly what it would feel like if you were driving an elegant new car. If you repeat the image often, your subconscious won't know the difference between *pretending* that you're driving the car, and actually driving it. You'll drive that car 100 more times in your mind. Soon, you'll have a new image of reality—a new picture of the car that's "good enough for me."

Once you compare your *new* image of "reality"—the elegant new car—with your *old* image of reality—last year's model, you throw your system out of order and become discontent with the old. Anything less than the new car that you visualize will not satisfy you. Eventually, you will invent a way to get the new car. You'll rationalize, "With the money I save from the new tires I'll need to buy next year, and with the better gas mileage and the better resale value of the new car, it'll pay for itself. In fact, I'd be stupid *not* to buy it!"

By setting goals, you mentally produce your own commercials. You deliberately throw your system out of order to stimulate the creative energy you need to resolve the conflict or achieve the goal. But you must imprint the image of the new into your subconscious so vividly that it is stronger than the way things presently are. The vision must be so strong that you can't stand the *old car* anymore. If it isn't strong, you'll return to your currently dominant picture.

The aspiration creates the appetite for growth. No goal, no appetite. You first create the appetite, and then you grow.

As you change the inner construct to the new way, your senses may say, "Ah, it's a lie. You say it's there, but it's not. You say it's done, but it's not." Now you're out of your comfort zone. Now your senses are saying, "You're out of place." And so you correct by changing the present environment to look like the new one. The inner picture changes first, and then your senses trigger the drive, motivation, and creativity to correct the problem. Goal orientation is deliberately causing a problem for yourself, deliberately causing disorder, chaos, or temporary insanity by throwing your system out of order to create a new, better order.

As you visualize the new, you become dissatisfied with the old. No dissatisfaction, no growth. How do you become dissatisfied with the way your house looks, with your health, with your present income, or with how some people are treated? You do it by becoming goal oriented, and that dissatisfaction naturally triggers the creativity and the motivation to complete the task.

You and I are always working for order in our minds. Your senses are always asking, "Where am I? How am I? How does this look, feel, taste, smell, or sound to me?" When your idea of how things are supposed to be does not match your present situation, you experience a conflict. Whenever you sense incongruence, you seek to clean up the mess. Goals, if set properly, stimulate creativity. So, your job is to disrupt the status quo by setting goals and then to imprint the *what* and the *why*. You need to write out the *what* and the *why* several times a day to imprint the new vision with emotion. It takes many repetitions to make that image so strong that *it's a done deal*. It takes clarity, strong emotion, and repetition to change the image in your mind to a new sense of the way things are supposed to be.

3. Avoid flattening out by setting goals *through*, not *up to*. Goal setting is not static; it must be a continuous process. Once we achieve a goal, our motivation tends to flatten out, and we relax and float. For example, as soon as you reach the level of performance that you're used to, you no longer have the motivation to get a *better* job or to make *more* money. You only do *what's good enough* to relieve the tension, no more. Once you've returned to *what's good enough* for you, your system shuts down. When our pictures match, we lose our motivation to excel and achieve. We have boundless creativity, drive, energy, and competence as long as we have a conflict to resolve.

What happens when parents set a goal to see the kids grown, married, and out of the house—and then the kids finally leave? The parents often stagnate, get depressed, lose energy and motivation. They may even get divorced.

Years ago, I taught a three-day seminar every month. My goal was to just get through that seminar and to get home so I could collapse on the couch. During that time, my daughter Nancy won a poster contest at her school with her drawing of what her dad did for a living. I went to school to receive the award with her. You know what the drawing was? *Her dad asleep on the couch!* "What does your dad do?" "He sleeps on the couch." That was her picture of me, because, at the time, my only goal was to get home and crash.

When I saw Nancy's drawing, I realized that if I wanted to have dinner with my family, and enjoy them after dinner, I had to learn how to goal-set *through* getting home, not just *up to* it.

Many people set goals to get through their work week. But then they get up on Saturday, and they can't get out of the house. They can't get off the chair to change the channel. They can't even get up to get a snack: "Bring me a sandwich. I'm too exhausted. I don't know what it is. I must be working too hard." Their goal was to get *to* the weekend, not *through* it.

Suppose a person sets a goal to start a dental practice and works diligently to open up the practice. But the person goes out of business shortly because his goal was to open a practice, not to manage it and keep it growing.

Once I worked with a large airplane manufacturing company on the East Coast. They gave their retiring executives 90 percent of their last three years' salary averaged out monthly for their retirement fund. I said, "That must cost you a great deal of money." They said, "No. We know we'll only need to make about 16 payments."

When you set a goal to retire but neglect to set new goals, you may die soon afterwards. You don't need to go into the same line of work, but you must set new goals, other than "I want to retire and do nothing." Remember Bear Bryant, the legendary Alabama football coach? He died less than a month after his retirement. He was known for his boundless energy and drive right to the end of his long career—but he apparently had nothing left after football.

The same thing can happen to you and me, unless we learn to create dynamic new goals, endure the creative dissonance, and ride the goals to higher plateaus of happiness and success.

If your goal is simply to "get there," you typically don't perform well once you reach that plateau. For example, individuals and teams that set goals to *get* to the Olympics rarely reach the standard of performance that got them there.

Once you arrive at a goal that you set, you stop your drive. To keep moving, you don't wait until you arrive; you set the goal past the one that you set. As you approach it, you set it out again. You don't wait until you arrive, if you expect to keep yourself alive. You need the goal, the imagery, the vision, and the affirmation to progress.

You shut down your own energy when you think you've arrived. You stop your appetite for growth. Your goal might have been to become vice president of your company. When you do, you get in the way of the growth of your company for the next 10 years.

High school students who work hard to *get through* high school and *get to* college, often flunk out before Thanksgiving. Why? Because their goal was only to *get* there, not to graduate. And college students who set a goal to graduate but forget to set a goal to start a career, may hang around your house for a year. What about someone who sets a goal to get hired by a company? They dress well and act bright to get the job. Then they're hired, but the company can't get them to work. What was their goal? To get *hired*. After that, it's "I *did* it. Now I can relax."

The natural growth process is to create tension and then to stimulate the creativity to restore order. The difference between what is supposed to be and what actually is causes tremendous anxiety or tension. Unless the new goal is deeply imprinted, when the tension occurs, you take away the goal through rationalization, and go back to the old way. You justify it through excuse making or rationalizing, because you're trying to prove that you weren't crazy for setting the goal. "I wasn't crazy. It wasn't absurd. Timing wasn't right. I didn't get the cooperation. The market wasn't right." Now, your goal isn't to reach the goal. Your goal is to get rid of the tension.

Tension and anxiety come with the discrepancy or conflict. By disrupting the status quo, you stimulate energy to fix the problem. By causing the problem you not only get energy, but you also get ideas; your creative subconscious seeks to resolve the conflict in the direction of the strongest picture, the most dominant picture or image. Now, this won't be an uptight, negative tension, but an adventuresome spirit, if you not only envision a positive outcome but also anticipate the joy and the excitement of the outcome.

4. Make the extraordinary ordinary. Some people say, "Thank goodness Christmas only comes once a year. Wouldn't it be hard if I had to be this nice *all year*?" If that's your picture, the answer is, "Yes, it *would* be hard. It would be extraordinary." On the other hand, suppose you saw yourself as an extraordinarily giving person. Suppose you repeatedly affirmed with your own self-talk, "I'm a very giving person. I enjoy giving of myself every day." Once that affirmation is burned into your subconscious, you will try to be a giving person *all year*.

Affirmations, visualization, and goal setting lead you to make the extraordinary ordinary. You look at all the special occasions, all the exciting travel and adventurous lifestyles that you once considered extraordinary, and assimilate the experiences into your subconscious so they become ordinary. You imprint them into your subconscious, and *that's* what you get used to.

A few years ago, I decided that Diane and I should have a big party on September 3 to celebrate our wedding anniversary. On past anniversaries, we'd had very nice parties with excellent entertainment. We'd always invited several people, but we hadn't decided on anything yet; all we started with was, "Let's have a big party on September 3."

I asked Diane, "What kind of party should we have?" She said, "I don't know. Let's just keep adding to it as we think about what we want." I said, "Okay."

Finally, we ended up with about 1,500 people, 18 kegs of beer, tepees, horses, covered wagons, mule rides, musket shooting, wine, roasted pigs, chili, popcorn wagons, country singers, community singers—and a two-day family *happening*. But all we started with was, "I think we'll have a party." We planned, we affirmed, we visualized, and ultimately Diane and I pulled off a party that we would originally have considered to be extraordinary—especially for an *ordinary* anniversary celebration. But as we repeatedly affirmed and visualized its reality, that extraordinary party became ordinary for us.

When you set your goals, you can assimilate the extraordinary so it becomes ordinary *for you*. This isn't just wishful thinking. It isn't just having positive thoughts; it isn't just hoping and wishing. You change your inner image of reality. ***Remember: All meaningful and lasting change starts first on the inside, and works its way out.*** It does not start on the outside and work its way in.

5. Take the chance, and don't leave yourself an out. some people think that it's better to avoid setting goals because they then avoid the risk and the responsibility that comes with having a goal. Their reluctance to set goals is then reinforced by their well-meaning friends who say, "Don't bite off more than you can chew. Don't reach beyond your grasp. You'll only be hurt or disappointed."

These people avoid setting goals because they can't stand the tension, stress, or anxiety. If they do set goals, they set them close so that they can't feel the sting of the creative dissonance. If you set a goal and don't get it, you feel uptight, you want to throw up, you can't sleep, you can't face people. So you say, "Well, I don't want to feel that way." Fine, don't set any goals. If you set a goal, go get it. If you don't get it now, get it the next time.

Some folks are reluctant to set goals and make decisions. They are overwhelmed with the choices: "I don't know which I like the best. There are so many to choose from." Subconsciously, they ask themselves, "Will I feel crazy for making this decision? What if I make the wrong decision? What if I don't meet the goal? I'll feel terrible!" To make things happen for yourself, you must recognize that it's all right to make a decision, even if it turns out to be wrong. If you are wrong, it will hurt. But it's okay to make mistakes. You just tell yourself, "That isn't like me," and move ahead. That's how to excel.

You also have people who don't want to limit themselves by setting any goals. They think that setting goals is like imposing limits. They want to be the best they can be, and yet they don't set goals.

When you've made a decision to do something—to take a new job, buy a new coat, sell your washing machine—later you've likely worried,

"Did I do a smart thing?" Buyers wonder: "Was I right to have bought this thing? Was this the right decision?" Did you ever go looking for a new car? You made up your mind which car you wanted, paid the money, signed the papers—and the moment the car was yours, you asked yourself, "Was I crazy for buying this car? Was this an absurd decision?" We all ask that.

Why is there a maid of honor and best man at weddings? To help kill the pre-dissonance. "Am I doing a smart thing?" the bride says. And the maid of honor says, "Oh, yes. It will be wonderful." Why does the reception line come *after* the wedding? So everybody will come by and say, "Congratulations, you'll make a lovely couple." And your subconscious will say, "Oh, thank God."

You can learn to control your self-talk through positive affirmations about your goal, and stay on course—if you have the guts to take the heat and stand the sting. You must tell yourself you are absolutely committed to achieving your goal. People say, "Let's not get married. Let's just live together in case it doesn't work out." When they feel the slightest dissonance, they break up and say, "It's a good thing we didn't get married." *But remember: We move toward, and we become like, that which we think about*. If you do get married, you're fully committed because there are no easy "outs." When the dissonance hits, instead of giving up on the goal, you will most likely work at straightening up the mess. That's the way you must be when you set your goals: *No "outs," no back door*.

6. Choose what's good enough for you. To engage your creative genius, you must constantly upgrade the picture of what's "good enough" for you. If you believe you're a C student and then surprise yourself by getting an A on one exam, you may find it hard to get another A because you think, "Hey, look how good I did. That isn't like me." Your subconscious finds a way to correct for the "mistake." It might convince you that, "I can flunk the next two tests and still get my C." Why? Because your expectations are "I'm a C student, not an A student. Don't expect me to get A's all the time. That's too tough for me."

It's almost impossible for you to motivate yourself beyond your expectations. But if you raise the level of your expectations, you can raise the level of your performance. Change your picture of what you believe, and you automatically change what you achieve. Since you rarely excel beyond your expectations, you must raise your expectations. You create energy when you have a problem that needs resolution. Can you see why you should think and work in ideals and why you should measure from where you are in relationship to your ideal rather than from where you started to where you are now? You shut off your drive when you think, "Look how far we've come. Look at how well we've done. This is better than we've ever had it. I don't know why I've got to work so hard to keep it up." Once you arrive at a goal you set, you lose your drive and energy.

As you walk around your home, your yard, your world, ask yourself, "What have I gotten used to?" And then set goals; otherwise, you lose the power for growth and change.

Goal setting is deliberately deciding what you're going to get used to in the future—and then assimilating that standard into your mind. Then you will not only see what needs to be, you will do something about it. As you visualize the new, you become very dissatisfied with the old. If you don't visualize the new, change almost must fall on you from the sky.

So look upon areas where you'd like to improve and visualize a new reality. For example, suppose you see a new kitchen in a magazine, and then when you cook again in your own kitchen, you begin to alter your image of reality. As you visualize the new, you become dissatisfied with the old. You now notice that the paint looks dirty, the counter is scarred, the flooring is worn, the dishwasher doesn't work right. And soon you say, "I refuse to cook in this mess until it's fixed. We're eating out." But it was all right three weeks ago. In fact, it didn't even bother you.

If you're single and you visualize yourself being married to someone, you can hardly wait until you're together. But if you're together and you start seeing yourself apart, you find fault with each other. Those faults have always been there. You've accepted them; you've lived with them. Visualization works to bring you together or split you apart.

7. Grow into the goal. Start with a goal out there that's bigger than you are. And rather than adjust it back to where you presently are, grow into the goal.

How do you know if your goal is too big for you? You and I have been taught to think *realistically*. We've been taught the concept of *realism* by teachers, counselors, and other people who have never had a job other than to go to school. And yet they tell us about what we can do. They talk to us about being *realistic,* and they say, "Why don't you reduce your aspiration to match your present appraisal of how good you are?" And so you limit your goals because you have a limited picture of the way things should be.

Start with the stretch goal and keep growing, until you're much bigger than you presently are, and you're not intimidated by it. Intimidation means you're frightened by your goal to start with. I think that it's okay to be intimidated, but it's not okay to stay intimidated. You can learn to handle the problem.

How big do you set your goals? You don't let yourself want what you don't believe you can cause. For example, how much would you normally spend on lunch? $2.50. Now add a zero to that, a $25 lunch. What would you eat? What would you pay for shoes? $60. Add a zero, a $600 pair of shoes. What would you look at? What would you pay for a theater show? $50. Add a zero, $500. What would you pay $500 to see? What would you pay for a car? You might feel comfortable with a $5,000 car, but very uncomfortable with a $50,000 car.

Consider what would be a stretch for you by adding a zero to your current budget. Let your mind stretch to what it would be like. Of course, that's harder to do when you're being held accountable for outcomes. Does your vision affect the outcomes? Sure it does. The restrictions you set affect where you go and how you grow. So I think there is value in imagining that $500 evening, without judging yourself or comparing yourself to others.

It does no good to covet. All that does is create envy, not healthy tension or discrepancy. So don't say to your spouse, "Look what our neighbors have," or tell your child, "Why aren't you more like your brother or sister?"

What limits the size of your aspiration or dream? If dreaming is what it's all about, if visualizing properly is what it's all about, why don't you just visualize yourself doing great things? *Because you don't let yourself want what you don't believe you can cause.* In fact, you don't even think about it. You don't even get the idea, even though you have the potential inside of you. You need the aspiration to work and grow through perspiration.

8. Don't worry about the resources. When you set a goal, you declare that some things are more significant than others. You define what's important to you. Until that time, resources and information that could help you achieve the end result could be right in front of you, but you block them out because you consider them nonessential. You see them once you set the goal.

"Do we have the money?"

"No, but let's find it."

"Do we have the people?"

"No, but let's find them."

Don't limit your aspirations, goals, and dreams based upon the resources available to you now. These resources may surround you, without your knowing they are there, because they're not important to you at the moment. But as soon as you declare them significant, suddenly they appear. You think you're lucky. You think it's coincidence. But it's not. You first set the goal, and then you perceive the resources.

Often I have set a goal without even the slightest idea of how I was going to achieve it. I didn't have what I needed. It gave me great confidence to set *unrealistic* expectations. I was often thought of as being an unreasonable person. I guess I still am.

Now, you may be thinking, "But I don't have the skills; I don't have the knowledge; I don't have the money; I don't know how to get from here to there." I know. But don't be too concerned about the material, money, and means.

If you set goals correctly, creating healthy dissatisfaction with the current reality, you will find the way. If you invent the *what* and the *why,* you'll find the *how.* You'll discover resources—or they will find you. You won't even know from whence they come.

Your primary task is to create the problem. You don't want to limit yourself by getting stuck in current reality. You must think in ideals. You think about the ideal way you want it. You don't need to know how. You'll learn how. You'll read books; you'll go to school; you'll find other people; you'll develop yourself; you'll save money. So you don't need to know how when you begin—just set the goal and then find. For example, suppose that you decide to buy a refrigerator. As soon as you clearly set that goal, you go through the paper and see refrigerators on sale. Chances are they've been advertised every week in the newspaper. But you don't see the solution until you need it. ***Remember: You do not perceive until you need. Goal setting is establishing the need.***

In theology, this is called faith, belief without evidence. Many people have little faith, because they need evidence to build their belief. They say, "Show me, prove it to me, and then I'll set a goal." That is one way of doing it, but if you just set the goal, you allow yourself to perceive. That's exercising faith. The goal comes first, and then you perceive.

The more specific that you make the desired outcome, the more it activates your awareness system. The more detail you imagine, the easier you detect the clues that lead toward the goal. Your subconscious looks for clues—clues that will lead you toward new business—or even a *parking spot.*

If you clarify where you want to park and program that into your mind with real intent, as you drive into town you look for clues through your senses. Your subconscious won't just look for the parking spot. It looks for heads in cars up ahead two blocks away. You start scanning for clues because heads in cars indicate they may be leaving. You see red lights flashing. That's not a parking spot, that's a clue. You see exhaust from cars coming. That's not a parking spot, that's a clue. You see people approaching cars. That's not a parking spot, that's a clue. Your subconscious looks for clues.

But you need to clarify what you're looking for to activate this system inside that allows you to stretch and to achieve goals that are always bigger than you.

When people around you ask, "Where are you going to find the resources? Where are you going to find the business? Where are you going to find the people?" simply reply, "Out there." This isn't magic or luck. It is knowing how your mind works. You attach physiology with psychology, and you start looking at how you function and how you can use that knowledge to improve your environment, yourself, your family, your business.

When I started putting on rodeos at our ranch, I encouraged our staff people in Seattle to organize them. At first they didn't know where to look to find Brahma bulls, rodeo riders, calf ropers, and all that goes with it. But once they started makings some calls, they found rodeo cowboys and animals all over the place. They didn't know there were so many of them. At first they didn't know there were *any* of them.

And then when I said, "We're going to Australia to find business," the response was, "Okay, no big deal. If we can find Brahma bulls in Seattle, I'm sure we can find business in Australia."

So practice on fun things. When you go on a scavenger hunt, you list a bunch of ridiculous things, but then you see them. So the goal comes first, and then you see.

For example, take a moment and draw a picture of your watch and all the details on the face of it. Draw the picture from memory without looking at it. After you've drawn the picture of your watch in all the detail you can remember, have another person correct your paper. Show them your drawing and your watch and see how you did. Why can you look at your watch several times a day and not see many of the details? Because detail is usually not significant. What is significant is the time. The detail doesn't get through because you don't need to notice it.

Finding resources, people, and information could be as obvious as the details of your watch. It could be right in front of you. But you don't know it's there. How many times have you started to set an aspiration or goal for yourself, and then been asked, "Well, where are you going to find it?" "I don't know. Maybe I ought to change my mind."

Don't ask how, where, and when at the same time you set the goal. There needs to be time delays in this. Put yourself out into the environment and watch for clues. They are there, but you won't see them unless you need them.

Now, write down exactly what time your watch said the last time you looked at it. After you guess, check your answer. Why is it that you did not know what time it was? Because the last time you looked at your watch you were checking the detail. Only significant information at the moment gets through. The information you need to reach the goal could be there, but you won't see it until you set the goal. Once you set the goal, the information screams through. It's all over the place. You set the goal, and then you find. But you won't see what you don't perceive you need.

Teach your children, students, employees, and team members to be great finders of information and resources. Encourage them to set clear goals and define specific outcomes so that they know what they're looking for. If you ask daily in the morning, "What am I looking for today?" you increase your resource awareness immensely. Previously unseen resources jump out at you.

You are already limited in your sensory perception, but you're limited even more when you fail to set specific goals. A lack of goal orientation shuts down your awareness. Having a goal orientation keeps you moving. You become a person who goes after what you want. You don't judge whether you have the resources now. You know that what you're looking for is out there, somewhere, and that when you set a goal, you will begin to see the resources.

c h a p t e r   9

WRITING AND AFFIRMING GOALS

NOW that you understand the importance of goal orientation, you are ready to learn how to set goals for growth and change. You are ready to learn how to affirm and imprint them in your subconscious belief system, often and vividly, until your future goal becomes your present reality.

When I left high school teaching, I couldn't imagine myself living or thinking the way I do now. It would have been way out of my comfort zone. You see, I grew up in poverty. My dad died when I was 12, so I had to help raise our family. I sold newspapers, and did all kinds of odd jobs just to eat. By the time I left teaching to start my own business, my vision of the future was very narrow. In fact, all I could imagine at the time was making enough money to survive. As I said before, Diane and I had $1,000 in the bank, bills to pay, nine kids to feed, and one seminar with seven people—and most of them were relatives. I thought, "If I can just make twice as much as when I was teaching, I can run my business and feed my family." But because I started setting bigger goals and affirming them, I have continually managed to stretch my comfort zone and expand what is *realistic* for me.

Affirmations are simply a blueprint for growth and change. Transforming imagery into written affirmations is a reliable way of programming your subconscious mind to anticipate desired changes as if they have already happened.

Here's how it's done.

1. *Consider where to change.* Before setting goals, consider how and how much you would like to grow and change. Maybe you want to improve in an area you're already good at. Perhaps you want to try something new. Maybe you want to alter some personality or character traits, or some behavioral habits, or some outdated attitudes. Or maybe you'd like to enhance yourself-image, self-esteem, and self-confidence, naturally, so you create a new picture of you. You might want to improve your financial situation. Or maybe you want to improve your memory, your concentration, or your stamina. You might want to sharpen your views on education, politics, religion. Maybe you'd like to exercise regularly, read more books, or cultivate a garden. You might wish to show more love to your kids. In any case, the first step is to give some thought to *where* you would like to grow and change.

2. *Write goals down.* Why write your goals in the form of affirmations? First, so you don't forget them. Second, you remove them from the realm of chance. Rather than passively wishing, hoping, or intending to change and leaving it to circumstance, you write affirmations to start *deliberately* changing *the way things are supposed to be* for you. Third, by writing affirmations, you can achieve goals effortlessly and safely, without the stress of *trying hard* and *enduring pain.*

A written goal prompts vivid imagery of an end result. That imagery, along with the emotions it stimulates, imprints the goal in the subconscious as if the goal is already accomplished. The subconscious doesn't know the difference between something real and something vividly imagined.

Suppose you set a goal to build a home. Once you select a lot and a basic plan, then, in your mind's eye, you visualize the end result: the finished home. Through repetition and anticipation, you imprint the vivid image of the home so powerfully that you can almost walk right in the front door. Now you start anticipating the pleasure of living in it: "I can hardly wait to move into our new home." At this point, even though you have only changed your picture *inside*, you feel as if you've already moved. Then, when you perceive that you don't *have* a new home yet, you create the energy and motivation you need to build it.

Now, the emotion—the "I can hardly wait" anticipation—is essential to this process. Without that anticipation, your goals turn into halfhearted intentions that never happen. *Writing goals* starts the process of targeting your goals by imagining them vividly. Wishing, hoping, or intending to change is like waiting for the Fairy Godmother to transform you into a prince or princess. She isn't coming, and neither are your desired changes—unless you deliberately write your goals and follow through on them.

3. *Now write one or more short affirmations for each goal.* Written affirmations are goals about *the way things are supposed to be* in the future: "This is the way my life is supposed to be," "This is the way my family is supposed to be," "This is the way I am supposed to look." An affirmation is a way of stretching present reality by imagining a new *supposed to be*. If you have many areas in which you want to grow, you might feel overwhelmed. Then you might end up setting goals haphazardly, leaving them to chance. One way to commit yourself to setting new goals regularly is to write them down in clear, concise definitions.

A two-sentence goal statement, as opposed to a paragraph or a whole page, provides a manageable definition that is easy to visualize and imprint into your subconscious mind. ***Remember: It isn't the writing that makes the change; it's the process of visualizing with feeling, and then imprinting.*** So it is essential that each goal, or each aspect of a goal, be written simply, clearly, concretely.

You don't need to limit yourself to just *one* brief affirmation per goal, because some goals will be more complex than others. If you are working on an elaborate change in one area of your life, you may need *several* brief affirmations, each one covering a particular quality or characteristic.

For example, suppose you want to affirm an overall improvement in your personal relationships. You can write a broad, general affirmation like "I am receptive and friendly toward all the people I meet. I treat everyone with respect and consideration." If you want to set specific goals within that category, you can write additional affirmations for each one. For instance, "I am thoughtful and patient with my mother." "I am sensitive to my brother." "I listen to my daughter with care and interest, especially when she talks about herself."

Or suppose you want to improve your golf game. You might want one affirmation for your short game, another one for your long game, another one for handling pressure.

How could you describe, in just one brief goal statement, what kind of parent you want to be? You might need one affirmation to cover your overall attitude on parenting, and another on improving your relationship with your son, another on relating to your daughter, another for their education, another for the emotional support you want to provide at home. If each aspect of the overall goal is written in a one- or two-sentence definition, it will aid in the imprinting process because each one will imprint separately and distinctly.

4. *Trigger experiential imagery.* In writing affirmations, you want to trigger an experiential image of you doing, having, being something, as though it's actually happening right now. Whenever we vividly imagine something and we hold it long enough in our mind, it becomes reality on the subconscious level. So you want to visualize your goal in such vivid imagery that it creates a new reality in your belief system.

When you trigger experiential imagery, your mind becomes a simulator. You create such powerful imagery in your mind that you actually feel as though you're living the experience. Only then will your subconscious record the imagined event, or goal, as if it was actually *happening*.

A properly written affirmation triggers experiential images which stimulate the right emotions. These eventually imprint in your belief system as your new present reality. It works like the car commercials where the camera places you in the driver's seat. You *experience* the feeling of driving, and you record, "This is *my* car. I own it."

For example, do you know of anyone who has bungy-jumped and has recorded the jump on video? If so, you could watch that video 100 times— or even observe the person doing it 100 times—and still have no desire to make a bungy-jump, unless you imagine *yourself* doing it. It does no good to have someone show us a model of what this company runs like, or that person lives their life like, unless we can see it happening to us.

What limits how far you can stretch is how far you can see yourself experiencing what you want to have, do, or be. You must not only see it, but you must see it with positive emotion. If you force yourself to imagine the jump, you will fill yourself with terror. Now every time you envision it, you don't need to experience the jump to feel terror—you simply imagine it. You record the negative emotion. So, when the real event occurs, the stored emotion comes out, which causes you to engage in avoidant behavior. You create reasons why you should not do it.

So it isn't just what you visualize, it is the emotion with which you visualize that has a lot to do with whether you're going to positively seek or negatively avoid the vision or goal that you have the potential to reach.

The experiential imagery must feature *you* at the center. In visualizing your own goals, you don't see someone else achieving them, you see yourself achieving them. Did you ever point out to your kid, "Look at how those other children behave. Why can't you behave like them?" Well, one reason might be, "Oh, I can see how *they* behave. But I can't see *me* doing that."

What would happen if the car commercial showed *someone else* driving the car? Instead of feeling "It's *my* car," you'd feel "It's *their* new car"—and that wouldn't create the motivation for you to buy the new car. That's why the imagery must be personal and experiential. If just any image worked, all we would do is observe someone, and we'd immediately become just like them. But it doesn't happen that way.

Years ago, I was in Arizona visiting a friend who had just bought a beautiful new home at the edge of a golf course in Phoenix. We went to see this house and I said, "I'm happy for you. I'm glad you have this new home." But as I was driving away, I told myself, "I will *never* have a house like that if I keep talking this way." I realized that I could see my *friend* in that house, but not myself. I always wanted to live like that, but I couldn't see myself into that situation yet. So I knew I had to work on seeing *me* into my goals, not somebody else. Otherwise, instead of creating the change, I'd end up creating envy, wishes, or idle dreams.

The imagery triggered by your affirmation must stimulate strong experiential emotion that tells your subconscious, "This is happening to *me.*" Until you see *you* doing, having, being something, it doesn't affect your present image of reality.

5. *Record specific details*. Your goal-setting affirmations must convey specific and detailed imagery, so your subconscious can record the goal concretely. You can set a goal, for example, to wake up in the morning. But that goal is too narrow. You can improve it by adding small details: "I am going to awaken at 6 a.m. full of energy and enthusiasm, feeling strong and looking forward to my work."

You must set clear, concrete goals. If you say, "I am a nice person," that will be difficult for you to visualize. If you say, "I am a strong leader," that still isn't specific enough. Pinpoint exactly what you choose to be, and how you choose to be it. Otherwise, it will be like telling the waiter in a restaurant, "Bring me some food." The waiter has no idea what you want because *you* don't know.

Having an accurately defined target is essential for both individual and group goal-setting. You and your people could goal-set for your company to have "a good year." But why would you only want to have a "good" year? If you are vague about your target, you won't get any *feedback*, and if you don't get feedback, your system won't know when you're off target.

If you don't have feedback, you don't get the tension; on the other hand, you also don't get the *motivation* to attain your goal. That's why coaches say, "It's going to be a building year." Or someone asks a supervisor, "How do you think business will be this year?" and the supervisor says, "Oh, better." These statements mean *"Keep the heat off me."* It's like someone who doesn't want to exercise saying, "I'll do a little jogging." You know how much "a little" is? Maybe 50 feet. You must pinpoint what you want—the exact distance, the exact amount of new business, the exact income, the exact career—because then your subconscious holds you accountable, gives you feedback, and makes you act as you believe yourself to be.

Effective goal-setting means deliberately determining what is important. As soon as you determine what is most important to you, you become very *lucky*. Your mind opens up and filters through the pertinent information. The less specific the visualization, the less information gets through. For example, if you go shopping for *something* for your children for Christmas, you probably won't find anything. How do you visualize *something*? But if you're looking for a 24-inch trail bike with quick-release wheels, you'll find one!

Years ago, I decided I wanted a swimming pool. But I was a teacher and football coach; I couldn't afford it. So I decided to get a swimming pool *for free*. As soon as I decided, information about swimming pools started coming through. I saw them, I heard about them, I read about them—but none were free. So I asked an informed friend, "Where can I get a swimming pool for free?" He immediately took me to the north end of the Seattle-Tacoma Airport where they were extending the runway. Workers were preparing to move a big brick home, which had a nice swimming pool. My friend said, "You can probably get that one for nothing." How did I move the swimming pool? That's another story. But, believe me, I found a way.

6. *Use positive images*. A key to effective goal-setting is affirming your goals in the positive. Always write your goals based upon what you *want*, not what you don't want. It's a process of moving away from the negative, away from restrictive and coercive motivation, away from the flames of hell. The images in your goal statements must be positive images of something you want to possess. Instead of visualizing your old impatience, you visualize distinct situations in which you act patient; instead of visualizing short, bitten fingernails, you visualize long, elegant fingernails; instead of affirming, "I don't want to drop the football when the pressure is on," you affirm, "I always catch the football when the pressure is on."

Suppose you think, "I've got this terrible temper." That is your problem. So you ask yourself, "How would it be if I didn't have my terrible temper?" And you might answer, "I would remain cool, calm, and poised under pressure." From that, you develop your positive goal statement for any given circumstance: "Whenever the kids fight with each other, I am always cool, calm, and poised." "Whenever a crisis at the office occurs, I am always cool, calm and poised." It's that easy.

Or suppose your problem is "I don't have any money." If you affirm the problem, what happens? Your subconscious confirms that reality— "Okay, if that's the way you want it"—and it keeps you in poverty. But suppose you ask yourself, "What would it be like if I had enough money to live happily for a few years?" Then, instead of affirming the *problem* ("I'm broke"), you affirm the *solution:* "Money flows toward me."

It's the difference between negatively affirming the *problem:* "My teenage sister and I don't get along" and positively affirming the *solu-*

tion: "Because of the caring way I treat my teenage sister, we get along like best friends."

The key is to trigger positive images of what you want, not negative images of what you don't want, even though you haven't the slightest idea *how* you will accomplish the goal. Creating the positive image of what you want, and looking at the way things are now creates the motivation to make the pictures match.

7. *Set realistic goals*. What is *realistic*? If you can vividly see and feel yourself experientially attaining the goal, then it's realistic for you. If not, then you need to back it up a little closer to your vision. If you're 50 pounds overweight at age 50, you can't realistically imagine yourself being as slim as you were at 20. If you can't imagine your goal vividly, *experientially*, with the right emotion, your subconscious will know it's unrealistic, and the goal won't imprint in your mind.

How far into the future can you see yourself doing, having, or being what you want? You can't just say you want to be something and change your picture. If you can't realistically visualize yourself as a billionaire, nothing will happen. How do billionaires think and act? What do their homes look like inside? Where do they shop? Where do they eat? Who are their friends? Can you see yourself as a billionaire? I can't. I don't know what they do or how they live. But I *can* see myself doubling my present income. Like a lot of people, I feel as though I'm *spending* that much now!

Visualize your goal close enough so you can see yourself into it. If you set your goals *too* close, you will lose motivation, energy, drive. So set your goals with about 50 percent believability for now. Later, when you are more proficient, you'll gauge how far into your future you can see. Setting *realistic* goals doesn't mean your goals can't stretch you—it just means one stretch at a time.

Being realistic when visualizing the future may seem contradictory. But remember: It's the gap between the two which creates the internal tension that you need to stimulate change. The gap between current reality and your vision causes your system to say, "You've got a problem!" The problem might be the difference between your vision of the career you want and the career you currently have; between your vision of the income you *want* and the income you currently have; between your vision of the way you *want* to get along with your family and the way you get along with them now. That gap is the dissonance in your system that eventually drives you to achieve the goal. But because of that same uncomfortable tension, people sometimes won't set stretch goals.

Be honest with yourself; did you ever dream about having, doing, or being something new, and feel miserable just thinking about it?

That's the dissonance of current reality—that's the problem. But remember: Don't shut it off. You *want* the problem. That's what will bring out the best in you. What you must do is learn how to make the vision in your imagination *stronger* than the sting of current reality. If you can do that—through affirmations, visualization, and proper imprinting of your goal—eventually you will attain your goal. But if you shut it off, you won't realistically see yourself into the change.

8. *Write your goals in first person, present tense*. Write all of your goals with you at the center: "I am a warm, compassionate mother." "I am a decisive father." "I treat everybody fairly." "I am a leader in my company." It may sound selfish, but it's necessary if you want to change your picture. You can't affirm to change someone else; you can only affirm to change yourself. I only have the power to affirm changes in *me*, not in you.

If you want your goals to imprint your belief system, you must affirm them in the present tense—in the *now*—as though you already *are* that person: "I *am* the new manager." "I *am* friendly and outgoing." You affirm that you already live in the new house, even though you still live in the old one; that you've already won the game before it's played; that you have enough money to take that vacation, even though you only have $20 in the bank. If you weigh 140 pounds and you want to weight 120, you might write an affirmation like "I look young and feel confident and attractive at 120 pounds." You write the goal as though it is already achieved, even though it isn't. If you trigger the right imagery and emotion, your subconscious will believe you.

You aren't lying to yourself. You are simply altering your image of reality. Affirmations are neither moral nor immoral. They are amoral or neutral. They are just the trigger tools for creating the right imagery for change. By using first-person, present-tense affirmations, you deliberately trigger a conflict to stimulate the impetus and make the pictures match.

Goal-setting is simply a process of constantly stretching what is presently *just like me*. Write your affirmations in the present tense; otherwise, you end up affirming *ability* or *potential*. For example, if instead of affirming, "I *am* patient with my kids," you affirm, "I *can be* patient with my kids," nothing happens. You have nothing to change because you already possess the ability to be patient with your kids.

In affirming your potential, you don't create any drive for change. When you think, "I *can be*" or "I *intend to be*" or "I'd *like to be*," you also think, *"but right now, I'm not."* And when you affirm, "I *can be* a nice person," it records, "I *can be* a nice person, *but right now I'm a jerk*." See? "I *can be* rich, *but right now I'm poor*." "I'd *like to be* brave, *but right now I'm scared*."

Affirming your ability or potential doesn't alter your present reality. You must affirm *achievement*: "I *am* a loving father." "I *am* a winning athlete." "I *am* a dynamic leader."

If you don't affirm in the present tense, you won't create the motivation to achieve the end result that you want. And you will end up wondering, "Why can't I change?"

If you don't affirm in the present tense, you might get trapped affirming the past, the way things used to be, while immersed in the present, the way things are. You complain, "This is awful." And your self-talk affirms: "Things are crummy. People are mean. Values are dead." What will your tomorrow look like if this is how you describe today?

What blocks most change? People keep reproducing, in their minds, the way things are now, or the way things used to be. What about the people around you—family, friends, business associates? What are *they* talking and thinking about? History or the future? High-performance people think future tense as though it's done: "The money's earned." "The game is won." "The house is built." They continually invent their own future *before* it happens. **Remember: The future is now. So affirm all your goals in the present tense—or your tomorrow will look like your yesterday.**

9. *Make no comparisons.* If you feel you can only grow by comparing yourself to somebody else, you will always think that somebody else is better than you or worse than you. If you feel they're better, that's like adding a negative weight to your shoulders: "I am not as handsome as he is." "I'm not as pretty as she is." "He's a better hitter." "She's a better doctor." That's restrictive motivation. Instead of feeling, "I *choose to* set this goal for my own personal growth," you always feel you "*have to*" become better than someone else. Or, if you feel they're worse, you relieve your dissonance, not by getting what you want, but by finding someone who has even less. Comparing is like saying, "I'll achieve *their* goal, only I have to do it better than they do." It's negative, ineffective goal-setting.

You don't grow by comparisons. Why would you want, or need, to be better than somebody else? You have your own unique visions, fears, comfort zones, attitudes, goals, dreams, desires, talents and tests that other people don't know about. It does no good to compare yourself with somebody else when it is you who must do the growing and changing. You must choose to grow for more significant reasons than just to beat somebody else.

There is a place for a healthy competitiveness. For example, I work a lot with college and professional athletes. They need a competitive mentality to achieve their personal and team goals—to be better than their opponents so they can win. That's different than competing with family members, with friends, or with fellow employees. The very nature of putting together a winning athletic team demands competition with other teams, whereas competing against family members produces only disharmony and discontent. Competing against friends might ruin friendships. Competing against fellow employees in a company can breed selfish attitudes and habits that will be counterproductive to the overall company goals.

The best salesperson in any particular company may not be very good. So if you are better than that person, you might still be mediocre. Yet, if your goal is not to be the best salesperson you can possibly be, but rather to merely be better than the *company's* best salesperson, you might feel satisfied with beating the company's best. The danger in that goal-setting is that you can *flatten out* in mediocrity, thinking you're the best.

You are in the business of personal growth and change—for your *own* reasons. You already have enough *internal* competition that can detour your growth: your own restrictive motivation; your own flat worlds; your own blocks, traps, and lids. You are trying to become the best possible you, and to improve your personal relationships with everyone in your own world. So a healthy, personal goal-setting attitude would be "I am trying to build a better world and a better me."

There is a healthy, positive way to incorporate in your own goal-setting whatever you admire in others. You can observe people you admire and try to emulate them. You can tell yourself, "I like the way she treats her family." "I like the way they run their company." "I like that quality." "I like that attitude." "I like—." That is not comparing yourself to somebody else. You are just observing qualities you like, and making affirmations to assimilate them into your own belief system.

10. *Guard your spirit of intent.* Written affirmations will have no power to change your belief system unless they are buttressed by a strong spirit of commitment. Just as when you compliment someone else with genuine feeling, it is the spirit of genuine and deliberate intent in your own affirmations that creates the dynamic change inside of you. Words that are empty of commitment are merely worthless platitudes.

When you invest as much credibility in your own word to yourself as you've invested in the words of the *experts* in your life, you will not need to keep repeating your affirmations until your picture changes. When you really get good at this, one affirmation—like the "I do" wedding vow—will be enough to make the change.

Affirmations make you more aware of the immense power of words. You will discover that sometimes, when you set a goal, you will be unconsciously kidding yourself. You won't be seriously committed to your goal. Eventually, if you want to grow and change, you will stop using words idly both to yourself and to others. Words are only seeds. They have to be nourished with your intent to transform you from within. Some people will need to repeat their affirmations often to talk themselves into it. Some will visualize and affirm often to build up their sense of worthiness before they are willing to believe, "It's over, it's done." Some already feel worthy enough to immediately believe, "It's mine." It is all a matter of how good your word is to you and to everyone else.

Years ago, I was about 30 pounds overweight, but I didn't really care. Every so often, I would half-heartedly make an affirmation about losing some weight, but nothing would happen. Sometimes, I would get up in the morning, glance in the mirror and say to myself, "Today's the day." Of course, what I meant was, "Today's the day—if nothing gets in the way." You know what got in the way? Lunch. Or, if I skipped lunch, two dinners would get in the way to correct for the mistake. It was funny. I could make all kinds of things happen in my personal and professional worlds with just one affirmation, yet when it came to losing weight, I had affirmation cards stacked as high as a table. I wonder why.

Obviously, my word on that issue was worthless to me. Yet there I was at the office, talking about bouncing information off satellites, doing business in many parts of the world, and starting this and venturing into that. I had to sometimes ask myself, "Hey, is this nonsense, too?"

Finally, a few summers ago, I decided to quit fooling around. I said, "Okay, that's it. No more." And I lost 30 pounds in six weeks. I wasn't hungry even once. What was the difference between 15 years of affirming "Today's the day," and one morning of affirming "No more fooling myself"? *My spirit of intent.*

All of your well-meaning goals are worthless without the spirit of total commitment behind them. But if you combine real intent with properly written affirmations, nothing can get in your way. You can change belief and you can change your life. It's that easy. Do you know why I finally decided to lose that weight? I wanted to make myself tougher so I could move on to bigger accomplishments in life—like helping millions of other people build a better world. I wanted it so powerfully that I now believe I can do just about anything.

So when you say, "I think I'll quit smoking," or "I think I'll be a better person," I say, "Save your breath." One thing you might consider, in fact, is affirming the power of your own word to yourself. That could be your first affirmation: granting yourself the ability to do what you say you will do.

11. *Keep your goals private at first.* When you set private goals, keep them to yourself. You might want to share some mutual goals with family members, teammates, or fellow employees. If so, share them only with those people who will help you achieve them. Do not share your goals with people who will work against you. Only you know who those people are.

Sometimes when we tell people about our goals, we start to feel as though we can't back out: "Well, I said it. Now I *have* to do it." You don't need that kind of restrictive motivation. Set all your goals on a *want to, like to, choose to* basis. Otherwise, you will feel coerced into achieving them. Another pitfall might be losing your flexibility to attain the goal.

I remember when we told our children that we were moving to a new home—*before* we found one. We sold the old one and prepared to move out. Our daughter, Nancy, was only in second grade at the time, and we thought she would be unhappy about having to move away from her friends. So we assured her that we would rent a house in the neighborhood until we found a house to buy, and she could stay in her old school. I will never forget her reaction. She said, "No! I'll run away!" I said, "Run away? The kids *love* you at school." She said, "I'm running away!" I said, "Why?" She said, "I told everyone we were moving, and they gave me a going-away party. I can't go back!" See, once we shared the goal, we lost our flexibility in terms of the timing. When you keep your goal to yourself, you have greater flexibility, and the timing is always in your control.

Also, the people with whom you share your goal might not be very supportive. Suppose you affirm a goal about being more patient with your spouse, and you tell him or her about it. If you have a temporary setback, your spouse might say, "Well, this stuff isn't working, is it? I thought you were going to be patient." Then *your* attitude might change, to, "Well, I was. But I'll be darned if I will now!"

Or, the people who love you might try to talk you out of your goals because, as you change, you are changing *their* reality, too: "What are you moving for?" "Are you studying French so you can be better than I am?" "Why did you invest in that business? You should have saved the money to fix up the house." Change can threaten people who have grown accustomed to *the way things are supposed to be* for you. Those closest to you may give you all kinds of advice: "Why don't you just be satisfied with what you've got? Don't try to reach too high or you'll get hurt. I'm just trying to protect you because I love you." See? You don't want that aggravation. They don't mean to do it, but you are changing their comfort zones, so they're fighting for their own sanity. That's why it might be best to set your goals silently, and let the changes speak for themselves.

12. Align and balance your goals and affirmations with your life mission. You need to ask yourself, "All of this goal-setting, company expanding, career enhancing, business promoting, how does it all fit? Is it based on fairness, on justice, on an ethical value system?" Try to get the big picture. Visualize in your mind the life goals you want to achieve, including the kind of person you want to become. Are you under- or over-emphasizing important aspects of your life? If you set out goals in just one area, say business, you can get quickly out of balance. To achieve life balance, your goals should cover the major aspects of your life.

Look at your life as a round wheel. If you place your goals and affirmations in just one area, you quickly get out of the round. Your wheel will only go around so far before it becomes stuck. Your happiness and fulfillment depend on balance in your life. *Balance* means an emphasis in each area that is rewarding to you and to the important people in your life: professional, spiritual, family, health, social, community, etc.

A bar of iron has many uses even though its molecules go in all directions. When an electric current was passed through it, the molecules were aligned and the iron, without losing any of its old strengths, gained a new one: It became magnetic.

We can achieve some goals in diverging directions, but we can achieve many more with less effort when the goals are aligned with our personal vision and our mission in life. When our goals are aligned, we generate tremendous power. Lack of alignment causes energy diffusion. Our personal goals should also be consistent with our family, team, and corporate goals.

Smart goals are balanced, aligned, clear, focused, specific, and constructive. The more vividly we visualize our intent, the more commanding is the call to action. Smart goals are measurable, attainable, structured, relevant, and written. Writing your goals and affirmations gives them precision. Imprinting gives them strength.

Writing affirmations is not magic. It is only one step in a conscious, deliberate process of change. The *imprinting* of your goals is what makes the difference. In the next chapter, we'll talk more about imprinting goals and affirmations.

c h a p t e r   1 0

IMPRINTING NEW GOALS, CHANGING OLD ONES

C LOSE your eyes and relax. Imagine yourself going purposefully into your kitchen to find a fresh lemon. Start walking to the refrigerator. Open the refrigerator door and pull out the fruit bin. Reach into the bin for a firm, yellow lemon. Close the door and take the lemon to the counter. Roll the lemon back and forth until it starts to soften. Reach in the cutlery drawer for a knife, and slice the juicy lemon in half. Take one half of the lemon and slowly bring it to your mouth. Smell the juice before you put the lemon in your mouth. You can practically *taste* it. Now, take a big, juicy bite.

Okay, open your eyes. Did you actually taste the lemon in your mouth? Could you feel the tartness on your tongue? Yet *there was no lemon*. What made it so real was your vivid visualization of finding, rolling, slicing, and biting into a juicy lemon. As I pointed out earlier, an event need not actually occur for you to *experience* and record it subconsciously. You must simply imagine it vividly, as if it *were* occurring. The vividly imagined experience of biting into a lemon is recorded in your subconscious *as if it really happened* because your subconscious can't tell the difference. And, in the future, every time you summon this same imagery in your mind, you will react physiologically as if you were biting into a real lemon.

The Imprinting Process

Once you write your goal in the form of an affirmation, you now need to imprint it. The imprinting process follows the formula:

I x V = R (Imagination times Vividness equals Reality)

A written affirmation creates clear, vivid images, which stimulate the correct emotions, which imprint in your subconscious as the new reality. Every time you write your affirmations correctly, with vivid, experiential imagery, and then go through the imprinting process, you record the imagined event in your subconscious as if it is actually happening to you right now.

The imprinting process takes three steps: 1) *read* the words of your affirmation to trigger the imagery in your mind; 2) *picture* the images triggered by the words; and 3) *feel* the emotion stirred by the images, and *experience* the affirmation as if it were actually happening to you now.

After you write an affirmation, visualize yourself being or doing what you are affirming. Seeing yourself driving the new car makes a very powerful imprint—even though you may not be aware of it. But it wouldn't make an imprint if you didn't see *yourself* behind the wheel. The television term *subjective camera angle* applies here.

To imprint properly, you must visualize your goal from a subjective camera angle, as if it is happening to *you*, not somebody else. That's why just watching TV or a movie, or merely observing people doing something, won't change you. That's why I can watch *other* people parachute from a plane without it causing me to want to jump, too. For my reality to be affected, I must vividly visualize myself jumping from a plane—I must see the chute unfurling above me; feel the tug of the lines and the wind blasting into me; see my feet dangling beneath me, the clouds above, and the earth coming up fast. If I just write down an affirmation to jump from a plane and then read the words without visualizing the situation experientially, it won't imprint in my subconscious mind.

The angle at which you visualize yourself into your goal situation is vital to the imprinting process. You must imagine the event exactly the way you would actually experience it. That means you must see yourself, not from a detached, *outside looking in* angle, but from a close-up, subjective, *inside looking out* angle. For example, if you imagined yourself biting into a lemon exactly the way you would really do it, you wouldn't see your back, your face, or the refrigerator behind you. In fact, unless you observed yourself in a mirror, you wouldn't even see the lemon going into your mouth. You'd only see your hands raising the lemon toward your face. Using the subjective camera angle, you'd see only what you would see if you were participating in the actual event.

See Yourself in the Situation

Suppose you set a goal to improve your skiing. You then write an affirmation, "It's easy and exhilarating for me to ski on my new skis."

Then you close your eyes and try to mentally *experience* skiing on the new skis. What would you see if you were actually skiing? You would see the slope, the surrounding scenery, perhaps other skiers around you, your chest, arms, legs, boots, and the front of your skis. You would feel the wind on your face, you would smell the trees, you would hear the snow crunching beneath you, you would feel yourself shifting your weight and working your poles as you slice down the slopes. In other words, you would experience the kinesthetic feel of skiing, as if you were really doing it.

You might wonder, "What if I have trouble picturing, or *experiencing,* affirmations in my mind?" One thing you can do is talk yourself through it. Explain to yourself where you are, vividly describe your surroundings, tell yourself why you're there. Ask yourself, "Who am I with? What am I doing? How do I feel?" If you still have difficulty painting clear images, it may be because you aren't relaxed enough. If you are under tension or stress, the picture will be fuzzy. Or perhaps your words are too general. You must be very specific and concrete. You don't want to affirm something vague like, "I am a good leader." How can you paint a picture of that? Instead, you want to affirm something specific like, "I am a calm and resourceful leader whenever my teammates lose their composure on the field." Or you could be more precise: "I always make the big defensive play or get the crucial hit when my teammates are down and the game is on the line." Then you envision a game situation, and picture yourself leading your team through it.

The most vital aspect of imprinting is *feeling the emotion* triggered by the words. If you've written your affirmation correctly, with descriptive, experiential words, you will *feel* the excitement; you will *feel* the joy; you will *feel* the anticipation; you will *feel* the love; you will *feel* the thrill that your affirmation triggers. The correct words will stimulate that *"I can hardly wait!"* emotion and anticipation. *Any* old emotion won't work. You must imprint the *correct* emotion. Otherwise, like preparing the five-year-old for the first day of kindergarten by saying, "Your teacher's a monster," you will record the *wrong* emotion, and block yourself from attaining your goal. Your affirmations must provide positive, *emotion* words: "I *love to* —," "I *proudly* —," "I *enthusiastically* —," "I *eagerly* —." You want to imprint the love, the pride, the enthusiasm, the eagerness, not the tension, anxiety, or fear.

Flick Back, Flick Up

To build the specific emotion that you want when imprinting a goal, try the *Flick Back, Flick Up* technique. This practice is especially useful when fear feedback—fear of heights, fear of public speaking, fear of meeting new people—blocks you from trying new situations. Remember how your subconscious works when you perceive a new situation? You *associate*, "Have I experienced anything like this before?" If so, you say, "Uh-huh." Then you *evaluate*, "What is this probably leading me toward?" If the past experience was negative, you think, "Nothing good"—and you get inventive finding ways to avoid raking the leaves.

How can I prepare myself *beforehand* for going into the wrong restroom? Well, mentally, I can *flick back* to a triumphant situation in my past, *borrow* the positive feelings that it recorded in my subconscious, *flick up* those same feelings that it recorded in my subconscious, and *flick up* those same feelings into my current situation.

With this technique, you don't leave the outcome to chance. You deliberately program it in beforehand. You just *flick back* and *flick up*— maybe 10 times, maybe 20 times, maybe 50—whatever works best for you through trial and error. You can use this method to prepare for a new social event, traveling to a new country, or having an important talk with your children—anything new for you. You just *borrow* from the old and drop it into the new to create that feeling of positive anticipation: "I can hardy wait. I'll blow them away. It's easy. It's over. It's mine."

Of course, there's a flip side to this technique. I didn't mention all the *negative* things that happened to me in the past—all the emotionally traumatic situations: the disappointments, embarrassments, failures, mistakes. Like most people, I've experienced my share of tragedy—awful events that I couldn't control. For instance, when I was coaching one time, I had a little boy drop dead right in front of me. And I remember breaking the news to his father. It was devastating for both of us. I have other traumas recorded in my subconscious. Sometimes, inadvertently, I'll lock out options by anticipating a traumatic situation and telling myself, "No thanks. I've had my share of hell." So it can work against you, too.

Instead of locking out options, you must learn to lock out the disappointments, the embarrassments, the failures, the mistakes. You take the hit, learn, and move on. Lock out all the jobs you didn't get, all the failed relationships, all the times you fell on your face. Otherwise, without realizing it, you might prepare yourself for an upcoming situation by *borrowing* a negative emotion. So, like high-performance people, you learn to control your emotional preparation by disciplining yourself to dwell only on past successes. And *that's* what you project into the new event.

The idea is to always prepare to be at your best. When we work with college athletes, we use *Flick Back, Flick Up* to prepare a whole team for a winning outcome.

The beauty of *Flick Back, Flick Up* is that you can use it to deliberately prepare, emotionally, for any situation coming up next week, next month, even next year. It will allow you to go into new situations with confidence and poise. And once you master it yourself, you can help people you love to do it, too. For example, you parents can use it to help your young children. At night, before your children fall asleep, sit on their beds and ask them, "Tell me what you did today that was great fun. What did you do that made you feel proud of yourself?" Then let them talk about it and feel the emotions all over again. Then you say, "And what are you looking forward to tomorrow?"

By doing this, you're helping them to unconsciously affirm a tomorrow that will be just as much fun as today. We know that's how high-performance people think; one vital thought pattern is *"I have pride in my past performance and a positive expectancy of winning big in the future."* And that's how you can train your children to think. If you do that for them every day, you will help them develop that high-performance pattern for adulthood. As adults, they will be more inclined to attack life every day with that positive expectancy. They will be ready to go places in life they would never have considered before. And when they get there, they'll think, "This is déjà vu!" They will absolutely *own* the situation.

You can build a storehouse of self-esteem for yourself, too, if every day you take some time, privately, to dwell on something you did well in the past, and relive that experience. What you will be doing is re-recording all those positive emotions, as if they're happening again right now. Then you just *borrow* those emotions and *flick* them forward into an anticipated situation in the future. It's a way of looking forward constructively in an *I can, I want to, I will* mode.

You can also use the *Flick Back, Flick Up* technique to build the right emotion into an affirmation or into a situation. For example, if you are afraid of heights or enclosed places or flying in an airplane or meeting new people or giving a speech, your fear feedback won't allow you to go into those situations comfortably. What you want is to have the right emotional response when you get there.

Remember, when you perceive a situation, you first associate it: "Have I seen anything like this before?" You then evaluate: "What will this lead me toward?" And then you decide whether to get involved: "Should I do this?"

How do you overcome negative fear feedback? You prepare emotionally for some outcome or situation that you anticipate in the near future. You can then go in with confidence.

Even today, when I'm scheduled to give a speech and want to be at my best, I may *flick back* to the third grade when the teacher, Mr. Anderson, left me in charge of the class on the playground. For me that was a big-time responsibility. I got to boss all the other kids. He would go off to have coffee, but I thought he had some important business to do.

Now, how did I feel at that time? It was a major esteem event. I can reflect back now, remember what it was like, and then project that into where I'm going to give my talk. I'll get a picture of where I'm going to give my talk—an actual photograph—and imagine what it might look like full of people. So I try to get as close to the situation as I can, building a simulator in my mind, like an airplane pilot. I then conjure up in my mind the emotion of success, the emotion of high esteem. As I visualize this new situation, I take the third-grade emotion and drop it right in.

Now, what will happen? You think about the speech and get all frightened in your mind. You've got to stop the emotion, because you'll record the frightened emotion. You've got to *flick back* to your own golden moments, and let the emotion of success come up. As soon as you get the emotion, you drop it right into the new situation. Now, if you vividly do that and borrow the emotion and drop it in, it's as if you were there with that strong, warm or confident emotion.

I might *flick back* to the sixth grade when I was captain of the safety patrol and president of the boys' club. Wow, did I think I was important. It sounds silly to say now, but I still borrow from that experience. I borrow that emotion, let it fill up inside me, then I project that into where I'll be giving the talk. I *flick back* and *flick up* into the new.

And I'll go back into the seventh grade when I was captain of the football team. I thought I was important and big time. I'll borrow the emotion from that time and project it into where I'll be giving the talk. And I'll *flick back* to when I was a senior in high school. Several things occurred that I wanted to make happen, and so I'll let that feeling well up inside and then drop it right out into where I'll be giving that talk.

I might go back to when I wanted something in college and got it, and I'll drop it right into the new situation. Or, I'll remember some of my best speeches and let that emotion well up, and drop it right on out into that same event.

Or, I'll remember when I graduated from college, went after a certain job I wanted, and got it. It was an ecstatic moment, so I'll just take emotion and drop it right into a new situation.

I *flick back* to allow the emotion of success to come in, and then I deliberately project it into where I'm going. I might do that 50 or 100 times. And so I've been through that event 100 times with successful emotion before I even get there. Now that greatly enhances my chances of succeeding, no question about it.

Of course, I also prepare the night before, and prepare while I'm flying. I don't leave it to accident. It is not accidental that I have the emotion of success, and a powerful delivery. I don't use notes, and so it has to flow out. I've got to be in my comfort zone. Otherwise, nothing will come out, even though it's in there. Anytime you go into something new for you, use the flick back, borrow from the old, and project it into the new. Block out all the dumb things, all the emotionally bad things that have happened —all the disappointments, the jobs you didn't get. I've had very tragic things happen to me that I didn't want to have happen. If you dwell on all the disappointments, you could carelessly prepare yourself with the wrong emotion.

As a professional, you can learn to control your emotional preparation by allowing yourself only to dwell on your success and project it into the new event. If you don't, what are you looking forward to? "I'm looking forward to that job—no, it'll make me sick. Looking forward to giving that talk—no it'll make me sick. Looking forward to going to that interview—no, it will make me sick. Looking forward to that sale—no, it will make me sick." You don't allow that to happen. You prepare yourself emotionally to be at your best. You project yourself into the situation with the right emotion, and you go in with the right confidence every time.

Imprinting Questions & Answers

How long should I visualize my affirmations?

If you're affirming and visualizing internal changes in your attitudes or habits, or the enhancement of character traits, it shouldn't take longer than 30 seconds. But if you're affirming and visualizing external changes, like a new income level, a merger in your company, an athletic performance, or a new skill or routine that has multiple affirmations, you will need to spend more time.

How many affirmations should I make?

Make no more than about 30 affirmations at a time. There's no magic number; it depends on how much time you spend on each one. If it takes 30 seconds an affirmation, 30 affirmations will take 15 minutes. I suggest that you go through the *read-picture-feel* process at least twice a day for a total of 30 minutes.

How often must I repeat my affirmations before I see a change?

You may need to repeat an affirmation 100 times before the goal imprints and changes your picture. But don't be discouraged; the actual change takes time. Remember how the process activates change: Each time you imprint a goal in your subconscious, you are recording it once as if it's actually happened. And since your subconscious can't tell the difference between a vividly imagined experience and the real thing, eventually, through repetition—with the proper imagery and spirit of intent—your inner picture will change. And even though you first only change the picture *inside*, once you perceive that you haven't yet changed *outside*, your subconscious will correct for the mistake.

If you are 30 pounds overweight at 190 pounds, you might affirm, "I feel attractive, healthy, and energetic at 160 pounds." Then you repeatedly read the affirmation, close your eyes, and *experience* how you feel, physically and emotionally, at 160 pounds. You see yourself at 160—wearing new clothes, doing new activities, looking great. You hear people telling you how great you look. You might even imagine stepping on the scale or looking at yourself in the mirror to see how slim you are. Once that slimmed-down image imprints, you *really* step on the scale, and you realize you *haven't* lost the weight, your system creates the dissonance that keeps you on target until you *do*. It keeps you act- ing like the person you believe yourself to be—someone who now weighs 160, not 190. So don't be impatient. Through repetition over time, the new picture assimilates into your subconscious mind.

Will repetition alone be enough to imprint goals?

No, mere repetition will not be enough to imprint goals. Regimented repetition can become hypnotic, which causes it to lose its power. You might end up reading your goals indifferently, like reciting from rote. There's very little conviction in that. Words alone are empty of value or power. It is the *intent* behind the words that makes the difference.

If you lack genuine intent, you might find that you are repeating your affirmations because you've become dependent on them: "Well, I don't really mean it, but I'd better say it anyway because I know I should change." That's what happened when, for so many years, I kept affirming to lose weight. The repetition was worthless because I didn't mean it. For all those years, I just repeated the affirmation because I was dependent on it. I told myself, "Well, at least I'm *trying*." But I wasn't trying. I never *intended* to lose weight at the time. I just repeated the affirmation in case it might work like magic.

When repeating your affirmations, continually clarify them with more specific details and a fresh investment of emotion. When you read and visualize your affirmations, keep adding to them. That way, the repetition more finely focuses your goals. If you only repeat for repetition's sake, you are wasting your time. It sometimes takes only one heartfelt affirmation—like a sincere "I do"—to change your belief system. Repetition in and of itself has no value.

As you continue to improve your imprinting technique, you will learn which of your affirmations you are most sincere about, and which require more commitment and repetition.

Also, if your affirmations aren't bolstered by a strong desire and commitment, the repetition may actually imply *doubt* to your subconscious. You might be repeating an affirmation only to convince yourself that you really want it, or that you can really attain it. At first, you might affirm, "I am a nonsmoker?" as if you were asking a question, because you're not sure you want it. And your self-talk will kill you: "No, you're not. You're lying. You don't really want to stop smoking." And you'll keep trying to affirm it: "I look better when I don't smoke. And I feel better. And I —." But your self-talk will battle back: "You don't really care about that. You really want to smoke." So sometimes you must use repetition—"I *am* a nonsmoker because—," "I *am* a nonsmoker because —," "I *am* a nonsmoker because —"—to keep convincing yourself that you are the kind of person you're *affirming* you are. Or that you really *want* what you're affirming.

At first, you may not feel you're worthy of your affirmations: "Am I *worthy* of that new job?" "Am I really *worthy* of earning more money?" "Am I *worthy* of a new house like that?" Those thoughts once troubled me, too. When you first start using this technique, it's like you're trying on a new fashion: "I'm not sure I look right in this." It takes time to get comfortable with it. Until then, though, some doubt can creep in. You might laugh at yourself, "No, this is ridiculous." But the more you keep repeating your affirmations—"I *am* a nonsmoker," "I *am* a strong teacher," "I *am* a good parent,"—the more you believe, "I *can* attain that goal." But once you decide you *are* worthy, then you declare, "That's it. I've got it. It's mine." And you won't ever need to affirm for those things again. So an affirmation that you are worthy of your goal may be one of the most important affirmations you make.

When is the best time to do my affirmations?

Just before you fall asleep at night, and again upon awakening in the morning—times when your brain is most susceptible to suggestion. Make your affirmations during some quiet, private time when you won't be disturbed. And make one of your first affirmations, "I enjoy writing and visualizing my affirmations daily because of the positive results." Write your affirmations on 3 x 5 cards; keep one set with you, and one set at home. When you read them, close your eyes and visualize. Or use a tape recorder or tape deck in your car to better use your time. On the way to and from your job, listen to your affirmations.

How long do I keep affirming for something I want?

Internal goals might only take a couple of weeks. External goals will probably take longer because they involve other internal changes as well. But don't be impatient. If you affirm, visualize, and imprint correctly, I guarantee you that in a relatively short time, you will notice a change. It's like planting a seed and waiting for the flower to grow. When you plant a seed, you trust and believe that the flower will grow from it. You know that this growth will begin with the roots in the soil, out of sight. You trust that the shoot will soon appear; you don't keep digging up the soil to see if the roots are growing.

How can I change old vows and goals that no longer work for me and imprint new ones?

Did you ever make a vow? Perhaps you just got engaged or married. That's a major vow. Did you make any vows when you were a child?

As a child, I was raised in a very negative environment. My mother was not mentally healthy. When things would go wrong, she'd be mad for a week, violent sometimes. So I made a vow: "I'll never be like her; I'll be happy when I grow up." I said it many times. It was a positive vow for negative circumstances. I wonder why psychology looked good to me when I got to the university. The vow I had made was driving me.

Also, the house I lived in was junk. The outside of the house and the yard were a disgrace. I was embarrassed to have anybody come to our house, so I would never invite anybody over. I was ashamed of where I lived. The housing projects were nicer than our home.

So I made a vow: "When I grow up, I'll have the nicest house in Seattle." That's what I said, and I meant it with strong emotion.

I now have a very nice home, one of the nicest in Seattle. And I have a ranch home that is even nicer than my Seattle home. And we're building a six-floor condominium complex with the nicest view of Seattle.

Do I need it? No. What motivates me? What's driving me? What am I trying to prove? Who am I trying to impress? That vow was a healthy vow at one time, but it's not necessarily healthy now.

You need to know what drives you. Identify your inner vows; otherwise, you could be driven to acquire more houses, more money, more fame. "I got to the top; I showed them." Nobody even cares. But that inner vow still drives you.

How do you change a goal that gets in the way of new growth? How do you change a vow that has outlived its purpose? The processes of affirmation and visualization allow you to alter vows that no longer serve you and change what drives you.

To correct those vows inside of me that are inappropriate and stop me from being the person I'm capable of being, I use the affirmation process, which is part of internal goal setting. I say to myself, "I'm not buying this home for an investment. My real reason is that I was ashamed of my house when I was a kid. But it's now a dumb reason. I keep buying houses for the wrong reasons. I don't need them. It's not a wise choice. It's an unconscious compulsion that causes me to accumulate things that I don't need."

We're still going to have the six-floor condominium, but it's going to be for a different reason. It's an investment. And it's the right reason. It's a mature reason. I know why I'm doing it, and it's okay.

When my father died, we thought my grandfather would help out. He didn't. As a teenager, I was mad at him, and I made a vow: "I'll never be like him. I'll always take care of my family." I made that vow many times.

One of our adopted sons is still incarcerated. He's attempted murder more than once. He's dangerous to himself and society.

We visited him one day at the institution. After our visit, the psychiatrists said they wanted to talk to Diane and me for a moment. They asked, "Why would you two adoptive parents stick by this kid who has caused the world so much trouble, when most natural parents wouldn't do so?" I gave them a flippant answer because I didn't know the real answer. I just said, "Well, I never thought not to."

Driving home, I said to Diane, "I bet it was my grandfather. It was that vow I made about taking care of my family."

That vow has served me well. But in building this company over 20 years, I created an extended family and brought in a lot of friends. Some of them quit growing. But I didn't fire them. I just built systems around them. So that vow got in the way of the growth of our company. "I'll always take care of my family." So while it served me well in one way, it did not serve me well in another. If you don't recognize that, you will wonder why you're not the leader you could be.

You've been conditioned by your past experiences, your *born with it or without it* attitudes, and your flat-world thinking. Limiting forces cause you to believe and act according to how you were taught and reared. You accepted other people's versions of reality as *the truth*, and you accumulated a lot of junk that might still be part of the way you view yourself and the world.

For example, when you were a kid, you may have vowed, "I hate liver and onions. It tastes awful." Your subconscious accepted your affirmations literally. So it said, "Okay, whenever you eat liver and onions, it'll taste awful. You'll hate it." Sure enough, you hated it. When you grew older, you didn't need to remember the vow; you automatically acted like it. That one-time affirmation keeps working—and you don't question why.

As kids, we make many vows: "I'm scared to death of heights," or "I'm afraid of the dark." When we get older, we're still scared of those same things simply because we said we were. That's the power of words to build belief. So, if you talked yourself into believing your own vows about "the truth," whose vows did you believe? What did your brother or sister tell you about reality that you believed? What did your parents tell you that shaped your self-image? How about your grandparents, your relatives, teachers, employers, coaches, friends? How many of *their* vows have you digested without a second thought?

For example, I am a Catholic. When I was a kid, what I learned was taught through fear. You didn't do something because you wanted to, you did it because you were afraid *not* to. You feared the punishment. It was a sort of "or else" motivation: "Either you do it this way, *or else*." In my school, I was taught to believe that you couldn't eat meat on Friday, or else you'd go to hell. The nuns who taught me that painted a picture of hell that frightened me.

They painted it so vividly that I *knew* if I so much as nibbled meat on Friday, I'd be hurled into the fire pits of hell. But most kids in my neighborhood weren't Catholic. So every Friday, someone would say, "You wanna come over to my house for dinner?" I'd always ask, "What are you having?" They'd say, "Hamburgers." And I'd think, "You maybe, but not me. *You* can go to hell if you want to, but *I* ain't going."

Then, along came Pope John XXIII, and he made a few changes. One change he made was "It's okay. You can eat meat on Friday now. It's your choice." That was so sudden. After centuries, now we had permission to eat meat on Friday? I thought of the people who'd already gone to hell for that, and I said to myself, "Oh no. *You* eat it!" But, eventually, I gave in. And when I finally did eat meat on Friday, it tasted like the flames of hell! That sensation lasted for weeks. With every bite, I wondered, "Is he *sure*?" Even though I had the Pope's permission to choose, my *conditioned fear* wouldn't allow me to change comfortably.

It takes effective visualizing, affirming, and imprinting to overcome powerful, past conditioning.

DIANE'S STORY

Part IV: I Was Still Me

LOU: Diane continued to make her own decisions by choosing to take chemotherapy, which was devastating. Her hair started coming out in clumps. At first, this really bothered her. So we got her the finest wig made. But she wouldn't wear it. She insisted, "No, I'll just look like I look. I want to be myself."

Eventually, she lost all her hair. But the amazing thing was that she looked absolutely radiant and beautiful anyway. You would look at her and think: "Oh, Diane's trying a fashionable new hairstyle." And she continued to dress beautifully, just like before. So, to Diane, it was never a negative. She thought of herself, and she *looked* happy and glowingly healthy. So everybody around her started seeing that, too. It was never, "Oh my God. You poor thing. You've got cancer." It was always, "Boy, Diane, you look fantastic!"

DIANE: In the hospital, I had my lipstick and mascara in my little nightstand. I thought, "If I wore lipstick and my mascara yesterday, I'm going to wear it today. I'm in the hospital, but I'm not going to look sick and pale."

I decided I was still me, and that *still me* should be the dominant picture. I remember how when Lou and I were just married and I was in the hospital with kidney problems, I got up the day after surgery and took a stroll because I couldn't think of myself as *hospitalized.* I dragged all over the hospital, and I felt much better doing that. The staff was aghast. They found out that I wouldn't allow myself to fall into a passive patient's role: "I'm ill. I can't do anything but lie here and hope for the best." Instead, my attitude was, "I'm getting better and better. What good is in store for me today?"

I always look to the future. In November, Lou was going to have his 50th birthday, but he wasn't up to doing anything. So I decided to arrange a big party. To do that, I had to reschedule my next chemotherapy session in advance because, afterwards, I knew I'd be too weak to do anything fun for about four or five days. Well, everybody pitched in to help and we reserved the Garden Court Room and Spanish Ballroom at the Four Seasons Hotel for Lou's party. I was bald at the time, but I got dressed up anyway and had a wonderful time. So it wasn't, "Well, I have cancer. I'm too sick to celebrate my husband's birthday." In fact, planning the party, getting dressed up for it, and enjoying it was very life-affirming for me.

LOU: During this difficult period, Diane was so focused on the future that she designed and helped build the 15,000-square-foot Tice Lodge in the mountains; went to Europe twice and brought back two container loads of antique furniture; decorated and furnished the lodge; threw parties, went shopping, entertained friends, and helped run our company. She changed her diet. Diane started exercising, even though sometimes she could barely walk. She went to a psychiatrist in case there was some undetected stress involved. In other words, she changed her entire life.

She also sought out unconventional people, like healers, whom other doctors referred to as "quacks." Doctors implored her, "Why would you go to somebody like that?" Without very high self-esteem, that might have imprinted doubt in her mind. But she decided not to rule out any possibility. She felt that research and decision-making were creative processes. And she knew that the creative process is very stimulating to your total system. So, for Diane, seeking options wasn't just a diversion; it was a stimulation of the total person.

She also had to make some very powerful decisions. At one point, she decided *not* to take radiation, even though the doctor said that radiation was absolutely essential because the cancer had broken loose in her system. It was a tough decision. She had to fight her own mind, she had to think independently, she had to become a risk-taker. A key factor throughout was that Diane took accountability for being sick. She chose not to torture herself with blame or guilt, and not to wallow in self-pity. Instead, she said, "Look, I helped cause the disease. I can help cause the wellness."

DIANE: Causing my own wellness now became very important to me. I read Dr. Bernie Siegel's book, *Love, Medicine and Miracles,* about his work with exceptional cancer patients. I began to understand that you don't so much *get* cancer as you *develop* it. I found out that cancerous cells are present in everyone to greater or lesser degrees. But we have powerful immune systems to keep things stable. If your immune system becomes depressed, it functions at less than optimal levels, and the cancer—or abnormal cells—can proliferate.

Around this time, I also found Dr. Glenn Warner, who was not only an oncologist—a cancer doctor—but he also believed in building up the immune system to fight the cancer. He helped me understand how my immune system might have become depressed over many years. What drew me to him was that his approach was more *total,* and he addressed the body's own fighting mechanisms. Back in medieval times, they talked about treatments for catastrophic diseases only in terms of "cut, burn, and poison." Well, today, what is the most modern treatment for cancer? Cut, poison, and burn. He saw much further than that.

His approach dovetailed perfectly with the concepts that we teach. My reflective thinking was that the immune system was part of me, so building it up would give me a personal feeling of accountability in the fight. I felt that if I built up my immune system, I could control the cancer. But I didn't give up the surgery and other traditional approaches. I just added a whole bunch of other options. This is significant. I think too many people deny unorthodox or nontraditional options. I'm not suggesting that you should give up surgery or chemotherapy. But neither should you rely only on traditional methods without also exploring as many complimentary methods as possible.

So, even while I was undergoing chemotherapy treatments with one doctor, I continued seeing an extraordinary healer who was able to describe very accurately the cancer cell activity in my body. At the same time, I kept following the regimen of Dr. Warner, who provided megadose vitamins, an exercise program, and a diet that helped build my immune system and depress the cancer. I also intensified my own research to find out about carcinogenic foods that you shouldn't eat, and immune-building foods that you should eat. I remember discovering little tips here and there, like the idea that cancer cells are weak cells that thrive in a saline environment in your body but wither in a potassium environment. That's how I discovered it was best to cut out extra salt in my diet and add more potassium.

I ate mainly fresh vegetables, fresh fruits, whole grains, and limited amounts of lean meat, such as turkey and some wild game and chicken—but not chicken which is full of hormones. I had immune-stimulating shots, I took special vitamins every day—beta carotene, vitamin A, vitamin C, vitamin E—and I took vitamin B_{12} shots once a month. The vitamins had an ironic side effect; they helped my fingernails grow long! That was the accidental realization of a lifelong dream.

I learned why the immune system gets stressed by researching the work of Dr. Carl Simonton. In his book, *Getting Well Again,* he explains the cancer healing process in terms of positive thinking, visualization, and affirmations. I sent for his report entitled " Psychology of the exceptional cancer patient," which inspired me to make a list of *superstar* affirmations, including:

I am a non-conformist. I am a fighter. I am psychologically aggressive. I have ego strength. I have a strong sense of reality. I have feelings of personal adequacy and vitality.

I treat all people with dignity and respect. I laugh at myself and don't take life too seriously. I am free each moment to choose my direction. My body has a built-in mechanism to fight disease and to return to a condition of health. I seek new worlds to conquer. My daily exercise retards tumor growth. I seek my priorities daily. I am learning to receive. I have freedom from conventionality. I seek information about my disease. I seek the finest medical treatment as well as other cures. I am physically active at work and play. I grow intellectually and emotionally.

I combat events in my life that cause life to lose meaning. I have psychological insight. I enjoy great flexibility in my life.

I found out that positive thinking is an excellent immune system booster, because the mind and the immune system are strongly linked. Studies show that what happens in the mind invariably affects the body. It's exactly like the placebo effect: If you can get sick on a negative placebo, you can get well on a positive placebo.

I worked on my weak areas. I was always an easygoing person, so I especially needed to affirm my assertiveness. Well, finally, I became more assertive than necessary. At a party, during the period when I was still having chemotherapy, Lou took me aside gently and said, "Diane, your affirmations on assertiveness are working beautifully. But could you add a little something about *tact* in there, too?"

Continued on page 227.

STEP 4:
Take Action, Correct Course

AS powerful as all these "mind games" are, sooner or later you have to take to the field. In this section, you will see why you should take to the field as soon as your mind and heart are right. You will learn along the way, especially from your mistakes. But take heart, make corrections, and keep going. You can't lose.

SMART TALK AFFIRMATION
I am, I do.

1. Clarify vision, mission, values, motives, attitudes
2. Engage in constructive self-talk
3. Set and imprint goals
4. Take action, correct course
5. Build people & teams

Chapter 11 deals with taking action. The *big time* is now, so don't wait to be perfect. Start developing your causative power by taking small, successful steps—seeing and seizing opportunity—while overcoming resistance and avoiding self-sabotage.

Chapter 12 tells how you can increase efficacy and stretch your comfort zones by using the tools of constructive imagination to change your idea of where you belong. You become dissatisfied with the old, break free from cultural binds, give yourself permission to grow, and take the path of obvious opportunity.

Chapter 13 deals with aligning mental and physical habits. Knowing that you can is half the battle, but you must still get past the bad habits of avoidant behavior, fears, rationalizations, and awkward situations. You do that by ridding yourself of the victim mind-set and developing resiliency.

Chapter 14 shows you how to receive feedback and make course corrections. Obtaining accurate feedback and accepting it are two different matters. So-called *negative feedback* causes tension and anxiety. But you can deal with the tyranny of the unfamiliar through the power of suggestion.

Chapter 15 tells you to challenge status quo and expand your comfort zones. We tend to regress to old, familiar comfort zones as we experience the symptoms of leaving them. But we can learn how to self-regulate at higher levels by adjusting what we consider to be *good enough*. As we imagine the new situation, we move relatively effortlessly and painlessly ahead. Having a "Board of Advisors" will keep us on track.

c h a p t e r   1 1

START TAKING ACTION

TAKING action is what leadership of self and others is all about. You need to develop your ability to cause good things to happen in your life. I call it *Smart Walk*—it's walking your smart self-talk.

You can sit and watch a master perform all day long without improving your performance, unless you move out of where you are and try something new that you saw the master do. Don't wait until you're good before you start. Start where you are, and then you get good.

In this chapter, I break this action step into seven smart behaviors that can become habitual.

1. Preview performance in simulation mode. Several years ago, I was seated in a fully loaded DC-10 as we taxied down a Honolulu airstrip. As we raced down the runway to lift off, all of a sudden I heard a loud noise—pow! We blew out tires on the left side of the jet. The captain held the nose of the plane down and veered to the left, gouging a 1,000-foot rut in the runway and bringing the aircraft to a halt just before it dumped into the ocean. Everybody breathed a sigh of relief. The captain calmly announced, "Well, folks, looks like we got a flat tire."

Flat tire? We almost *died!*

How could that captain be so calm and cool under such stress—and still get the job done right? Was it luck? Was he born with it? No, of course not. It was *habit*. He'd programmed in the anticipated recovery from that kind of emergency so often and so thoroughly that he didn't need to think about it. He just reacted as he'd trained himself to react.

Pilots train in flight simulators, full-scale replica cockpits with authentic instruments, and they *fly* the simulators without ever leaving the ground. They learn, "If this happens, here's what you do. If that happens, here's what you do." They visualize situations vividly, then rehearse them over and over until their reactions become routine.

But they don't rehearse the accident; they rehearse the recovery. If they do that often enough, with the right imagery, when the emergency happens, they act like they believe themselves to be. When they perceive the danger signals, their simulator habits kick right in. They hold the nose down and keep the plane on the runway.

Deliberate preparation for a predetermined outcome results in high performance. You accomplish a goal hundreds of times in your mind (your simulator) *before* you try to do it. You program habits into your subconscious mind with visualization—you anticipate the changes in your business, you anticipate what the new house will be like, you anticipate expected crises. Then, when the tires suddenly *do* blow out, you're in control.

You and I can do the same thing in our work. Before every speaking engagement, I prepare myself mentally by projecting myself into the situation. I learn about the audience, looking for things to admire about them. I learn to genuinely like them and look forward to being with them.

Do you mentally prepare for your day? Do you mentally prepare for the important events in your life? Do you mentally prepare for meetings? Do you prepare on the inside for the outcome you want on the outside? You may think that you are too busy, so you just rush right in, gamble, play it by ear, and take whatever happens. Foolish, indeed, is the person who rushes in unprepared.

You can prepare yourself for any situation by mentally preparing yourself in advance and by anticipating the event with positive emotion. When you go into a situation—mentally prepared and with positive expectancy—you naturally create success.

Positive forethought is a habit of highly successful, causative people. They see the outcome as constructive; they reiterate it over and over in their minds, and then they go out and create it.

2. Start here and now: don't wait for the big time. Just as pilots don't merely *talk* their way through simulated emergencies, you don't merely *say* your affirmations. You rehearse and start taking action.

You don't wait for the big time—the big time is where you are at the moment. You don't wait until you develop fully before you take action. You take action on the level you're living presently. Or you will never take action. You do things at whatever level, at whatever place of work, in your community, in your family. You've got to turn and face the challenge now, and then you'll turn and face bigger problems and challenges later.

I wasn't ready 20 years ago to do what we are doing today. If I had waited until I was as good as I am now, I would never have started. I was as good as I could be when I started, but I needed to get better every day.

In fact, I feel that I'm not ready now for the things that I'll do in the future. It's a constant process of growing inside, an ongoing daily process of preparing yourself for the future by changing an attitude or habit or shortcoming, and by taking action now.

It's a mistake to keep waiting until you're *good and ready* before you take action because only by taking action now will you get better as you go. So you don't wait until you're great. Daily you improve. You intend to, you want to, and you do. As Diane reminds me, "Contemplation without action is being unjust to yourself." Many people are unjust to themselves. When they go to a self-improvement course, they think, "Okay, I've been to that one." They scan a book and say, "Now I've read this book." Goodness gracious, what a waste of time.

Having knowledge isn't enough. Universities are full of people who have the knowledge, but who haven't changed a bit in years. They haven't done much to improve the community in years. They don't even believe they can. They don't know how to take action. You grow in causative power as you apply what you know, as you apply it to what you want to do at the moment. As you apply it, you find the way to become more every day. If you envision great dreams but take no action, you get no growth.

Again, a word to the wise: *Allow yourself some time to assimilate your bold ambitions before you jump in.* When I learned years ago that I could be just as happy giving as receiving, Diane and I decided we would adopt a child. We didn't have any children of our own at the time, and so we adopted Bonnie. The first day that I had that little two-month-old baby around me, I just danced all over the living room floor with her in my arms. That baby gave me so much happiness, and yet she wasn't able to give.

Well, the case worker thought we were an easy touch, and so she brought us three more children within one month. We went from zero to four adopted kids just like that. They were 5, 6, and 7 years of age, and holy terrors. We threw ourselves out of our comfort zone. Instead of having nine months to assimilate a new baby coming into our lives, we had nine days.

Imagine us driving around town in an old Rambler with one door wired shut, and these kids screaming and yelling and fighting. The kids were just driving us nuts. Still, when I would come home and the kids would say, "Daddy's home, daddy's home." That would make me feel super. When I came home driving the MG and Thunderbird I had before the kids, I never had that feeling.

So, allow yourself time to assimilate your important goals. Visualize yourself at the next plateau, and gradually adjust your comfort zone.

3. Give and keep your word. How do you gain the power to make things happen? Strength comes from being able to give and keep your word. Have you ever been around people who say, "Have a nice day," but don't mean it? "Good to see you," and they don't care? "Let's get together someday," but they don't ever call you? Words in themselves have no power, except what you the sender and the receiver give them.

You can believe some people when they say that they will do something. You know that it will occur. And yet you know other people who when they say things are going to happen, you have an element of doubt, even if they use the same words.

One of my partners in Australia, Denis Horgan, has various business ventures going. Anything Denis touches seems to be successful. When we started doing business with Denis, I knew that anything he ever said he would do for us was done; I could just count on it.

Once when I returned from Australia after visiting Denis, I told my staff, "Anytime we promise Denis anything, make sure it happens, at any cost. He has the right to expect from us what we expect from him."

One time we promised to send Denis a $20 package by a certain date, but we forgot to send the package until he called to ask about it just two days before the promised delivery date. Since Australia is a day ahead of us, we couldn't mail it. Diane was the only one who had her visa ready, and so she flew it over at a cost of $4,000—and that has happened twice to us.

Now, $4,000 is a lot of money, and I wouldn't want to incur charges like that all the time. But it's that important to me to keep my word because my word is power. I don't want to let people down. I don't want to let my company down. My affirmation is "People can depend and rely on me if I give them my word." So if I'm not going to do it, I'm not going to say it. If I give my word, I expect to keep it.

Sometimes I'm strong, and sometimes I'm not. For instance, one time, Diane and I were sitting around planning our future. And Diane said to me, "I think you ought to forget about setting goals." I looked at her quizzically. She said, "Unless you take better care of your health and lose weight, you might as well forget about what you want in the future."

And all of a sudden I said to her, "Okay, no more excuses." That's when I lost 30 pounds in six weeks. But, for 15 or 20 years I was overweight, and my word on weight was no good to me.

If you don't mean it, don't say it. All you do is lessen your power. When you don't keep your word, you lose causative and creative power. When you say "I do" in a wedding vow, and then keep your promise, you have power—power to be resilient in tough times. If your affirmations aren't working for you, and if good things aren't happening around you, it could be that your word is not much good to you. The ideal might be to make a one-time affirmation like "I quit smoking" and do it. Imagine affirming almost anything just one time, and then being or doing it. But for the most part, our word is not that strong. And so those one-time affirmations don't work for us. But we can use the affirmation process to assimilate it to where we expect it and we believe it. Power comes from how good your word is to yourself.

4. See and seize opportunity. An opportunity must be seen to be seized. By visualizing the new significance, you open your mind to the abundant opportunity around you. You've got to see it to seize it. And as you increase your seeing power, you've got to be willing to seize opportunity when it comes.

You will grow as you see and seize opportunities. They're all over the place. You can also create your own opportunities. You will see and seize obvious opportunities when you have a strong vision and goal. When those are very clear—many opportunities just jump out at you. You need not be consciously alert to the obvious opportunities, they'll just be there; in fact, some of them will slap you in the face.

Our mission statement at The Pacific Institute sets the tone for our ability to see opportunity: "We affirm the right of all individuals to achieve their God-given potential. The application of our education empowers people to recognize their ability to choose growth, freedom, and personal excellence. We commit ourselves to providing this education through all means that are just and appropriate."

That mission statement requires us to have eyes for fresh opportunities and hands to seize them. For example, at times I accept speaking engagements simply because I sense that they will lead to greater opportunities to fulfill our mission.

5. Go ahead—make a mistake. Many people are blocked by the need to be perfect. They fear failure. The total quality dictum is *zero defects*. The boss says, "Don't make a mistake." But that can freeze the culture and stun many people into inactivity. "I don't want to be embarrassed. I don't want to make a fool of myself. I don't want to fail. I think I'll wait. I'm not taking any chances." Several folks have tried to get me to play golf. I respond in jest, "I think I'll wait until I know how before I try it." I'll need to change my attitude to use my potential.

Education without application is virtually useless. You need to take small, successful steps from your view of where you are now toward where you want to be. All those tiny steps develop your ability or efficacy, especially when you relive and reiterate them. You are strengthened inside. You have the resolve to move forward. And your purposes and projects get bigger and deeper. My success, and the success of many others, has been found on the far side of failure. As Mark Twain suggested, one should never let school interfere with his education. Mistakes are a big part of learning in the school of hard knocks.

6. Groove the right behaviors. Habits are automatic, free-flowing actions that we don't have to consciously think about. They allow us to comfortably do several tasks at the same time. We can talk while we drive. We can breathe while we eat. If we had to stop to consciously think about how we breathe, how we digest food, or how we drive a car, we'd have difficulty *doing* it.

When I was a high school teacher, I taught driver's training. That's how I lost my hair. I would first get the kids frozen in that ten-and-two position on the steering wheel, driving cars with automatic transmissions, and then I'd teach them how to drive cars with stick shift or manual transmissions. Now they'd have to use a clutch. It'd be one foot on the clutch, the other on the gas. At first, they'd always kill the engine.

But, after a few weeks and what seems like endless repetition, that same kid would be going 70 miles an hour in a 30-mile-per-hour zone, with one hand on the wheel, the other around his girlfriend, listening to the radio, watching for the highway patrol in the rearview mirror, and looking for more girls alongside the road. Now, how could they do all that when just weeks before they could hardly get out of the parking lot? They turned driving over to the subconscious. And then they'd just free-flow.

So, habits are good in the sense that they allow us to free-flow. But with change happening so fast around us, the patterns that we have set may not get us to where we want to go. And yet we still free-flow out of habit if we don't alter the pattern.

So, you have some people working for you who can wake up, go through their morning routine of getting ready for work, drive to work, take the elevator up to the right floor, and not wake up until eleven o'clock. They've got the routine down well; they just free-flow through the morning. But interrupt their pattern, give them a different pattern, or change their task or even the location of their desk, and they are bothered beyond belief. Most people who get into ruts and routines don't like change. Because the change disrupts their ability to be lazy, both mentally and physically.

Habits are fine, as long as everything stays the same. A habit that might have served us nicely three years ago might hinder us today. Some of our habits require updating. We must keep making habits *current* if we expect to change and grow. We must change our habits as our marriage changes, as our children change, as our business changes, as our own needs change.

Changing old habits and developing new ones is a challenge. Our subconscious may lock out a new routine, even if it would help us achieve 10 times more than what we do now. We feel more comfortable with old habits because we don't have to think about them. In fact, once you have a habit, if you bring it back to the conscious level, you mess up the automatic flow. Have you ever been asked to spell a familiar word? You might say, "Give me a pen. I have to write it out." You *know* the word perfectly, but having to *think* about it causes you to be unsure.

For example, have you ever tried to teach somebody how to dance? You can suddenly be awkward, uncertain. You wonder, "Do I really *know* this dance?" You know it, but you know it best *subconsciously.* Bring it to the conscious level, and you need to think it out.

Suppose you're golfing with a friend. On the 10th tee, when your friend is ready to swing, ask: "I was wondering: Do you inhale or exhale on your backswing?" If he stops to think about it, he'll probably mess it up. He'll shank it, maybe miss it altogether. I've seen it happen, even *made* it happen! How? By bringing the habit to the conscious level.

You get a great deal of resistance to change from organizations, teams, families, even from friends when you ask them whether they inhale or exhale on their backswing. You're asking them for conscious effort, and they don't like the uncomfortable feeling: "Stop it," they say. "You're irritating me. I don't want to think about it."

"Well, I would like to stop it, but the competition won't wait for us. We can't keep doing things in the same old way."

So, how do you get yourself, your spouse, your company to change old habits that are hindering growth? You use visualization, affirmation, and goal-setting to imprint new responses. Then, when the time comes for the actual change, you can do it *automatically.*

7. Be authentic and accountable. When I was a high school teacher at Highline High School, I was a pain for the administration. Now, I wasn't always right, but I always expressed my opinion, even if my opinion was different from the opinion of the principal or other teachers. Right in front of everybody, I'd say, "I think you're wrong about this," even though it might cost me a future in teaching. But it was more important for me to be authentic than it was to be pleasing.

Today, some people in my own company tell me, "Lou, you act as if you don't care if we stay with you. You come in and tell us some things that make us mad."

"Well, I don't tell you these things to make you mad, but if they make you mad, so be it. I'm not going to come in and act nice if I'm mad. If I'm upset, do you want me to come in and pretend that I'm not? I try to be authentic, even at the risk of losing you as a friend or losing you as a business partner."

And when I teach and speak, I hope to be very authentic with the audience. I seek integrity between who I am and what I say.

You can't *will* your way into being authentic and accountable. You can't use your willpower to override the subconscious self-image, pitting your conscious will against the way you presently are. That use of willpower is counterproductive, because you don't want to be coerced or forced against your will. Why can't you just let go of willpower, coercion, and *have to* motivation? Because much of what you do is not your idea, and so your work is not on a *want to, choose to, like to, love to* basis.

You can't be authentic without being accountable, and you won't want to be accountable if you feel that you *have to* do what you do. You won't say, "If it's to be, it's up to me." In fact, you may say, "I hope it's not up to me. Isn't there somebody more capable?" I confess that I've thought that way, and maybe you think the same way: "I hope it's not up to me. I know every place I ever screwed up and every mistake I ever made. There must be somebody better out there who can tell me what to do."

Well, there may be. But don't you think it would be better if you searched inside yourself, designed your own future, found your own path, and went after what you really want out of life? How long has it been since you felt that sense of accomplishment you felt as a child when you first ventured out of the neighborhood on your own, or when you took the bus to school all by yourself, or when you went downtown all by yourself? Look what you're missing out of life if you don't take charge and do those things on your own. If you don't do them on your own, then you lose your power. Because, you're waiting for somebody or something outside of yourself to act, which keeps you a child in an adult's body.

I was 36 years old before I honestly learned how to tie my own necktie. Diane always tied it. We started going together at 16, got married at 18, and there was nobody else to tie it. I just had Diane tie it, and never learned how to do it myself. If she wasn't around, I would just pull it around my neck and cinch it up halfway. Isn't that ridiculous?

And, you know, my mother used to cut my meat for me, even when I was a grown man. I was 30-something, and she would come to dinner and slice my meat into little bites, so that I wouldn't have to cut my meat for myself.

"But Mother, I can do it myself."

"That's okay," she said, "I do it for your other brothers too."

She meant well, but keeping me as a child in an adult body was doing me no good. Would you want your mother to come over to your house and cut your meat? No, you want to cut it. But if she is forceful, then you may let her have her way. But what you do is give up accountability for your own future.

It's very important that you decide what you want. You need to ask yourself, "It isn't what my mother wants for me, nor what the boss wants for me, nor what other people say that matter. What do I want?"

That's what Diane and I try to do. We make choices and decisions about what we want, and we are willing to take the consequences for our decisions. That's being accountable. Some people want rights without responsibility, or responsibility without accountability.

"Oh, give me that promotion."

"Okay, if you accept the responsibility."

"But I don't want added responsibility."

"What you want, then, is reward without risk. I'm sorry, but it does not work that way. If you take the risks, there's a chance you'll lose. And what happens if you lose? Well, you may have to sell your house and pay off the bills."

"I don't want to do that."

"Then you really don't want the promotion."

Do what you want to do, but accept the consequences of your choices and decisions. That's the way life is. But isn't it wonderful that we have free will? Isn't it better than being a bird or dog or cow and going along with your nature? The challenge of choice is a wonderful one.

The difference between amateurs and professionals is that amateurs are constantly coping with the new and unexpected. Professionals anticipate situations and prepare, first in simulators and then on the field, to program in the new habits that they need to succeed.

c h a p t e r   1 2

INCREASING EFFICACY

I was 35 years old before I first flew in an airplane. I didn't need to fly in an airplane where I went. I never left Seattle. When Diane and I would plan a vacation, we thought of going to Portland, Oregon, 150 miles away, and staying with somebody we knew there. Going to a hotel never came to our minds.

You don't let yourself think about what you believe you can't cause or accomplish.

For years, I was stuck—stuck in poverty; stuck in Burien, a suburb of Seattle; stuck in just hoping, wishing, and dreaming; stuck in wanting to win the lottery. I would think, "How can I be what I see other people being? They must be born that way—I can't be like that. I can't earn money. I can't grow in character and wisdom. I can't be rich, and still be a good person."

Those were my rationalizations for not getting myself out of my rut. But one day Diane and I decided to set out on a journey to develop our inner strength. We constantly worked on the inside so that we could be more and do more on the outside.

As you develop your inner strength, your dreams get bigger, your aspirations get bigger, your goals get bigger, and what you expect of yourself gets bigger. You want to attack bigger problems and face bigger challenges. You want to become more every day through study, learning, changing your beliefs, overcoming your fears, changing your attitudes, developing relationships. As you build inner strength, you say, "I think I can do that. I think I can do this." You get bigger ideas, creating greater discrepancy between your *here* and *there*.

Causative Power

Efficacy refers to the ability to cause and make happen. As you increase your power to cause and make happen what you want to make happen, you gain the courage and confidence to say, "Give me the next one, give me the next one." You begin to see bigger and better ideals, and more options and possibilities. And you begin to see yourself in new conditions and situations.

While it's important to know that you can learn, to know that you are bright and capable, you need more than self-knowledge to create self-efficacy and to boost your causative power. You must know how to change your attitudes and habits, how to motivate yourself constructively, how to rid yourself of negative thinking, and how to reject invalid ideas. You must know how because bad attitudes, habits, and ideas override good intentions and high ideals.

To achieve your stretch goals, you will need to increase the causative power not only in yourself but also in the people around you—in your family, in your company, and in your community. To develop your causative power, you use imagination and affirmation to develop your inner strength.

Developing efficacy is possible at every age and stage of life. Looking at how things are, current reality, while holding an ideal in your mind causes the energy and ideas you need to gain closure. The discrepancy between *here* and *there* is what creates the appetite. The dream or vision creates the appetite or aspiration.

Consider: How do you develop efficacy or causative power in a child? In the early months, you can hang a mobile over the crib—the kind that won't move unless the baby hits it. She thinks, "I caused that movement to happen. What else can I do?" Next, put a little toy just outside her reach, so she has to wiggle to get it. "Ah, I got that. Now, what's next?"

Efficacy is about knowing that you can cause and make things happen for yourself. So you should not only teach first graders how to read and how to write, but also teach them to believe when they come out of the first grade, "I'm smart. I can succeed in the second grade." That's the attitude of self-efficacy.

When you set a goal, you naturally appraise your efficacy. You wonder, "Is this too big for me? Or, am I bigger than it?"

You hear people say, "Well, can we afford it? Could I do it? Could I learn it?" Inefficacious appraisals are when you set a goal and then you talk yourself out of it. You tell yourself you can't do it. You don't believe you can do it. So you set the aspiration or the goal and then wonder: "Is this bigger than I am ? Can I afford it? Can I do it? Can I cause it?"

You've got to know the barriers that cause avoidant behavior. You've got to get past what I call your *optical illusions*, but you might call your *obstacle illusions.* You create illusionary obstacles, and you won't let yourself get past them. They become as real as any physical barrier.

Creative Power. You build your efficacy by building inner power. The more you know you can cause, the more you know you can create.

Now, I'm not talking about taking the place of God. But I am talking about being co-responsible. I believe that we are created in the image and likeness of God. And if God is a creative being, so are you and I. You and I have the creative power to build better communication systems, better highways, better health care.

But you don't just sit and wait for things to come to you. If you want good things to happen on the outside, make good things happen on the inside. Is the change inside you or outside you? Do you feel like a victim? Do you feel like the world has pounced upon you? Do you feel that you can't cause anything to happen? Do you have to wait for the right sign? Do you rely on superstition? Do you say, "There's nothing I can do about it"?

Or, do you feel like "I don't like where I am, but I'm going to change it. I don't like the way the company is running, but I'll fix it. I don't like my financial setting, but I'll cause it to be better. I don't like how my marriage is going, but I'll repair it."

I used to be a person who would just sit and gripe about things, saying, "Why don't they fix it?"

My self-talk would respond, "Why don't *you* fix it?"

"They won't listen to me."

"So make yourself somebody they'll listen to or get out."

As a high school teacher, I wanted to cause the school to leap into greatness. But I wasn't credible enough to change things. So I just complained and fixed the blame on the outside.

When I finally decided to do something about it, I knew that I first had to fix me. And so Diane and I started a lifetime journey to become better, stronger, more influential. Now we're not only good, we're good for something. We can now influence the high school system on a national level. We can influence people worldwide.

So can you. But it's up to you to change you. As you improve yourself, your life improves. You don't just wait for circumstances outside to get better. You cause them to get better.

You may have been raised to think that good things happen from the outside. "Grandpa or Grandma makes them happen, or Santa Claus brings them. But surely I don't cause them myself."

How were you raised? What is your attitude? What is the attitude of your people? Do you have a victim mind-set, or do you have a causative mind-set?

Please understand, I didn't always have a causative mind-set. I had to learn how to build my inner strength and change my behavior. As I strengthened my inner self, my efficacy, and my outlook, I strengthened my output. Now I don't sit and wait; I cause.

Be careful how you speak to people around you about what you or they can or cannot do. You create an impression of your causative power. What you affirm, your subconscious assimilates. It accepts what you tell it. So continually work to develop the efficacy in the people around you, because the tasks and goals you need to accomplish in five years are going to be more than what you're capable of doing now. You can't do it with the same efficacy you have now. You must keep developing.

And so when you walk down the street and your child says, "Daddy, can we get a car like that?" you don't say, "We can't afford it," because you're giving that child the idea that "we're incapable of doing it." You say, "We have a better place for our money now. There's something else we choose to do. We could take all of our money and sell our house to buy that car, but we choose not to—we have other things to do."

Remember: authentic, progressive, effective. Progressive means constantly developing day by day, constantly improving day by day. It is affirmation at work; it is study at work. It's constantly working to develop yourself. Why dream bigger? To accomplish more. To cause more results in your world.

Bite Off More

Many people quit learning and growing when they graduate from school or when they get their first job. Most schools create an inefficacious mind-set by telling kids what's wrong with them, where they make mistakes. So they believe they're incapable and not causative. We are counseled by people who shouldn't be counseling because they don't know how to grow. When we start talking about our dreams and aspirations and what we want to be when we grow up, they listen and tell us, "Now, let's be realistic," or "Let's not think that way." And the reason they tell us that is because they don't want us to feel like failures or to be disappointed. They're afraid that we'll get hurt.

We can't be afraid. We've got to allow our kids to get hurt, and then help them to recover. We've got to build resiliency and toughness in them, and in us.

People will sometimes say to me, "Well, this goal-setting stuff is all right, but this vision-and-mission stuff is pie-in-the-sky. I'm a realist.

What happens if I set big goals, or invite others to set big goals, and fail to reach them? We'll crash."

"Yes," I say, "you might fall. But you're tough, and you'll get right back up and go after it again. And if you learn from mistakes, you'll get it next time."

The reason we tell people not to dream big is because we already expect them to fail. Our expectations determine outcomes—it's like a self-fulfilling prophecy. If you communicate low expectations to people all around you, you undermine them. You can even do it with body language. You can do it by the way you treat people. You can do it in many subtle ways you're not even aware of.

So what happens when you don't accomplish a goal? You still have the dissonance. And so you throw up, don't sleep, and don't want to face people. And then you say with conviction: "So be happy with what you have, my dear. That's good enough for you. If you expect too much, it will only make you sick. It's because I love you that I'm telling you this. If I didn't care, I'd let you go out with big aspirations and dreams."

Honestly, that's told to so many people. Corporations run that way; teams run that way. They don't even know why they run that way. They think it's the way to be. It is not the way to be.

"But aren't you biting off more than you can chew?"

"Yes, you are supposed to. Bite it off, and grow into it."

"And what happens if you fail?"

"You cry. It hurts. But you get up and go again. You learn to build resiliency in yourself, resiliency in your children, resiliency in your people."

You might even celebrate some of your so-called losses and failures, especially if you learn some valuable lessons. And you can also brag about the recovery.

For instance, you might tell a child who tried out for the team but didn't make it: "I'm so proud of you, Mary. You tried out last year and didn't make the team, but you stuck with it. This year you came back and tried again. Wow, you're tough. You can do anything now." Mary will hear that, whether you say it directly to her or say it in her presence to another person, and she'll build resiliency. She'll then say, "Give me the next challenge."

Efficacy is *can do* causative power.

"Oh," you say, "I don't have the skill."

"Yes, but you can learn it, and then take on the challenge." That's the way we train military strike forces, superstar athletes, and peak performing professionals. We give them the skills and then give them the task. And when they know they can do it, they are not intimidated.

When you're intimidated and try to compete, you can't think right and you can't use your skills. ***Remember: It's not what you know; it's what you can use of what you know under unusual and difficult circumstances—the skills and knowledge you can use when you're stretching your comfort zone.*** If you prepare yourself well beforehand, you can use the knowledge and the skills that you have to succeed in events against competitors that once intimidated you.

For example, fighter pilots learn that it isn't what you know, it's what you can use of what you know when you're being shot at. It isn't what you can do in practice; it's what you can do when you're being tracked by a missile or when you're flying toward that target and artillery is coming at you.

If you're not at your efficacious best, you're dead. You may have been very good in rehearsal, but it doesn't matter. When you take the test, can you retrieve what you need, or do anxiety and pressure keep you from being successful? It isn't just what you learned in school, it's what you can get out when you're in the job interview and what you can deliver on the job. You won't fail or make a fool of yourself in those situations if you stretch your comfort zone and place yourself into that environment many times before you get there.

I won't go into a tough new situation unless I've already been there in my mind 100 times; then I can go there safely. I draw on successes of the past, and they don't need to be similar. If they are similar, so be it. I let that feeling well up inside of me, and then drop that feeling into the coming event. I go back and come forward. I go back and come forward. Now I can walk into that new environment and be good under pressure. Because I've already been there so many times successfully.

This same process will allow you to leave the familiar and to travel where you've never been before. Just reiterate a performance you are proud of and assimilate it with emotion: "Ah, good for you." Highly efficacious, causative people look forward and see success. Inefficacious people look forward and scare themselves to death. The difference is the control of forethought.

Releasing Potential

We don't know how much potential we have, but we all have much more potential than we develop and use. So act as though your potential is unlimited, just largely untapped.

How do we release our potential? Let me answer by telling a story. One time Diane and I were flying from London to Seattle, a 10-hour flight. Not wanting to waste the time, we talked about what we wanted to do in the next year and set some goals. I wrote my list, and Diane wrote her list. We looked at each other's list, and realized that it was basically the same list we had last year. Our lists indicated that we hadn't grown much on the inside during the year.

You don't make bigger goals than what you think you can accomplish. Your goals reflect your efficacy appraisal; they are accurate indicators of your growth, your skills, your knowledge, your causative power, your relationships. Have you grown in recent months? As you grow on the inside, your goals get bigger. If you don't grow, your goals remain the same.

So Diane said, "Let's not set any goals for a while. We'll spend the next six months developing our efficacy, and then we'll set goals. If we set goals now, they would be too small for us."

Inner strength creates outer reality. If you develop on the inside, you won't just wait for somebody to throw a party for you, promote you, or discover you. You won't just wait for good fortune; instead, you will cause it.

There's a direct relationship between the way your life is going and the way you think, talk, and walk. Some time ago, a friend of mine was involved in a float plane crash and almost died. As she started her recovery, she was depressed, thinking "Nothing in life matters now." Gradually, she gained more strength and stopped feeling sorry for herself. Her smart talk became, "Look, you're here to enjoy life. You could die any time. So enjoy it all."

At every age and stage in life, we can come up with reasons or rationalizations why we can't do something. Or, we can come up with reasons why we can do something. For example, in Ireland, I once met an impressive young man, age 25, who was attending an executive program. Most participants were 40 to 60 years old. I observed, "You seem to feel that you belong here." He said, "Why not? Alexander the Great was 17 when he took over command of his country's army." Another example: at age 89, Ruth Stafford Peale took over the management of The Peale Center, a major business and ministry, following the death of her famous husband, Norman Vincent Peale. She said, "Oh, I feel younger than ever. I'm excited. This is a new job for me. But I'm ready for it." I'm impressed by such people because they don't feel that they are too young or too old to do what they want to do. They reject the rationalizations common to their age.

On to Bigger and Better Things

If you blame your lack of growth on the people and events outside of you, you don't grow. Part of efficacy is knowing that you can know, that you can learn, that you can do, that you can unfold options and create a new reality.

As you increase your efficacy, you'll turn and face challenges, even dangers, in your community and your workplace. You'll have the strength to go toward the problem, to turn toward bigger challenges when you feel that it's the right thing to do and you're capable of doing it. Your *there* will get bigger than your family, your neighborhood, your school, your home town. Sure, you start there, but then you ask, "What could I do for all the kids around me? What could I do for the community?" And the spiral gets bigger. "Now, what do I want for China?" Your wants just get bigger.

Now, as you try to take other people with you to go where you need to go in a competitive world, you may frighten some of them to death. To a point, this anxiety arousal is okay; but if you let it go unchecked, then you not only get uptight, but you also get negative ideas and avoidant behavior. Inefficacious anxiety arousal by you or your people is the root cause of avoidant behavior. You talk yourself out of what you're capable of doing. And to you they're not excuses, they're good reasons. If you won't quit on one good reason, your subconscious gives you two; and if you won't quit on two, it gives you 200.

To get from *here* to *there,* you will need to release your potential. You stretch your internal comfort zone first using visualization and imagination. It's a deliberate process of seeing yourself into the next level—socially, financially, environmentally. When you do it properly, you change the picture in your mind. As you visualize the new, you become dissatisfied with the old. And that causes you to automatically move, to motivate, to get creative, to go to the next level.

If you're in a team effort and expect to bring your team with you, they need to change their internal image too, or all they do is drag you back. They're not bad people—they're just uncomfortable with your growth. So they keep pulling you back. They find reasons why "it won't work." They subtly sabotage your growth, because they're fighting for sanity.

I know what a struggle it is to transcend your culture and to operate on a more global level. And so I praise people who transcend the culture inside their own organization or community, people who are fighting the battle on the street. The constant challenge is to help change the culture that we are in now, whether it be a home, a high school, or a major corporation. It is the same problem, the same challenge, and it takes the same courage for the second grader as it does the *big time* executive. The big time is where you are at the present moment. It is some child in the second grade standing up against oppression; it is some kid taking a lead inside a community against drugs or crime—it has nothing to do with whether you happen to be in the big time.

The *big time* is where you are at the present moment. It takes courage for a high school teacher to take a stand against the injustice going on at the school. It takes courage to challenge injustice wherever you are. Transcending a culture is just going against the way things presently are in the environment. It isn't some grand thing reserved for those people *out there.*

Some big-salary entertainers, athletes, executives, and celebrities who allegedly affect millions of people aren't doing as much good as some *small people* are doing by helping the homeless get food and shelter or by helping sexually abused children. That, too, is making a difference. Whether you make a difference with two or two million, who's to say which is better? Is more always better? Is bigger always better?

Who are the truly great people? Those who act most courageous, most giving, most loving. The best leaders honestly don't believe that they are more important than anyone else in the organization. They're fighting the same problems. And in the process, they grow, progress, improve, increase their causative power, and prepare for the future. In seeking a new opportunity, a new world, a new life, they often transcend their childhood culture. They leave the homes and towns and professions of their parents and go where they can make a major contribution with their talents.

By contrast, if you put inefficacious people into a new culture or environment where they can't go back, they tend to recreate their old environment.

How do you grow beyond the image that you hold in your mind of how the old country was or how the old way was? What allows you to break free from entrapment and from past history?

As you change your internal picture of where you belong, you'll encounter attitudes, beliefs, forces, and habits that hold you back. You may find that some of your cherished beliefs are false: "This is all that man can do." "The world is flat." If you hold on to false beliefs, you remain a prisoner. You must free yourself from the fears, the ignorance, the ambivalence. Believe you can change, want to change, decide where you want to go and grow, and create some deep emotion about it. Identify one or two areas to start with and start building efficacy in that one area.

That's the way I did it. I started only wanting to win more football games. I was just trying to improve the way I coached. And I said, "But it will work here, and it will work there." Before long I talked myself right out of coaching football. And yet now, I coach other coaches and players. My life is very different from the way I thought it would be.

Your success may not come the way you thought it would either. But if you stop and reflect back, you may say with me, "Well, what do you know, I am a coach." So, be careful that you don't map the way to some of your big ideals. Don't lock on to some method or means. Keep the end in mind, but be flexible about ways and means.

Obvious Opportunity

Roy Vaughn, one of my mentors, was once head of the Texas Exes, the University of Texas alumni association. When he spent a few days at our ranch, he asked me, "What do you think the shortest route between two points is?"

I said, "I think it's a straight line."

He said, "What if you want to take the shortest route from your ranch to Seattle? If you draw a straight line between the two sites, would that be the shortest route? Look at those rugged Cascade Mountains in between. You would have quite a trip if you stuck to your straight-line strategy. So, if you don't go in a straight line, what's another way?"

"I guess I could always drive around."

He said, "It's the path of obvious opportunity. You always want to be alert to the path of obvious opportunity. You may opt to take a jet plane, a helicopter, raft the river, or follow a trail. You examine all options, looking for the path of obvious opportunity. When you find it, you seize the opportunity."

What is the straight line between you and foreign markets? It's the path of obvious opportunity. It may not be traditional. It may not be the path of least resistance. It's the one of obvious opportunity.

That's the way I go into other countries, that's the way I go into prisons, that's the way I work with governments.

Once I had an ideal to make a difference in the political leadership. We worked a little bit here and there, and soon we had an appointment in Washington, D.C., to meet Jim Wright, who was then the majority leader. He didn't know me from a rock. I sat in his office for a 1 p.m. appointment until it was 5 p.m. When Diane and I finally got into his office, he said, "What can I do for you two nice people?"

I said, "You can't do anything for me. Quite frankly, I don't know why I'm here. But I think that I'm supposed to do something for you. I don't know what it is."

And he said, "I want you to put on a seminar for me and a few of my colleagues." And he said, "I want to pay for the whole thing. What will it cost?"

I said, "This is what it costs."

He was shocked.

Then I said, "Or, it's free. You just take care of expenses and it's free. I'm not here to make money."

He then got seven young congressmen together, and that led to several other chances to influence political leaders, including an invitation to give the keynote address to 240 Democratic congressmen at their annual leadership conference.

I'm alert to opportunity, and I seize it. I have the end result in mind. I don't know where opportunity will surface. But when it surfaces, I get it. I get it in the path of obvious opportunity.

Make an affirmation: "I am very creative, alert to opportunities, and eager to seize them." Remain calm, alert, eager, and ready. And when opportunity calls (or knocks), you're ready. Just follow the path of obvious opportunity.

I'm always looking for a way to go to the front of the line without making anyone mad. I look for ways to bypass bureaucracy, forego tradition, find the way. Sometimes, I just show up and let the spirit work through me. I go with the faith and confidence that I can cause good things to happen.

Once I found myself in the castles at Heidelberg with our top generals of the European campaign, talking to them about leadership. "Me?" That's what goes through my mind. But I know I'm supposed to be there, and I know that I'll make a significant difference in their lives. Another time I found myself in Anton Rupert's home in Johannesburg to see if we could make a significant change in South Africa so that they could implement their first New Constitution with a Bill of Human Rights attached to it.

"Me? How did I get there?" The path of obvious opportunity.

You won't know how you'll get there when you start the journey, but if you're alert to opportunity, you will find the path of obvious opportunity. You will know when you're supposed to go someplace. You may not have the slightest idea what you're going to do when you get there, but you will discover a purpose.

Most people don't recognize an opportunity until they see it working for somebody else. If you're going to get *there* from *here* and make a difference, you need to see and seize opportunity. Everything you do doesn't need to be bold and big. It's little, everyday things that you do.

Out of the Rain, Off the Plane

Once I went to a concert in Perth, Australia, for Denis Horgan's 50th birthday. He brought in a Philharmonic orchestra to the Outback. This was out in the middle of nowhere, and yet there were 6,000 people, all dressed in tuxedos. He had one of the world's best opera singers and James Galway, the world's best flutist. So this big deal was going on, and everybody was dressed up, sitting on lawn chairs and holding umbrellas, because it was threatening rain. All of a sudden, a downpour hit, and everybody put up their umbrellas. Meanwhile, the orchestra played on.

Now Diane and I were sitting on the grass, and with the umbrellas up, we couldn't see a thing. So I said to Diane, "I'm going to get out of this rain and go where I can see."

She said, "You've got to walk through 5,000 people."

I said, "I know it, but I can't see."

She said, "Why don't you just shut up? You don't see music anyway; all you do is hear it."

I said, "But I want to see and hear it." So, I got up and walked through several thousand people toward cover under a balcony. Kevin, one of the Horgan brothers, saw me coming, with Diane following close behind. So he called out, "Lou, Diane, come sit here, under the balcony." And so we sat where we could be dry and see the concert. Kevin even brought us two bottles of chardonnay while we were sitting there.

See, you've got to get yourself out of the rain. Take charge of the situation. Feel that you can do something about the situation. You can't alter the rain, but you can seek shelter. No big deal—it's just an attitude. You don't sit and let it rain on you.

Now, our daughter Nancy and her friend David were with us, and Diane said, "Do you think we should walk down and get Nancy and David out of the rain?"

I said, "No, let them get wet if they aren't going to get themselves out of the rain."

Nancy is a little like me in this way, and soon, she and David came to join us. And now we had four bottles of wine. Jack MacMillan, the chairman of Nordstrom, and his wife, Loyal, were traveling with us, and Diane and I and the kids were sitting there having a bottle of wine and feeling sorry for them. Diane asked, "Do you think we should get Jack and Loyal out of the rain?"

I said, "Let them get wet. If they don't have the sense to get themselves out of the rain."

Soon here came Jack and Loyal. They saw that we weren't around, and looked for shelter. Now we had six bottles of wine. And we were all dry, enjoying the concert, being served hors d'oeuvres, and watching 6,000 people get rained on.

Another time, we went to South Africa. In Johannesburg, we were sitting in a British Airways 747 about ready to take off. But the pilots could not get the engines started. Now, security at that time in Johannesburg required us to stay onboard. The plane was hot, and people were sweating. It smelled bad. Over the PA, the captain said, "Our engines are too hot. We'll need to wait about 45 minutes before we can try again."

Now, we couldn't get off the plane, but the doors were open on both sides and a breeze was going through. So I got up, went out and sat on the stairs, without permission. I was all by myself out there. And the steward came and gave me a glass of wine. He didn't kick me off the stairs or say I shouldn't be there. Here I was, in a nice breeze in the shade with a glass of wine, while the rest of the people on that 747 were sweating, complaining, and hating every minute of it.

And I thought, "I'd better get Diane." So I went back and asked her if she wanted to sit on the stairs. We then had two glasses of wine. She said, "Do you think we should get Nancy and David and Jack and Loyal? Before long, six of us were sitting out on the stairs with glasses of wine. We waited there for about an hour, until the captain got the engines started again.

Don't Ask for Permission All the Time

If you get out of the mind-set "Will they let me?" you can take control of situations, become accountable, and accept the consequences of your decisions and actions. Don't get conditioned and trapped constantly by waiting for permission to take charge of your life. You may be asking for permission when you don't even need permission. I've learned not to ask for permission.

We're so conditioned to ask permission, starting in the first grade. "Will they pass me to the second grade? Oh, I hope so. Oh, thank you." And then you go to the sixth grade, "I wonder if they'll let me go to junior high school? Oh, thank you." "I wonder if I can graduate from junior high school and go to high school? Oh, thank you for letting me go." "I wonder if they'll let me make the team? Oh, thank you." "I wonder if I can graduate from high school. Oh, thank you." "Will they admit me to college? Oh, thank you." "Will I be able to graduate? Oh, thank you."

We constantly sit around and wait in long lines, hoping someone will grant us permission to move forward in life. We may feel trapped in an environment, unable to move, but if you exercise your efficacy, your causative power, you can start your own business, start your own life, start your own career. Start where you need to start. Quit waiting for permission. Take charge. Through Smart Talk, give yourself permission, and then walk. That attitude is essential to achieve what you want and get from *here* to *there*.

Often I'm not qualified to do what I do, as determined by those who set the qualifying criteria. There are people significantly more qualified. And yet I'm the keynote speaker, and I'm wondering, "What am I doing here? I've never even been in the Army, and yet here I am speaking to the chancellor of West Point. What am I doing here?"

You've got to learn to give yourself permission. It's an efficacious attitude. And you quit waiting for the sanction of those in authority. You've got to go to the head of the line, without making people mad. Don't just wait in line.

Sure, it's easier to move when people grant you approval and sanction. One big deterrent to your personal growth is that you wait for people to give you permission and tell you that you're qualified. Learn how to qualify and sanction yourself. Give yourself permission to take the next step, to go into this business, or to move into this market. If necessary, create your own rites of passage and credentials.

Of course, in some societies and situations, certifications are a must. But don't get trapped or stop your growth because you're sitting around waiting for somebody to make you a vice president. Maybe you ought to start your own company. Maybe you need to get out of your current environment. Maybe you won't achieve in the traditional manner. You may need to get out of the system and adopt an attitude of full accountability, of sanctioning yourself, of not getting trapped, of not waiting for people's approval to bless you and give you permission to take the next step.

c h a p t e r   1 3

ALIGN MENTAL AND PHYSICAL HABITS

Y OU can speed up the acquisition of a new habit by using the affirmation process to routinize your mental, emotional, and behavioral patterns.

I learned this when I was coaching football in high school. I put in a multiple offense ahead of time. Once I gave them the new patterns on the practice field, I would have the players groove them by making mental affirmations while they were home or in study hall. They were grooving a pattern or skill that they needed while they were waiting in the lunch line. They would go through the pattern several times in their minds, using odd times to rehearse, to speed the repetitions and groove themselves.

That's the way I gain new knowledge or practice skills. I practice the routine in my mind. I rehearse where I'll go, who I'll be with, what I'll be doing—I practice it all in my mind. And then I write it out in affirmation form and repeat them, because affirmation and repetition speed the acquisition and grooving of mental, emotional, and physical habits.

Groove Mental Habits

Take time out during the day to do mental rehearsing. You prepare ahead of time, before you're in the situation, by practicing your ideal mind-set, emotion, and behavior in your mind. Once you're in the event or game, you don't think about your performance consciously; you get focused, and you let yourself flow.

At night some people think about all the things that didn't go right during the day. No wonder they wake up feeling overwhelmed. You need to think about all the positive things that happened. It's okay to look at problems, but then say to yourself, "How will they look when they're fixed?" End with an image of how you want to solve the problem, then go to sleep. Let your subconscious work on it while you sleep. You might even tell your subconscious "I need the answer by 6 a.m."

You do the same when you tell yourself what time you want to wake up. Just tell your subconscious, and you'll wake up to the moment. Don't set the alarm clock, because your subconscious knows it has an out. Don't give it an out. Trust it. Tell yourself, "I know if I don't wake up, I might lose out, but I'm trusting my subconscious to come through, and so I'm not setting the alarm."

Where else don't you trust? Where else do you put safeguards around yourself because you don't allow yourself to flow? Where else do you set the alarm, just in case?

I encourage you to keep a journal as a way to monitor your affirmations and attitudes every day. I also encourage you to put your affirmations on audiocassette, and listen to your family and relationship affirmations frequently, thinking about how you're going to be with your spouse, children, and friends when you are home. And then listen to your work-related affirmations on the way to work. If you prepare yourself during the slow periods, you will use your time more effectively. Program in what you'll do, how you'll be, where you want to grow.

Groove Emotional Habits

A decorated veteran of the Vietnam War and a master in martial arts once told me that the North Vietnamese were effective fighters because they kept their emotions as cool as ice water. What we learned from them was "three slow, one super quick." *Slow, slow, slow, hit.* He said they practiced the slow, slow, slow so that they could then strike super-fast.

You can achieve spectacular awareness and effectiveness by applying the same principle—*prepare, prepare, prepare—flow.*

Many of us are *go, go, go—miss,* and then we wonder why things don't improve. Part of the *slow, slow, slow* will be your affirmation, affirmation, affirmation—and then let it happen.

In other words, you put in the right information, right knowledge, right habits, right skills, and the right emotions, and then trust in the right end result. You program and prepare your subconscious mind on the conscious level. Emotional preparation is a deliberate, intentional, conscious act.

*Remember: Use the words **up till now** and **the next time** to help you groove desired emotional habits.* "Up till now I lost my temper, but the next time I won't." Don't drag negative emotion into the future. Shut down that negative emotion. Since your present thoughts and emotions determine your future, you will want to monitor them.

Many people beat themselves up emotionally with dumb self-talk, such as, "I should have, I would have, I could have, if only, what's the matter with me anyway, how could I have been so stupid, there I go again."

Not only do they say these things to themselves, but they say them to others: "What's the matter with you anyway? How could you do this again? Haven't I told you a hundred times, if I've told you once? What will it take for you to get it through your thick head? Didn't I show you where you were screwing up? Don't you care?"

They are constantly telling you what you're doing wrong, repeating it for you, which embellishes the negative picture and emotion and almost guarantees that you'll re-create it next time.

So, when you are rehearsing a desired habitual movement or behavior, groove it with the right emotion. Rehearse it with the right emotion. If you want calmness, put it in with calmness. If you want excitement, put it in with excitement.

Affirm in your mind the desired emotional state. For example, if you get frightened in an enclosed place, you might say to yourself, "This is no longer like me. I see myself being as calm in this enclosed place as if I were in my own living room."

This is an important piece of reaching the goal. Too often we set a goal to *just do it*. At least, we think about doing it, or try to do it. And then we give up: "I can't seem to get myself to do it." Attitudes, habits, and emotions all need to be grooved.

If you want to speak in a constructive, positive way, you need to think and feel in a constructive way. You want to practice new habits in your mind with the right emotional response. Think about how you're going to treat people, how you're going to greet people. Everything that you're learning—new knowledge, skills, and behaviors—can be routinized with the right emotional response using affirmations.

For example, the best coaches rarely need to get their players emotionally *up* for the game. More commonly, they say, "Just go be yourselves. That's good enough. Just don't be less than best. Just go out and be like you. You're already good enough." No hype, no cheerleading, no pep assemblies, no motivational speakers.

The lesson is this: Don't try to *get up* emotionally for an important event, rather *be up*. Change your internal standard in your mind ahead of time as to what it will take to be best of class, best in the league you want to be in—socially, financially, professionally. You've got to have the model of what it takes and then practice it during every spare moment. That's the *slow, slow, slow, flow* approach. *Easy, easy, easy, flow.* You just adjust your inner standard of excellence and put it on an automatic level.

People ask me, "Do you get yourself up when you speak or teach?"
"No," I say, "I am up. I'm just myself."
"But don't you get nervous?"
"No. Why should I get nervous? This is me. I only get nervous when I try not to be me: I lose my memory; I get uptight; I start to perspire; and I'm not sensitive to my audience."

Before a speech, I anticipate the level of emotion that I need to have and I rehearse it in my mind until it's routinized, until it's assimilated. Then I *relax, relax, relax, and flow.*

Don't try hard to be what you're not. If you need to change who you are, your self-image, do that the same way you built it in the first place—through the words, pictures, and emotion of our self-talk. Smart Talk is positive, affirmative talk about the way you intend to be before you ever see it in your actions. You affirm that you are strong before you are. You affirm that you are relaxed before you are. You affirm that you are calm before you are.

Groove Behavioral Habits

The old approach to changing behavior was to tough it out, holding or repeating a new behavior long enough, if you could, until it became habitual. During this process, you were under tremendous stress because you were out of your comfort zone. In a sense, it was coercive, forced discipline.

My approach to changing behavior is first to change your self-image through Smart Talk; your behavior then follows. I feel that the key to maximizing potential is to alter your internal idea, your standard or self-image, how you are on the inside, and let your action flow from it. When you let go, you will act like the person you now know yourself to be. How we—you and I, and our children, friends, and co-workers—think of ourselves is reflected in our behavior. We behave, not like we're capable of, but like we know ourselves to be.

If you know you're no good, you act no good. You act like the person you know yourself to be. "You never listen." Oh. "You're always getting in trouble." Once you know that, if you're not consciously trying hard to be good, you must be bad for sanity. If your self-talk says, "I'm not a morning person," you won't be.

However, you can change your behavior by controlling your self-talk and image in the areas where you want to grow, and affirm them on a regular basis. I recommend that you not only affirm the behavior that you choose, but that you assimilate your affirmations regularly. You will then discipline your behavior with ease.

So you invest a few minutes in the morning and evening every day to make about 20 affirmations in the areas wherein you want to grow. If you don't affirm and assimilate, you tend to get busy and go back to the way you were. And if you can't get from *here* to *there* doing what you're doing, you need to change habit patterns.

Your current behavioral habit patterns represent restraining forces to achieving your aspirations and goals. You may set a new aspiration or goal, but you're so grooved in your daily routine that it's difficult for you to do what's essential. You think you need to do more, work more, get up earlier, stay up later—but what you need to do is to put in new patterns of movement, activity, or behavior.

Habits start on a conscious level with deliberate, conscious activity. But once a pattern is established, your behavior is turned over to the subconscious to flow. For example, after you play a particular song on the piano many times, it becomes an automatic part of your behavior. Many martial arts are about repetition, using imagery until the flowing motions become routine.

Many folks have life down to a routine. They can get up in the morning and get to work without really waking up until 10 a.m. They've got down what they do in their morning routine, what they do for breakfast, how they drive, where they park—it's all automated. Now, the problem is when you bring a subconscious pattern to the conscious level, it becomes bothersome. When new managers come into the organization, they become a bother because they disrupt your routine: "We're going to ask you to change patterns of what you do in the morning, what you do in the afternoon, how you go about your work." When you do something different in your pattern, it becomes difficult or bothersome. Coaches often bother their athletes by taking a subconscious skill and telling them to "focus on follow-through," or to "look at this, and do that."

We're at our best when we can let go and free flow. But when we start putting in new patterns, we go back to the conscious level. Most people don't like that. "Look, I've got my day down good. Don't give me something new to think about." Some people resist you when you ask them to move what was subconscious to the conscious. It's bothersome to people. "I had it down good, and all you're doing is disrupting the department. You're screwing things up."

If you want something to be habitual, get the new pattern down and practice it in your mind. For example, to improve your golf game, you need to go to a pro and groove the right kinesthetic pattern. Once you get the feel of the kinesthetic pattern and some feedback on your swing, you can then just practice perfection in your mind. You can routinize a great deal of what you want just by thinking about it. Affirm and then assimilate the new pattern while you're sitting at home or riding in a car. You don't need to be doing it onstage or in a practice session. In fact, the practice of imperfection gives you imperfection.

Don't try hard on the conscious level to be what you're affirming. Change your internal standard—your attitudes, beliefs, emotional response—and you automatically change your habits.

Your Automatic Pilot System

You have recorded, subconsciously, reality as you perceive it, in your attitudes, skills, knowledge, emotions, and self-image. Your self-image controls your performance when you let go of conscious control. It serves as an automatic pilot system, allowing you to free flow without conscious effort.

Again, you can consciously override the system by trying hard to be better than you are. But the moment you let go of conscious control, the subconscious takes over. So, how do you adjust your auto pilot?

You can try hard to be nicer, braver, smarter, and happier. But when you try hard, you override the subconscious, which causes stress in your system. When you try hard to be different than you know you are, you'll hear yourself or others say, "I've been under a lot of pressure lately." Pressure comes when you take conscious control over your behavior for a period of time. You override the natural system for weeks or months. For example, you may try hard to be nicer to the people in your family when you have company, but when the company leaves, you go back to being yourself.

People with a poor self-image don't grow because they keep affirming their old behavior. Their image is that they are not a good person; in fact, if they do something well and you praise them for their behavior, you'll hear them say, "No, that's not like me. I don't know what happened. I usually mess up. I'm not that good."

If you confront people with a reality that doesn't match their image, they reject it. If you get feedback that brings to your attention how good you are, it may be frightening. And so you tend to push away or deny that you're that good. When you mess up, you'll say, "Well, there I go again. That's like me. I've always been this way." Your self-talk reinforces your self-image, which causes you to act like it again.

If you do well but you perceive that you're just lucky, you say, "It was luck" or "It was in the stars" or it was something else. "I had nothing to do with it." You don't assimilate the success that causes the behavioral change.

When a coach tells a player, "You need to get up for this game. Do you know who we're playing?" the coach is saying, "If you play like yourself we'll get beat. So please be better than you are."

At the University of Texas years ago, when Earl Campbell and Johnnie Johnson were playing, I helped the team look at how good they needed to be to be number one in the nation. In the spring, the coaches programmed these standards, including the emotional component, into the players. They worked for several weeks to change their internal standards of how good they needed to be.

Affirmations are tools for adjusting the automatic pilot system. When you learn how to use them, you will grow and change in areas that allow you to get away from the familiar and to stretch and grow and mature for years to come.

As you observe your behavior or performance, your Smart Talk will affirm "that's like me" or "that's not like me." You learn to assimilate success when you do well by saying, "Yes, that is like me now." And when you mess up, you say, "Whoops, wait a minute. That's no longer like me to do that. I'm better than that. The next time I intend to—" and you go on to tell, write, and assimilate what you intend to do the next time until the image changes.

You need to use both written affirmations and Smart Talk because you may mess up several times. You monitor your behavior on the conscious level, "This isn't like me any longer. Maybe I was this way up until now, but from here forward, I intend to be—" And you simply self-correct until your behavior changes.

When other people exhibit behavior that isn't appropriate, you say, "Stop it. I won't tolerate the way you're behaving. You're too good for that. I see you as a better person."

You must give feedback as a leader or parent. The feedback, though, needs to be firm. Don't ever make the mistake that being positive is being weak or permissive. In fact, I think you become stronger and tougher when you do it right. You know the image, standards, and behaviors you're trying to make habits.

When I started using this as a coach, I was very firm, but very constructive. I would tell a player, "You stop that immediately. Next time step this way or run this pattern. Ah, you've got it. That's like you. You're good."

See, it used to be, "You dumb ass. There you go again. Didn't I show you on film what you're doing wrong? I'll run it over again for you until you get it down."

To stop the wrong behavior, tell others, "You're better than that." You affirm greatness in them. "You're very good." Now you need the positive picture. And the way to get the positive picture is simply by saying, "now next time," and you describe how you want it.

You've got to make this an automatic, natural way of correcting yourself and other people. When you do things very well, you affirm it quietly to yourself. When others do things well, you affirm it out loud to others. When you do things incorrectly, you say, "Well, that's no longer like me. The next time—," and then you trigger the desired behavior.

A good mentor. If you've ever had a good mentor, you could see the process at work. A mentor always saw more in you than you saw in yourself. And the mentor described it in word form so that you caught the dream. Mentors place you into the image. "I see you as being ..."

"Oh, you do? I don't see me that way."

"You remind me a lot of—"

"I do? Wow. They were good, weren't they?"

"Yes, but I think you could be even better."

"Really?"

The mentors see more in you than you presently are. They describe not your full potential, only what they can see in you or what they can get you to see in you. Usually they trigger mental imagery in the area that they are interested in—athletics, music, art, or business. But they may not work on your spiritual, social, or academic development. Using imagery, they create the discrepancy between what you are now and what you could be, and you work, develop, study, and practice until you meet their image of you in that area.

If you give up accountability for growth to your mentor—a manager, minister, teacher, parent, grandparent, uncle, or coach—when you graduate, leave the company, or move away, you're stuck. A friend told me, "My 19-year-old son doesn't always do things that I think are smart, and so I talk to him about it. Once he said, 'Dad, if you're going to be my conscience, I guess I don't need to listen to my own.'"

Are you going to self-regulate internally, or rely on external regulation? Who's going to control your behavior? Do you need a boss? Do you need a mentor? Are you responsible and accountable, or do you need somebody being your conscience?

Mentor yourself to greatness. You can learn to mentor yourself to greatness. Even when you don't have a mentor around, you can cause yourself to grow to the degree that you need to grow to achieve balance. The self-mentoring process is the same—it's a natural process for growth. Many people can help you to see the potential in yourself; they may even correct you when they hear you berating yourself. And you can do the same thing for yourself. You need to write out your goals and affirmations and trigger the imagery as if your mentor were speaking to you. You can do this in any area where you believe you have the potential to grow and you know it would make a positive difference in your life.

You never need to be stuck if you learn these basic skills of the self-mentoring process. You can set a goal, create the discrepancy, and create the appetite to take art lessons, create the appetite to lift the weights, create the appetite to practice. The dream of being creates the motivation or the drive to assimilate the skills or the habits necessary.

The dream comes first. It's more important that you dream the end result than that you have the skills or knowledge at the moment. It's more important that you expand your capacity for growth and groove the right mental, emotional, and behavioral habits. That's what the affirmation process does for you, if you do it right. Your self-affirmation almost becomes the mentor. It triggers the imagery over and over. And you move toward and become what you think about. If you think about your written affirmations several times a day, you will determine your future. If you think about your past mistakes, you will repeat them. To grow you must think of the future as if it were a done deal. Think of the future in the present tense.

That's what every great leader does; that's the way he or she talks. Read or listen to the speeches Winston Churchill made during World War II. He was a master at creating an image for people who were on the verge of defeat.

What inspires people? What causes people to grow? How can you talk to your children? How can you talk to your spouse? How can you talk to the people around you who you need to carry off the mission? You talk in terms of *It's a done deal.*

Now, where in your life have things been *a done deal* for you? For example, is it *a done deal* that you'll watch the Super Bowl game on television? Do you know where you'll watch it? It's almost as real as reality, is it? There's not much that will get in the way. And yet it hasn't arrived, it isn't real, it's only in your imagination. That's the way your goals need to be in every area wherein you want to grow.

Now sometimes it starts off laughably. Then you see others doing it, and soon you say, "I think I could do that." And then you say, "It's *a done deal.*"

Do you know where you'll take your next vacation? Do you know where you'll have Christmas dinner? These are other examples of things being *a done deal.* You may start planning months ahead to create the right environment in your mind—who will be there, what you'll do, what the place will look like, the music, the mood. You create the ambiance using imagery. That's controlling your forethought. And when you do it right, it's *a done deal,* and you know it weeks ahead. With the exception of some emergency, it will occur almost exactly as you plan it.

Remember: You get what you expect, not what you want. When you expect a certain level of performance and you affirm it, your subconscious automatically produces the expectation over and over until your behavior conforms to it. When a football team goes into a huddle, they use words and numbers to trigger an image in the mind of each participant. They then go to the line of scrimmage and execute the image. When they rehuddle, they set another goal and affirm it, using words that trigger pictures, and then execute. Then they rehuddle and do it again. But they've practiced and rehearsed many times before until they flow. It's habit.

You can do the same in your life. Look ahead six months. See the way you would like your life to be. Dream about it. And then place yourself there. What's it like? Imagine that the changes you want have already taken place. What's your life like then? Now write it down. And then bring that emotion back with you to the present moment. And now just read your affirmation, and you're there. Repeat it, and you're there. Repeat it over and over. That's the fast way to groove a habit and step ahead into your desired future.

chapter 1 4

SEEK FEEDBACK, MAKE CORRECTIONS

ONCE in Northern Ireland, I visited the shipyard in Belfast where the Titanic was made. I purchased a book and read about the maiden voyage of the Titanic. As you may recall, on that fateful night, five clear warnings of icebergs came from other ships. These were given to the captain of the *unsinkable* Titanic before the ship struck an iceberg. The last warning was ignored to the point that the Titanic basically signalled back, "Don't bother us. Who the hell are you to tell us anything?"

You know the rest of the story. Many a proud captain has gone down with the ship because he refused to listen to objective feedback and make course corrections. Invariably, the result is a disaster of Titanic proportions. Without a measure of humility and willingness to be open, flexible, and adaptive, you too can sink your dreams.

We All Need Feedback

A teleological mechanism operates on sound, like sonar; or on electronic waves, like radar; or on metallic attraction, like a magnet. But it doesn't stay on the beam; it self-corrects when it's off beam.

When you perceive yourself behaving beneath your moral standards, your conscience bothers you. And you correct your behavior. When you perceive your income beneath what you normally know you need to live on, you do things to correct the problem. When you perceive yourself being different than you know you are, you try to correct back to the standard.

Accurate, objective feedback triggers the correction process. If you perceive yourself beneath your target, you correct. And if you perceive yourself doing better than you think you should, you'll correct back. You get anxious and uptight when business isn't as good as you think it should be. But you also get anxious and uptight when business is better than you think it should be. Athletes not only get uptight when their performance is below their expectations, pressure comes when it's above their expectations. And they do things to correct back to what they think it should be.

If you want a higher quality of life, raise your internal idea, expectation, or standard of what is good enough for you. If you try to temporarily override the automatic feedback system, such as when you try hard to be nicer or neater when you have company, you invite stress. That's why when company leaves you, say "Now we can relax and be ourselves." So why aren't you nice and neat all the time? Perhaps because you think that it would be too hard or too much of a bother.

Watch for such dumb talk in your reflective thinking. Watch for times when you try hard to be non-authentic, or different from who you know yourself to be, just to put on a show. Where you are *trying hard* in your life is where you have taken conscious control of your behavior, and you're trying hard to override how you know you are. It's very telling on you because you put a lot of stress and pressure on your system.

If you're facing change and needing to improve, don't try to override the system. Just make the internal change through visualization and affirmation and then just be like you imagine yourself being. When you learn to change the internal system, you let this guidance system take care of itself.

If you know you're poor, you could win the lottery and still be poor; it won't take you long to correct for the *mistake* of wealth. For example, growing up I had poverty consciousness, and so I always spent more money than I made. I was always in debt. If you don't change your internal idea of being in debt, of always being a poor person, you can make $1,000,000 a year and spend $1,500,000. I would keep myself poor. I had to change my internal beliefs; otherwise, I just kept correcting for the *mistake* of having money.

A teleological mechanism has the ability to receive feedback and change directions after it's released. A teleological mechanism doesn't care where it started; it only cares where it is now in relation to where it intends to be.

When you hone in on a target, you ask yourself, "Where am I, where am I, where am I?" And the question is "Where am I in relation to where I want to go?"

Still, in spite of having a good scanning and guidance mechanism and receiving accurate sensory feedback, keeping on track is no easy task, primarily because we become experts at denying objective feedback. For example, you may look at a photo and say, "That doesn't look like me." Your friend then tells you, "Oh, it looks exactly like you." You then say, "No, it can't look like me because in this photo, I look too fat."

If you don't like the picture, you deny the feedback . . .unless you want the feedback to help you grow. Diane is like an angel on my shoulder. If it weren't for her, and for others who give me feedback, I'd miss a lot. And so will you, if you don't set up your own *board of advisors*. I have advisors from 20 years ago, and some new ones. But I don't even tell them they're on my board; that way I can let them go when I outgrow them. I select people whom I respect and admire when I know they have my best interests at heart. They tell me what I need to hear because they care for me. They see greatness in me, and they want me to do well. I also select people who are different than I am. They can see my scotomas. They have different filters than I have. People who are like me, can't see. They have the same scotomas. They're conditioned the same way.

You will welcome objective feedback, even seek it, when you understand that receiving and accepting accurate feedback greatly helps you to keep moving toward the target. You need this feedback to progress. Your senses are constantly scanning the environment for information to tell you how you are doing in relation to your target goals.

For example, once you become accustomed to receiving feedback as a driver, you feel uneasy driving a car without it. Try driving your car down the road without allowing your head to move to the left or right. You'll feel a tremendous urgency to turn it left or right because of your subconscious need to constantly orient yourself in relation to changing traffic and road conditions. Or, try looking only a few feet over the hood of your car and see how fast you can go. You need feedback to keep on the road, up to speed, and safe from accidents.

A missile doesn't move in a straight line. It pitches and yaws from side to side and up and down. If the target moves, the missile must track. So when the missile is off target, its sensory impulses and scanning devices send feedback to the guidance system: "We're too high! We're too low! We're a mile wide!" And the guidance system immediately adjusts the course.

Remember: We need feedback to adjust direction on the way to our goals. We get the feedback from our senses. Once we target a goal in our mind, our senses alert us to where we are in relation to the goal: "Where am I? How am I doing?" If we are off target, we get negative feedback in the form of tension or dissonance: "It doesn't look right." "It doesn't smell right." "It doesn't taste right." "It doesn't sound right." "It doesn't feel right." In other words, "You're off course in relation to what you have planned." You can then make adjustments.

Try this exercise. Get a 1,000-piece jigsaw puzzle and empty the pieces in front of you. Throw away the box cover with the picture of the completed puzzle. Now try to put the puzzle together. You can probably do the perimeter, but the rest will be very difficult. Why? Because the picture is your feedback. Without it, you can't accurately gauge: "Where am I? How am I doing?" You need the picture—the target—to adjust your progress: "Am I too high? Am I too low? Am I too wide?"

Receiving feedback isn't enough. To reach a target or goal, you must also accept the feedback. If you don't get objective feedback and correct course, you'll never get from *here* to *there*.

People with low self-esteem don't want to set goals because when they veer off course, the feedback stings too much. So they build scotomas to it. If you want to lose 20 pounds, you must step on the scale and accept the feedback. That triggers the creative dissonance to make corrections: "I'll add exercise to my diet and make *sure* I lose the weight." Otherwise, your subconscious will blind you to the numbers, and maintain your present picture of yourself as 20 pounds overweight.

Once you target, in your mind, the way you want things to be—the business merger that you want, the income that you want, the respect that you want, the environment that you want—allow yourself to look at the way things *are*: "We said we were going to deliver quality in our product, and we aren't delivering it." "We said the project would be completed by now, and it isn't finished." "I said I would stop yelling at home, and I haven't stopped." "How are we doing in our family relationships?" "How are we doing as a team?" "How is our marriage doing?" "Hey, you're out of line! You're off the target!" When you feel the anxiety and tension of being *off target*, that triggers your subconscious creativity: "Line it up! Line it up! Line it up!"

Measure Your Progress

If you deny feedback and fail to measure progress, you shut down the growth process. So measure your progress, from the ideal to where you are. If you measure progress from where you started to where you are now, you tend to get stuck.

Suppose that you need to lose 30 pounds. When you step on the scale, you see that you lost two pounds. You feel so good about yourself, you're so proud of yourself, you quit the diet.

How do you sustain your motivation? You don't do it by measuring from where you started to where you are. "My, you've come a long way. You've done well for you." You'll hear people say, "Aren't you proud of yourself? Look at how far you've come in the business. Look at how far you've grown."

If you measure from where you started to where you are, you kill the drive to go forward. But if you measure from the ideal that you have in your mind to where you are presently, you won't care so much where you started, because you still feel that tension, the drive to go forward.

A teleological mechanism, like a missile, doesn't care where it was launched—it only measures from where it is at the present moment to where it needs to be, the goal or target. It doesn't say, "My, I've come a long way! I'm so proud of myself."

If you measure from the ideal to where you presently are, when you run into an old friend who says, "My, look what you've done; you've done well for you. Why do you keep going?" you won't lose the drive to go forward. You won't get caught in that trap. You might say, "I've done well so far, but I still have a long way to go."

When you think about times when you tried but failed, or started but never finished, analyze why for a moment, without beating yourself. When you think of where you tripped, think, "What will I do next time to correct course? Think of mistakes as part of life. Growth is a process of correction, of keeping yourself on the beam, of keeping yourself moving forward.

When you achieve one goal, think what that next goal will be. See through the fog between you and your goal, and get clear about what you can do to move forward. Without clarity, you either won't move forward or you'll move forward in a different direction. For example, it's easy to focus on money and things, rather than on purposes and ideals. Often in the process of reaching a goal, in the middle of the journey, you lose the clear picture, and have to fight to get it back. You may start with the motive of helping people grow, but you lose sight of that and think, "I'm here to make money."

Remember the story of Pinocchio, the wooden puppet who wanted to be a real boy. On his way to school, he got sidetracked to the circus, something that was more enticing, more immediate, and more entertaining. The detour almost cost him his life—and the life of his father.

You experience the Pinocchio syndrome whenever you have an idea or an ideal, but you get off track. Your idea or vision isn't strong enough. Somebody comes up with what seems at the time to be a better suggestion. So you start listening. You tune into the rap, and you get into some crap. Soon you find yourself way off course. Why? You move toward what you think about. If you don't have a strong, compelling goal and purpose in front of you, you'll move toward whatever you're thinking about—or whatever is being suggested to you—and wonder why your life is wasted. From unclear visions, vague goals, and bad attitudes come bad habits and poor results. Your vision and mission will keep your motivation and direction in line.

Anxiety Feedback

When you're off line or off the beam (for you), you're going to get hit with anxiety or tension. You're supposed to get hit with this *negative* feedback because it causes you to correct course, to correct back to your idea of how things are supposed to be.

Don't be afraid of getting negative feedback. Learn to see the feedback as healthy as you go after the goal. When you are off the beam or off track as a leader, parent, or advisor, feedback is essential. Sometimes you don't want to hurt feelings or sound negative, but objectivity isn't the same as being negative.

Getting this anxiety, this tension in your system is necessary to keep yourself moving forward on beam. Your feedback mechanism tells you how you're doing and how to correct to get back on beam, the image of what you're trying to create. But feedback shouldn't stop when you're back on the beam. It goes past the beam to the next goal or milestone. Otherwise, you won't want feedback when you're on beam, because you're in your comfort zone. You don't get much comfort zone feedback.

This negative tension or anxiety feedback comes when you're out of your comfort zone, whenever your environment or your behavior doesn't match your internal idea of how things are supposed to be and how you're supposed to be and feel.

When you feel that you're out of line or out of place, in a new position or location, making changes or having change thrust upon you, you say to yourself, "My gosh, this can't be right." This tension or anxiety can cause a loss of memory; it can shut down your recall of the skills, knowledge, names of people, what you were going to say—and so you act as if you don't know what is happening to you. For example, you might know what you want to say, but when you get in front of a large group of people to talk, you can't get the words out. Or, you might attend an important social event where you know very few people, and you can't think of what to say. The information is inside of you, but you can't retrieve it when you feel that you're off beam from where you belong—from your idea of how the world is.

Not only does that feeling of being off beam or out of place limit your recall, it also blocks input. So somebody could be giving you directions on how to get somewhere or could be trying to give you instructions, but if you feel out of place for you, you block the input of information. You don't let it get in.

And sadly, you will mistake your inability to receive and recall information as a lack of potential or ability. You'll say, "Oh I must be dumb at this." You'll say, "Oh, I don't have the aptitude for this." But you're probably just out of place for you, and so you make the wrong conclusion about the use and development of your talent and potential.

Knowing how to receive and use feedback to make course corrections will give you a whole new appreciation of your talent and potential, and allow you to set bigger goals, to try new things, to venture out from your current situation. For example, you may think, "I didn't do well in that subject in school, so I can't learn it now." But perhaps you didn't learn it in school because you didn't control the anxiety arousal and couldn't release your potential to learn. Anxiety, pressure, or tension come when you detect that you are environmentally, personally, morally, socially, or financially acting outside of your comfort zone. You're off beam for you at the present moment. And so you not only block recall, you block input.

Many teachers program the wrong idea into the minds of children when they teach kids who are new or different that they're *not as bright as most kids* when the kids are just feeling out of place. Whenever people are outside their comfort zone, their ability to receive and recall information is limited.

When you perceive yourself being off beam, negative tension hits you and tightens your upper body; your breathing becomes difficult, and you say, "I've been feeling uptight lately." Tightening up impedes the use of your skills, and so you make more mistakes. You flub, make a fool of yourself, or become more accident-prone. And you tell yourself, "It isn't natural to live with all this pressure and stress. So, don't be stupid. Go back to the familiar. Go back to where you're good. Go back to where you're comfortable. Stay with who and what you know." Your subconscious stimulates creativity to guide you back to the old neighborhood, to the old job, to old friends, to *where you belong*. It creates reasons why you shouldn't take the step or go to the next level. You then misinterpret negative feedback, thinking negative is bad.

When you're off beam in relation to your goals and ideals, negative (objective) feedback isn't bad; in fact, the feedback that is most harmful is the truly negative thinking that tells you to avoid, retreat, move away from. It tells you why it won't work, why you shouldn't go, why you shouldn't invest, why you shouldn't grow the business, why you shouldn't get married and have children.

When you feel that you are off beam morally, financially, socially, racially, religiously, or environmentally, you say, "This is unfamiliar."

Your knees get shaky, you lose balance, your blood pressure increases, your pulse goes up, you perspire, you feel nauseated. "I've got a gut feeling about this." "This makes me sick to my stomach." All this feedback strikes when you're off beam.

So why set goals? Why seek feedback? Why cause a problem for yourself by creating a new vision, a desired ideal, and by looking at how you are now (the current reality) in relation to your ideal? Because the difference creates the drive. If you set a goal to lose weight, don't refuse to step on the scale. Don't deny yourself the feedback. Envision yourself at a new weight *and* step on the scale. Sure, every time you step on the scale, you feel terrible. I know. You're supposed to feel terrible. If you don't, you won't change.

Self-Correcting Course

Many people dream about living well in the future, but they don't look at how they live now. They dream about treating people well, but they don't observe how they treat them now.

You've got to hold the new way and observe how you are now, simultaneously. That creates the natural process for correction inside you. You cause yourself to correct and change in the direction of the strongest image. If you don't change the image in your mind first and make it the strongest image, you'll only create more anxiety. You will then likely solve the problem by giving up on your vision or goal and going back to the way things are because you're always working to maintain sanity inside yourself. So you correct backwards. Your goal is to get rid of the problem, to get rid of the tension, not to reach the goal.

Don't make the mistake of correcting back to old behavior just to relieve the tension that comes naturally when you set a standard or target in your mind. You may even correct back past your old behavior to a new low. "Your marriage is going too well; screw it up a little bit. Your golf game is better than you, so blow it in the next few holes." See, if life is going too well for you, you correct backwards.

As I've said one of my sons was badly abused as a child, before Diane and I adopted him. We placed him in a good environment, treated him very well; but the better we treated him, the more difficult, even dangerous, he was. If you know you're abused and now people are treating you well, you correct for the *mistake*. This boy was so badly abused and confused that at age four he tried to murder the man who was living with his mother. He tried to kill him when he was asleep.

Diane and I were trying to be the best mother and father anybody could be. But the kid started fires; every day was a crisis. We'd say,

"What's the matter with you? Why can't you behave yourself?" Well, we now understand that his self-image was, "I'm not a good person, so don't you treat me that way."

Self-sabotage occurs inside of you and me if we don't improve our image of what we deserve, which is part of our self-esteem. Why do I keep talking about improving self-esteem? Because if you don't make that change in your inner self, then even though opportunity comes to you, you'll push it away. You will correct for the *mistake* of too much business. You'll correct for the *mistake* of too much wealth. You'll correct for the *mistake* of things going too well for you. It happens to you, to me, to my adopted kids, to athletes.

Of the feedback you receive, you only accept, affirm and assimilate that which corresponds to your idea of how good you are. When things go better or worse than you think they should, you correct. And you don't do it consciously; it's a constant subconscious correction. But it's easy to see in athletics, in commissioned salespeople, in everyone. When you're doing *too well,* you say to yourself, "This is too good. I'm performing well above my capability."

Your self-conscious says, "Don't worry, I'll handle it." And over the next few weeks, you'll screw up. Your subconscious will handle it. You don't need to worry about doing *too well,* when you fail to change your image of how well you can perform.

You and I will self-correct and self-regulate around the dominant image of who we are and where we belong. If you want continuous improvement in yourself or your organization, change the picture on the inside first, then let your behavior catch up to the picture. Don't throw your behavior out in front of the picture. Change the picture on the inside first to create the appetite, and then grow into the picture.

The other way is to hire muscle, an intimidator, somebody who bullies you out of your comfort zone into the next plateau. Using fear and intimidation mixed with motivation, this bully may get you to use more of your potential at a higher level, at least for the time you are in his presence. He hopes that he can keep you performing at that level long enough for your inner picture to adjust to where you are. But the moment he lets go, you fall back.

The way I was trained to coach people was to intimidate them, bully them, coerce them, put fear into them, drive them past what they were capable of doing, and hold them at that mark until their image changed. I found that they might even stay at that level, but they wouldn't go to a higher one unless you applied more external force, pushing, motivating, and correcting people.

If you were raised that way, you don't know how to correct yourself. You wait for the minister to correct you, or the manager to correct you, or the coach to correct you because you got caught in the trap of having external motivation and correction.

What I'm saying in this chapter is that as you learn to self-correct by seeking objective feedback and correcting course, you won't be dependent on any other person for your continued growth, progress, and happiness.

c h a p t e r   1 5

EXPAND YOUR COMFORT ZONES

Y EARS ago, Diane and I escorted three Catholic nuns to a seminar in Portland. One was a philosophy professor at Seattle University, one the principal of a school in Alaska, one a second grade teacher in nearby Bellevue, Washington.

I remember that the second grade teacher was never hungry. She wouldn't come with us into any nice restaurants. She'd say, "Oh, no thanks. I'll just get a sandwich later."

On Saturday, the third day of the seminar, Diane took the three nuns window-shopping at some fashionable stores in a nice section of Portland. They paused to look at one elaborate storefront, and then started to go inside. But the second grade teacher said, "No, I don't have time. I have to get back to the hotel." So they all went back.

At the hotel, Diane asked her, "Why wouldn't you go into that lovely store with us? Why wouldn't you eat in those restaurants?" You know what the woman said? "They were too nice for me. I don't belong in places like that. I don't need to eat expensive food, and I don't need to wear those clothes."

When we stick to our environmental comfort zones, we don't allow ourselves to go into situations we believe are either not good enough or too good for us. Subliminally, we build a restrictive zone—*"This is good enough for me"*—and we don't go outside of it. ***Remember: Since we limit ourselves by the way we think, we must learn to think outside of our limitations.***

Good Enough for Me

Where and when do you feel out of place? With what people? In which business situations? During social activities? The beliefs you build with your own self-talk regulate your comfort zones. If you believe "I'll always be poor," then you'll probably stay poor, unless you learn how to see yourself at the next plateau. You might say, "No, I won't stay poor. I'll just gut it out." Go ahead—you might make it, but you also might die of the stress.

On the other hand, you could anticipate change like a kid looking forward to opening birthday gifts. That's better than being thrown into the situation and having to gut it out, waiting for the tension to strike. Using imagination, visualization, and affirmations, you create a picture in your mind of what the new situation will look like before you get there.

It helps to know exactly what you expect of yourself. So ask this question: *"What is good enough for me?"* That applies to all aspects of your life—emotional, physical, moral, educational, financial. If, for example, you average $3,000 a month in sales commissions, why can't you make $6,000? It's not that you *can't* make $6,000 every month; it's just that, in your mind, it would be stretching *what's good enough for me.* You resist: "Who needs the stress? Besides, I want to spend more time with my family." You think other people don't? "I want to have more free time for recreation." You think other people don't? "I'm concerned about my health." You think other people aren't? Watch how creative you get to stay inside your comfort zone.

Stress comes when you know you're a $3,000-a-month person and you try hard to earn $6,000. But if you believe you belong at the $6,000-a-month plateau, your system will create the motivation for you to make that every month—automatically, effortlessly, free-flowingly, without stress. *Remember: We only get the stress when we try to be what we "know" we're not—when we try hard to exceed our self-image.* So you can expand your comfort zone, and eliminate the stress, simply by altering, in your mind, what you believe is *good enough for me.*

Environmental Comfort Zones

Internal comfort zones regulate our emotions, making us feel either safe or afraid, competent or inept, happy or sad, loving or cold, disappointed or satisfied, meek or strong, proud or ashamed, aggressive or shy, smart or dumb, open-minded or locked-on. By defining what's good enough for us emotionally, ethically, and spiritually, our comfort zones control our internal reality.

But we also define *the way things are supposed to be externally.* We have an idea about the way our environment should look—whether we should live in the city or country, at the seashore or in the mountains, desert or rain forest. We know what our apartment or home should look like. We have an idea of the stores where we should shop, the car we should drive, the neighborhood we should live in, the work we should be in.

Environmental comfort zones aren't right or wrong. But once you get the picture in your mind, whenever you feel out of place for you, negative tension occurs. Have you ever been far away from home for a while and told yourself, "I'm homesick"? You probably got very creative finding ways to leave. Even if that vacation resort or home-away-from-home was a lot nicer, more fun, and more relaxing, you were still driven to get back home *where I belong.*

What happens when you're out of your environmental comfort zone and the tension hits to get you back where you belong—but you *can't* get back? Your subconscious will remind you to *stay with the familiar.* Re-create your familiar environment to relieve the negative stress.

When the Dutch left Holland, the English left England, and the French left France, they came to America, where they were completely out of their environmental comfort zones. What did they do? They re-created their picture here. That's why we have New Holland, New England, New Hampshire, New York, New Orleans. The negative tension feedback—"There's no one like me here"—was so powerful, it drove them to re-create their houses, their shops, their streets, their whole culture to feel more *at home.*

Look at Little Havana in Miami. Anti-Castro Cubans who fled their homeland for Florida clustered together in Miami and re-created Cuba. They hung signs: "Spanish spoken here." They renamed the streets the same as those in Havana. They ate Cuban food, played Cuban music, sold Cuban goods. See? *Stay with the familiar.* When you're out of place, you either get back to where you belong, or you re-create *the way things are supposed to be* right where you are.

Environmental comfort zones help you adapt to anything new. But they can also become mental prisons; they can put bars on your potential. They may keep you from venturing too far away from the familiar to experience the new. They might deter you from exploring new languages, new foods, new cultural traditions, or people of different races, colors, and creeds.

For example, many Americans who travel abroad prefer to stay at the Hilton or the Holiday Inn. They aren't comfortable staying at the local inns or hotels; they need to feel they have a familiar *home* base.

The American military understands the concept of environmental comfort zones. One U.S. Army barracks in America looks like every other U.S. Army barracks in Germany, Korea, or anyplace else abroad. The military knows that when you transfer troops to a new environment, you transfer their comfort zones. You re-create the barracks they had at Fort Dix or Fort Bragg or Fort Campbell. That relieves much of the negative stress in adjusting to a new comfort zone. Then you sell them

American products at duplicate PXs; feed them hamburgers, hot dogs, and beans; and provide American movies, newspapers, and magazines. Many of those kids seldom leave the barracks. When they do, they travel in packs of kids exactly like themselves, they don't go very far away, and they hustle right back. They tell each other, *"Hostile out there! Man, they don't even speak English!"* They fear stretching their comfort zones.

That's why some of us still cling to our old high school friends; why we won't leave our hometown; why we always listen to the same music; why we return, again and again, to the same vacation spots. *Stay with the familiar.* But if you want to fulfill your potential, if you want more excellence, more success, more variety in life, you must continually shift your picture of *the way things are supposed to be.*

What happens when an elderly person who's lived in the same house for 40 years is suddenly put in a rest home? That's tragically hard on them. Nothing's familiar; they feel out of their environmental comfort zone with no way back. The stress of the new environmental reality could literally kill them.

Ineffective leaders don't know why people resist change and growth, and so they fix the blame on their people for not growing.

Remember the programs started in the 1960s to help the undeveloped nations? Their founders had high ideals and unselfish motives, but little understanding of environmental comfort zones. They found cultures where people weren't using their potential—and decided to show them how. They said, "Let's shape them up. Let's teach them our language, our economic system, our agricultural and sanitation techniques. Let's put these people into a new situation so they can use their potential."

So they went down and *shaped them up*—according to *their* picture—and then left those people on their own. They returned 10 years later to see the fruits of their efforts. Why, those ungrateful wretches! They kept their animals in the *houses* that were built for them! They had their oxen pulling the *tractors*! What's the matter with those people? Don't they want to change?

Lasting change can't be imposed from the outside. You can *temporarily* change the environment, but the moment you let go, the momentum starts turning back again.

So how can you change your comfort zones? It's a matter of imprinting in your subconscious the image of the new before you ever get there. You visualize yourself in the new situation before it's part of your *reality.*

With all your major future goals, learn how to change on the subconscious level before you go after the goal. When you can do that, you will no longer be content with the old environment, living the same old way, staying only with the familiar. And yet you won't feel tense and uptight, nervous and sick. You can do *easy time* without gutting it out. Because you can learn how to take yourself out of your comfort zone *safely and deliberately*.

Deliberately venturing beyond your comfort zone stimulates within your system the creative tension and energy to resolve conflicts, accomplish new goals, expand comfort zones, and grow. Deliberately taking yourself out of your comfort zone is called *adventure*. You can create so much positive change in your life that adventure will become *the way things are supposed to be* for you from now on.

Where do you belong? The walls that surround your comfort zones are as real as the walls in your house. And since you won't let yourself crash through them, they restrict the use of your potential. It is an inside problem, not an outside problem. As you change on the inside, the outside expands. The quality and quantity of your thinking on the inside are manifest in your life on the outside. If you want the world to change outside, change on the inside. By setting personal goals, affirming them, controlling self-talk, and changing attitudes, you change the quality on the inside—and then life gets better on the outside.

I still have comfort zones. If you ask me, "Why don't you go to Russia?" I'll give you a hundred excuses. "Why don't you take your business here? Why don't you go there? Why don't you do that?" I don't call them excuses, I call them reasons. But you and I have got to know the difference between real reasons and subconscious *obstacle illusions*; otherwise, we're intimidated by the problem.

If you aren't honest with yourself—if you don't face what frightens you, where you start to sweat, why you won't go to the party, why you won't invest, why you won't grow, why you won't try—you won't grow much. So learn to capture your feelings and fears and face them.

Of course, you won't need to do any of this if you don't set a goal, because you're already camped in your comfort zone and you don't want any feedback. When some people say, "I don't feel that I'm out of my comfort zone," I think, "Of course, you're still in the same neighborhood, going to the same stores, doing the same shopping, playing cards with the same people, going bowling in the same place. You don't need this to stay the same." You do need this if you're starting a continuous improvement process to take yourself from *here* to *there*. As your *there* gets bigger, you keep asking, "Where can I go next?"

I know what stops me is not only my comfort zone, but also the comfort zones of the people I live and work with. What stops me is when the people around me get intimidated by an expansive or an expensive idea. You can't afford to associate with people who won't go where you want to go simply because it's outside of their comfort zone.

You have an inner image of where you belong. For example, if you need to use a public restroom at an airport or theater or ballgame, you know you belong in one or the other. If you walk into the right restroom, you feel free of tension and relaxed enough to use your potential. But try going into the opposite restroom and using your potential. You have the need, the desire, the know-how, and the ability, but you'll find it hard to use your potential when you're in the wrong restroom. You're out of your comfort zone.

You may feel that you're in the wrong rest room when you try to mix or work with people of different race, religion, nationality, industry, or even gender. You tend to join or create clubs, companies, and other environments to keep certain others out. You try to surround yourself with people of the same religion, color, vocation, income, and comfort zone.

In today's world, you must be comfortable with people from many nations, races and religions. You and I are not so different, as much as we make ourselves different. But the world is changing, and you've got to grow with it, until it becomes a boundaryless world for you and for your children, your company or organization.

Boundaries are the comfort zones fixed in your mind and in the minds of the people who work with you. But they are expandable, using constructive imagination. You can take yourself out of where you are into the next level, the next environment, the next adventure. You can travel safely there, first in your mind and then in your body.

I remember the first time I travelled from Seattle to Spokane, 300 miles away. That was a big trip for me then. Once, I went all the way to Colorado to work with Eddy Crowder, who then was the head coach at the University of Colorado. That was a big adventure for me. Now I may leave Seattle for Pittsburgh at midnight, make a presentation, and fly home for dinner.

You might say, "Oh, it's easy for you." But remember where I started. As a high school teacher and coach, I didn't get around. Diane was an art teacher, but I didn't go to art shows. My attitude was, "Who wants to be around artists? I mean, the women are all right, but *those men.*" I created thousands of rational, ugly reasons why I wouldn't go.

You don't wake up in the morning and ask, "Where can I go make a fool of myself? Oh, that's where I'll go." Your subconscious says, "No, don't go. You'll blow it. Stay with the familiar. Stay where you belong. Stay with who you know. Don't try to expand."

But you can learn to use your imagination and forethought to stretch your comfort zone, your idea of where you belong, to allow yourself to move safely to where you've never been before without the negative feedback that causes you to give up and go back.

When you are surprised by change and quickly dropped into the unfamiliar, your mind becomes an abundant source of negative synergy. You will come up with 10 reasons why *this won't work.* And you'll share those ideas with other people who have their own 10 ideas. Soon we have 1,000 ideas why we ought to shut this place down. "What do you think?" "Me too. Me too. Me too."

What's the *home field advantage* in athletics. The players who are traveling aren't cowards—the environment's different. And that causes them not to think effectively when they're on the road. They call the wrong plays. They forget plays. They tighten up. They drop the ball. They miss open shots. They do dumb things.

When you are *on the road*, you may try to get temporary results by gutting it out, overriding the system, forcing yourself to move ahead. But before long, you find reasons why you should bail out and go back: You don't want to move into the neighborhood, or go to the schools, or try the business. Any venture is *risky business* when you don't use your imagination correctly.

Growing Beyond Your Comfort Zone

When you take yourself in your imagination outside your comfort zone into things that are not natural for you, you get the same feedback as if you were there.

Certain signals tell you when you are out of your comfort zone. Your memory gets blocked. You suddenly become awkward, clumsy, accident-prone instead of being comfortable, easy-going, and relaxed, the way you are with close friends. You feel tense, your head starts pounding, your hands get sweaty, you feel sick to your stomach, your blood pressure rises, your pulse rate goes up, your knees get shaky, you lose your balance, your vocal cords tighten to make your voice sound funny.

Now, if every time you try something new, you suddenly feel uptight, and your head pounds, and your heart thumps, you start sweating, and your voice sounds like Donald Duck—what do you tell yourself? You say, "Are you nuts? Why are you doing this? Stick to the familiar!" So, you won't let yourself try new things, seek new friends, try new careers, find new recreation, change neighborhoods, or have adventures. You're more comfortable staying with the same routine, having the same friends, bowling the same night, eating the same foods.

It's the difference that makes the difference. Your subconscious isn't concerned with benefits or drawbacks. It is concerned with keeping you in line with *the way things are supposed to be* for you.

You can sit comfortably at home, talking to a few friends, and be very astute. But when you try to address the same subject in front of a conference of 5,000 people, your mind goes blank. You have the knowledge, desire, and potential—but nothing comes out.

You could easily walk across a six-inch-wide beam when the beam is placed on the floor. You could do it 10 times in a row; you could do it backwards, perhaps even blindfolded. But if I put that same beam 500 feet above the ground and challenge you to walk across, you may not do it, even for $1,000,000. Why not? It's the same beam. You have the skill, the balance, the potential. You've already done it backwards and blindfolded on the ground. Yes, but the difference makes the difference. You can't use your potential when you're suddenly 500 feet above ground. You're too far out of your comfort zone.

Tension feedback keeps us from wandering too far from our presently dominant self-image. It makes us stick closely to our present attitudes, habits, and opinions.

One time, my teenage son said to me, "Dad, you never show me that you love me."

I said, "What do you mean? Why do you think I adopted you?"

He said, "I didn't say that you don't love us. I said that you never show it."

Now, I had all the potential to be very loving and warm to my wife and daughters, but not so much to my sons. It wasn't part of my picture. My father died when I was 12, and I pretty much raised myself. Since there were no loving hugs from dad when I grew up, I thought, "I don't need that stuff. Besides, it isn't manly."

When I was a high school football coach, my idea of showing love to a boy was yelling at him: "What do you mean, I don't love you, son? I hollered at you yesterday! Don't you remember?"

"Oh, was that love, dad?"

"Well, certainly! What'd you think it was?"

After my son told me this, I tried harder to be loving and warm toward my boys. I'd come into the room, give them a quick hug, and say, "There, I love you. Now get out of here." Of course, it wouldn't *take*. I felt pressured and uptight. I was out of my comfort zone, and that's what came across. I couldn't be free-flowing with my love—even though I felt it, even though I wanted to show it, even though I had the potential to show it. Every time I tried hard to show love to my sons, nothing came out.

When you learn how to visualize and imprint the new situation in advance, making it part of your picture of *the way things are supposed to be* for you, you create a venturesome spirit and take yourself safely to the next level or the next situation.

Challenge the Status Quo

You need to challenge where you know this is *the way it is supposed to be*. Cliff Young, a 62-year-old fellow in Australia, once entered a race between Sidney and Melbourne, 600 kilometers, running against world-class runners. He showed up in Oshkosh overalls. Race officials didn't think he was qualified. But in his first race, Cliff beat all runners by a day and a half. How? He wasn't faster. They had locked on to knowing "the truth" that when you run 600 kilometers, you must sleep 6 hours and run 18.

Coming from the outback, Cliff never hung around the people who knew the truth. He didn't know you were supposed to sleep. So he ran while they were sleeping. People said, "No, you can't do that, it's physically impossible." But the guy was too far out in front to hear *the truth*. The next year, they broke his record.

You change the way you think, and you change the way you run your life. Your present beliefs entrap you in your own comfort zones and your own thinking. You manipulate your own senses.

An MBA student once told me: "Our teacher gave us a case study, told us corporate policy, and then said: 'Your goal is to improve efficiency by 800 percent, without laying anybody off.' We could all improve efficiency by 800 percent, but not without laying people off. Finally, the professor asked, 'Did you think to add a shift on weekends?' We said, 'No, it's against company policy,' to which he replied, 'But you could always change company policy.'"

To expand your current comfort zones and to get from *here* to *there* in your life, you've got to become an option thinker, an optimistic person with constructive inner dialogue.

As psychologist Martin Seligman points out, the test comes in two forms: 1) How do you think when good things happen? and 2) How do you think when bad things happen?

When bad things happen, the pessimist thinks, "It's all my fault; it's going to ruin everything; and the ill effects will last forever"—even when there is clearly nothing they could have done to change the outcome.

Optimists think when a bad thing happens that they're not accountable for all of it and that while it might ruin their day, it won't ruin their life. They isolate the ill effects.

When good things happen, the pessimist says, "I had nothing to do with it." The optimist says, "I caused it." The pessimist says, "It won't last." The optimist says, "It's going to last forever." The pessimist says, "But it was just in this one thing." The optimist says, "My luck in life is changing forever."

One of the best basketball coaches in the nation is a good friend of mine. His team had just beaten a Top Ten team, and so I called him on the phone and said, "Congratulations! Look what you did."

He said, "Lou, it was a miracle." And in the paper, he was quoted as saying, "It was just luck." Well, his team believed him. They dropped right out of the top ten, then out of the top 25, and struggled the rest of the season.

In effect, he told himself and his team, "We didn't cause it. We're not that good."

When you expand your comfort zone, you make some mistakes. But you don't let it damage your self-esteem. Don't dwell on it; don't worry about it. Just laugh about it, and say, "That's not me. I'm better than that. Next time I'll do it right." And you move on. You build resiliency, and you keep your ideals burning inside.

DIANE'S STORY

Part V: A Matter of Self-Esteem

DIANE: Getting well is so much a matter of self-esteem, self-worth, and self-assertiveness. If you feel good enough about yourself, you'll take care of yourself. If you don't feel good about yourself, you'll only do so much and that's enough. It's important to feel good enough about yourself that you'll go to extremes to get better—like learning about the crucifer winter vegetables that help increase the body's output of tumor-inhibiting enzymes, why you don't eat spinach and beets, and which foods provide immuno-stimulating nutrients.

I went all-out to build myself up psychologically and physically. I found out that oxygenation of the body is crucial to building strong cells. So I started doing vigorous exercise every day. When I was doing chemotherapy, it consisted of just walking downhill to the beach behind our house, because I was too weak to do more. But I knew that if I walked to the beach area, it would force me to walk back uphill to get back in the house—and that was enough exercise during those periods. Later, I started swimming at an athletic club. While I swam, I planned, in my mind, all the fun things I would do the rest of the day or the rest of that week, and I'd review my affirmations. At the time, we were building our ranch lodge in the mountains, so I would visualize the rooms and the furniture I wanted in each one, and where I would travel to find that furniture.

That was very beneficial because it was a creative project, which was energizing. But you don't need a project as expansive as that; you can just visualize simple things, like planting bulbs that will come up in the spring, and seeing the bulbs in bloom. I had a flower garden that was in poor shape, so I ordered a lot of lily bulbs that wouldn't come up until the next year, and I imagined what they'd look like when they came up.

I also visualized and planned for future family events: "Who's coming for Thanksgiving? What will we be doing at Christmas?" Even if something was eight months away, I visualized being part of it. I envisioned the decorations, the activities, the people we'd invite. I also made sure I called my sister regularly, so we could continue going out to lunch together. And I didn't give up on buying clothes; I went shopping a lot. If you have the idea that you won't be around very long, you aren't going to buy that winter suit you'll need for the next six months. So I deliberately included long-range goals like that in my daily planning, instead of subconsciously eliminating them by thinking: "Well, I don't need that anymore. I won't be here to use it." Instead, I'd think, "That's a beautiful winter coat. I'll wear that at the ranch this year."

I also wanted to have a psychological evaluation of my life to see what things I'd need to change. Early life traumas can subtly suppress your immune system over a long period of time, and gradually lead you downhill until you reach a point of low resistance. There's a song that says, "I made it through the rain." Well, you can make it through the rain if you make constructive psychological changes along the way. If you don't, it might just keep raining on you. If you don't get cancer, it will be something else.

My immunology doctor did lab tests every month to check the cancer cell activity and the strength of my immune system. Each month, I saw that the cancer cell activity was diminishing while my immune system grew stronger. I continued going to my healer, who reassured me about my blood chemistry and told me where I still had cancer, what stage it was in, and whether it was growing or not. He was an amazingly gifted person; everything he told me matched the lab reports—which he never saw. Eventually, I got him and my immunology doctor talking together, and I balanced what one told me against what I learned from the other. When I was through with chemotherapy, I *knew* I was getting well.

I also used visualization every day. I would first still my entire body, start deep breathing to relax, and then remind myself of the reality of the present moment—that there was still the possibility I had cancer in my body. I visualized the little spots of cancer that might still be present. Then I visualized an army of immune cells exploding like popcorn and multiplying, then attacking and devouring the cancer cells. I also visualized a little river that these cells flowed into, which ran the cancer spots out of my body.

Each time this happened, I would visualize myself walking up a hill and standing at the top. Then, as if I were outside myself, I would see myself looking through my body, which was lit up and transparent and totally clean. That was my symbol of total wellness; the transparency represented a cleaning out of the cancer. Every other visualization revolved around that central image.

I had to discipline myself to do these visualizations at least twice a day. I pretended it was a business appointment with myself. That made it a priority because I wouldn't lightly cancel a business appointment. You need to be undistracted when you do your visualizations, so I'd often drive to the park and do them in the car. I would visualize different states of wellness, energy, and strength. I would try to visualize the various *superstar* characteristics. For example, I'm a nonconformist, so I would visualize myself not conforming to certain expectations. Or for assertiveness, I'd sometimes imagine someone doing something unwise, and my making a point to say something about it.

Self-talk was also very important because I was alone a lot, especially during my chemotherapy period. Though many people spent time with me, I was the only one who stayed in the hospital while everyone went home at night. Driving home, I was the only one looking for places off the side of the road where I could throw up. When I was recovering at home, I was the only one lying in bed, feeling sick, while everyone left because they didn't want to bother me. For five days after chemotherapy, I would experience the sickness and all the throwing up. I needed to continually reinforce my optimism, or else I might have created a negative self-talk cycle of "Oh, I'm sick. I'm throwing up. I'm going to throw up again and again."

Through positive self-talk, I controlled post-chemotherapy sickness a lot, but I didn't totally eliminate it. My hair kept falling out. That didn't bother me so much, so I didn't bother to intensely visualize taking the treatment without my hair falling out. Maybe if I had done that, I could have controlled it a little more. But I didn't spend as much time and energy on those things as I did on just getting well.

Right after the last chemotherapy session, my surgeon told me that I should start periodical radiation treatments within three days, which meant I couldn't take my overseas trips. He was very explicit about all the possible negative side effects. He mentioned everything from permanent intestinal damage to effects on my sex life.

I thought, "I'm not going to let those things happen to me." So I didn't take the radiation. Three months later, he sent me a letter: "It has come to my attention that you did not follow my protocol. Don't you realize how serious this is?" He went on for two pages and said at the end, "Would you at least come in every six months so I can see how you're doing?"

My immunologist thought I needed radiation treatments, too. But I said, "The last tests showed that cancer cell activity is almost nil, and my immune system is growing steadily stronger. I don't think I need this treatment. I'll take my lab test every month and, if anything changes for the worse, I'll come in for radiation treatments." Also, my healer had been giving me feedback that indicated my immune system was killing off the cancer cells, so I figured my immune system was taking care of it. We left it at that.

My decision was right. For the last ten years, they haven't found any cancer cell activity, and my immune system is very strong. Recently, I took a CAT scan test to prove I was totally clean—and I am. I haven't even caught a cold.

LOU: When I think of this whole ordeal, I always think of the special moment between Diane and me when we were driving to Swedish Hospital for her last chemotherapy treatment. Since we were married at 16, we had gone through many setbacks, and we always told each other that whenever we stood up to those challenges, great things occurred on the other side. So, just as we approached the freeway, I said to her, "I can hardly wait for you and me to get through this. Because every time we've come through something, great things have happened on the other side. We have never faced something this devastating before, so it *has* to be good on the other side. I can hardly wait to get there."

As we pulled up to the hospital, I smiled at Diane, and she said, "Remember what I always say about adversity: '*When you come through a tough crisis, it just gives you longer legs for bigger strides.*'"

And with bigger strides, you can get from *here* to *there*, from this side of the problem to the other side, much faster.

STEP 5:
Build People and Teams

I F you want to tackle big chal- lenges, you need a winning team of high-performance people around you.

I remember well the "growing pains" in my life, as I transformed myself from a teacher and coach to an independent producer, to a team leader, to a busi- ness owner, to a mentor and manager, to a leader. But each step allowed me to have greater influence and greater fulfillment.

1. Clarify vision, mission, values, motives, attitudes

2. Engage in con- structive self-talk

5. Build people & teams

SMART TALK AFFIRMATION *I am, I do.*

4. Take action, correct course

3. Set and imprint goals

Chapter 16 recognizes the importance of reducing *restrictive zones* where you try to be the *Captain of the World.* You will learn how to create *constructive zones* that allow you to recruit people who share the same values and to progress past plateaus by working togeth- er to achieve goals.

Chapter 17 talks about boosting your credibility as a team leader. *Who Saids* of the Greatest Magnitude can limit the power of our belief. These false *Who Saids* and negative wizards only add to our self-defeating beliefs. You can turn the tables by becoming a *Who Said* for the causes you believe in.

Chapter 18 asks you to build other people by boosting team esteem. Groups also have self-talk. By creating relationships of trust and by affirming and praising performance, you raise the esteem of people. They begin to say, "Send me anywhere" and "Give me the ball." It also helps to make many happiness-producing events.

c h a p t e r   1 6

RESTRICTIVE VS. CONSTRUCTIVE ZONES

IN teams and organizations, you and I self-regulate at a shared standard of performance that operates like a thermostatic control in a building. You set the thermostat at a certain temperature. When the temperature rises, it triggers the air-conditioning unit to drop the temperature down. Should the temperature drop below the setting, the heater turns on.

Teams and organizations have cultural climate controls. Once you set a standard, you regulate to the standard. When you perceive yourself below the standard, you correct up. When you rise above your standard, you correct back. The key to team growth, very simply, is to change the setting closer to the potential of the group. You then self-regulate at a higher performance standard.

Co-Responsible Teams

What happens if the people in one department don't feel co-responsible for the quality of the final product? For example, suppose you have 10,000 people in a plant trying to build a quality car. If the people who work in the fender department or the transmission department or the tire department see something wrong, will they care enough to spot and fix a problem outside of their area? Or will they say, "Why don't *those guys* fix their own problems? When are *they* going to get *their* act together?"

It depends whether or not they feel co-responsible for the quality of the final product. In co-responsible teams, the feeling is, "Let's fix this problem. We're in this together. We're co-responsible for this product."

In the new self-directed team approach, it isn't just the person with the seniority who takes the lead—it's the one who can see the problem and knows how to fix it. It's the one who's got the right information and steps forward. That one person may be only 18 years old, not of your department, not of your experience. So, why listen to some young kid? Because your existence depends on it.

To compete in the global market, you need inventive, co-responsible people who have mutual respect for each other's differences. Your attitude is, "I don't see it; please show me." You create that environment when you treat people with class, dignity and respect. As long as you share the same vision and mission, you will even seek and value differences. Change and improvement are what you're after.

If you're a flexible leader, your attitude is, "I don't care how long you've been with this organization or in this industry. If you've got a bright idea, I want to hear it."

You empower people to step forward when you build their self-esteem, teach them how to set goals, and create a climate of trust in the organization. You disempower people when you get stuck in your comfort zone, lock on to old ways and means, and become blind to options.

What happens when you take people from different backgrounds and drop them into a task force? Even if they've never met or interacted before, they're inventing new stuff. Innovation is happening all over the place. These people are inventing, creating, sharing. How are you going to stay with them unless you give every person, at every level, the power, skills, attitudes, and self-esteem to create a more competitive organization?

Historically, the primary values in company, church, or society are *predictability* and *stability*. How is it where you're working? "This is the way it is in this company. This is the way it is, always was, and always will be."

To keep it that way, we pigeonhole people. We take people and say, "Okay, you're the secretary, you're the engineer, you're the salesman, you're the administrator, you're the electrician, you're the plumber, and you're it forever. Don't even think that you're anybody or anything else. That's it, because we want stability and predictability."

Another way we get stability and predictability is to take bright young hopefuls and send them away to the university or seminary, teach them history and law, and then drop them into the organization to lead us into the future. We just duplicate history, and preserve the hierarchy. *Off the wall* people typically don't get to go to the university or seminary.

In the Army, they have a saying, "You don't make a mistake, or you won't get to be a general." It takes 100 *atta boys* or pats on the back to overcome one *ah shit*. So you don't do the wrong thing. You step where the other one stepped.

Now, what happens to innovation, creativity and option thinking in that organization? It's stifled. People forget that creativity and option thinking are natural, that they're supposed to figure out better ways of doing things, better ways of running the business, better ways of teaching, better ways of learning.

In a high-trust culture, you have flexibility of leadership, flexibility of roles, flexibility of wealth. People want that today. Instead of predictability and stability, people want change, they want improvement, they want growth.

Your Growth as a Leader

As a self-directed leader, you can cause your department or organization to grow. You might say, "Well, I don't know if I'm a leader." You will be if you start visualizing, affirming, and acting the part. Many people will get on board, or they will try to hold you and the organization back because your vision will be too far out of their comfort zone to advance. They'll find fault with your proposals. So give others the chance to visualize the new and to grow with you.

You will also need to recognize the selfish, mean, and negative leaders in your environment who want to hold you back. You've been taught to respect authority, but not everyone in a position of leadership is worthy of your followership, especially when they are leading you backwards.

To grow as a leader, you may also need to leave some friends and family members behind. When I left high school teaching, I wanted a lot of my friends to come with me into this business. But it was out of their comfort zone, or they didn't want to. If I had waited for them and not moved until I could get the group to move, I wouldn't be doing what I'm doing today. I needed to go it alone.

Sometimes you're going to need to go it alone, because you can't take the whole group around you. Taking into account your mission and values, you've got to decide, "Who comes with me?"

I made a vow to Diane that she and I would stay together, and we hope to take our children with us. But we're not going to stop for our brothers and sisters or friends who might say, "What are you trying to do, be better than we are?"

"No, we're just trying to improve the quality of our lives; if you want to come, please come along."

As you grow, you'll find that you won't be socializing as you used to socialize; you won't be going to some places you were going; and you won't see some people as often as you once did. You don't do this intentionally; you just don't have the time, the interest or the connection.

As you stimulate tremendous growth in yourself, you will see that many people you know and love are, by comparison, *sleeping*. They're sleeping in school systems, in government, in business, and industry. Some of your family and friends are sleeping. People stop their progress when they feel victimized. How do you respond to them? Do you drag them along? Perhaps, if they are family or close friends. But don't let the others stop you. Try to love and enlist them to change the community or the environment that they're in.

Such *tough love* is a mature love, and effective leadership. You want the people around you to live the life that they deserve to live and are capable of living. Knowing how to help yourself grow, you know how to help other people grow.

None of us are independent performers; we have spouses, team-mates and colleagues who may or may not want us to change and who may become restraining forces along the way. How do we bring those people along with us?

We must decide whether to continue with them or without them; otherwise, we'll stop our own growth because we won't want to "leave our friends or family behind." So, we need to make some tough deci-sions. If we don't make the decisions, we'll just complain about those people. We'll resent them for holding us back.

You must be wise here. If you grow, but stop the people with you from growing, divorce, separation, and alienation occur. So who do you bring and how do you bring them along with you? And what do you value to the point where you're willing to leave people behind? Who would you leave behind?

Those are serious questions that Diane and I have tackled over the years. Who do you leave behind? It's not easy to leave people behind. But if they prevent us from using our tremendous potential to achieve our ideals, we must make some hard choices.

You naturally want to have your friends and family come with you as you grow and develop. Diane and I place high value on spouses attending our programs so that they set goals and grow together. Nobody could accuse us of setting one spouse against the other. To progress together, you must set some goals together and bring them about together.

You try your best to move ahead with the people you care about. We tried to do that with our children when they were in our care. But now that they're adults, they make their own choices. It's up to them. For many years, we slowed down for them. In some cases, we also slowed down for our extended family, at home and at work. And yet we still professed this mission, this aspiration, these goals. So, when someone asked, "Why aren't you doing it?" I would say, "Well, we started to do something about it, but when somebody didn't do what they said they would do, I never fired them. In fact, I would try to do it for them."

If we are passive and permissive, we soon plateau, and our progress stalls.

In fairness, I must accept the bulk of the blame for this. I had to grow as a leader. My attitude toward managing people needed to change. I would only allow my company to grow so big because I couldn't stand people calling me on the phone every night. I needed someone else to manage my company. But my attitude toward managers was that they just sit around and do nothing. I wanted doers! That was my attitude. I wouldn't let my company grow because everybody who was a doer was calling me on the phone day and night, and it drove me nuts. So, I finally decided that managers should get those phone calls. I decided I'd better change my attitude about managers if I wanted to expand my company. Once I changed my attitude toward management, we grew a lot faster.

Make Change an Adventure

When I was a schoolteacher and vice-principal years ago, I discovered how difficult it was to move 20-year teachers from the room they'd had into a better room. They would get angry about it.

"I taught these children's parents in this room."

"But you're going to get a better one."

"I don't want a better one."

Why do some people who are treated well in a hospital get sick again once they're released? So they can come back! Why are some older people who are uprooted from a retirement home and put into another environment, even if the environment is much better, so disturbed that they might even die from the move?

Why is it so difficult to get people to change? Because most people perceive change as a risk, a threat, a danger. They see only the negative side of the change.

Change becomes a positive adventure when we feel safe moving out of our environmental comfort zones, out of our narrow definitions of the way things are supposed to be. When we're taken out of our native environment and dropped into an environment where people look different, we don't feel right.

Our comfort zones have a lot to do with our idea of how things are supposed to be. We know the kind of restaurant we feel comfortable in. We know the kind of car we can drive, the kind of aircraft we can travel in, the kind of theater and shops we would go to. We want only certain people in our club or in our neighborhood. It has a lot to do with what we let ourselves do, where we let ourselves go, and who we let ourselves be.

Without knowing it, we create our own boundaries in our own minds. Because once we get assimilated into our minds the way the store looks, the way the house looks, the way the neighborhood looks, the way the environment looks, we're always bouncing our perception off of the environment.

When we sense differences from the way things are supposed to be, we feel tension or anxiety in our system. We feel out of place. We create boundaries around our lives or business. We need to start knocking down the walls, knocking down the boundaries, to allow ourselves to do business in India or South America or across the street with people who are different.

Building Teams

Why do you do what you do in your organization? Your power and energy come from your shared mission. It causes you to be resilient and fiercely committed. It keeps you from having a shallow, superficial life or partnership.

Most things in life can't be done by one person. You need, then, a group of people who are united behind a common goal, reason, or purpose. How can we develop collective efficacy in our organization?

When you try to build a co-responsible team, a team for the future that can take on change and challenge with a positive nature, you first need to look at the basic philosophy and beliefs of the organization.

Two styles are dominant—control and release. The release style—where leaders do all they can to create an open environment conducive to the expression of ideas and talents—is rather rare.

Most churches, governments, teams, corporations, and schools historically are control-oriented. In these organizations, imaginative, creative ideas are not welcomed. "We need to put in some checks and balances to shut down the imagination. We don't want your bright ideas, thank you. I've only got three years before I retire. Who are you to come in here with these smart, unclassified ideas?"

With the control orientation, you don't want ordinary human beings running around, messing up management's perfect world. Somebody has got to control them.

How do you best manage your team? Is control one of the dominant issues? Are you saying, "We've got to have controls here and there. Who's going to control this person and that person?"

Self-Appointed Captains

Some people try to control everybody's behavior by becoming a self-appointed "Captain of the World." They take it upon themselves to shape up the whole world—for the world's own good. Most rules in organizations aren't for the good of people as much as they are to get people to behave so they don't bother you.

As a vice principal, teacher, and football coach at Kennedy High School in Seattle, I was an interesting piece of work. I had about 35 rules for my classroom alone—all for the kids' own good, of course. "Don't chew gum!" "Sit up straight!" "Write your name on the *left* side of the page. Don't lean back in your chair." Every time a kid violated one of my rules, it made me so mad that I couldn't think straight. I was so busy enforcing rules, I hardly had any time left to teach.

I knew that parents were sending their kids to my school to be shaped up, and I knew that I was just the man to do it. And so I made all sorts of restrictive rules. We even had one-way halls! I'd get there at 7 in the morning to patrol kids, even though school didn't start until 8:30. If I saw a kid going the wrong way, I'd say, "Hold it. This is a one-way hall. Don't think you can beat it. Go that way." And then I would mutter, "Damn kids, always trying to get away with something."

To the girls, I'd say, "Your skirt's too short; your hair's too long; you're wearing too much makeup." And then I'd mutter, "Damn kids. They drive you nuts."

Do you think my job as *Captain of the World* ended with the 3 p.m. bell? Not at all. There was plenty of time left to shape up more people in my other job as football coach: "Pick up the towels." "Put your pads on right." "Run this way." "Pass that way." "Darn kids!" I loved that job, too.

And it didn't end at 6 p.m. There was still plenty of time to shape up people on the way home. After all, somebody was always violating my restrictive zone when I was driving: "Hey man, who taught *you* how to drive? Who's crowding in? I'll get you!" I couldn't even drive home without becoming a nervous wreck.

I'd go out of my way to get irritated at strangers. I'd be in my community, and I'd spot some kids leaning against their car, smoking cigarettes. I'd pull up beside them, get out, chase them down the block, grab their cigarettes, and throw them away. I'd say, "Go home. Where are your parents? Don't they care? Nobody cares but me!"

When I'd get home exhausted after a hard day's work, Diane would ask, "Why are you so upset? What's wrong with you?"

I'd say, "You can't imagine what I go through all day. I caught those same two kids smoking again tonight. Can you believe that? I don't even know who they are. It's a tough job shaping up the whole world. It's a jungle out there."

Why was I so upset? Not because those kids were behaving badly, but because they were irritating me by violating my restrictive zones. Were my rules constructive? Were they conducive to running a good class? Did they have anything to do with teaching school? Absolutely not. They were silly rules. Why did I impose them? "Oh, I can justify it. These kids have to learn how to behave when they get out into the *real* world. That's what I'm teaching them." No, I wasn't. I was teaching them to stay out of my restrictive zones—*or else!*

I resigned from the post of "Captain of the World" many years ago. And I want to thank those of you who have taken up that burden and responsibility for me. Because the world runs a whole lot better since I quit.

Management Zones

Many managers are so compulsive that they get jittery about things they can't control. So they create restrictions. These *restrictive zones* prevent them from being free and moving easily, effectively, flexibly, optionally, seizing opportunity. Avoid restrictive zones. If you're a compulsive punctual, you not only get upset when you're late, you get upset when anybody else is late. And so you set up rules and regulations to cause them to behave according to your rules, which makes you difficult to live with.

You need to use affirmations to undo all those stupid restrictive zones that ruin your life and the lives of people around you. Quit trying to shape everybody up and make them have a nice house or a clean yard. In many neighborhoods, people start off loving each other but end up hating each other because they violate each other's restrictive zones.

All of these things prevent you from exploring options and seizing the path of obvious opportunity. You start avoiding any environment where people might bother you. You won't place yourself into any world that is different.

Imagine you are a nonsmoker who used to be a smoker, and now you're trying to shape everybody up. You sit down to eat at a nice restaurant, and somebody puffs a cigarette clear across the room. You think, "Why are they smoking in this restaurant? That ticks me off. Don't they have a nonsmoking area?"

Whenever anyone violates your restrictive zones, you get irritated, anxious, upset. You let people bother you and ruin your day, don't you?

We may have one restrictive zone or thousands. The variety of restrictive patterns conditioned into us by our parents, teachers, coaches, bosses, and mentors are like exposed nerve endings. Every violation hurts: "Get your hand away from your face. You'll spread germs. Why do you think I bother to tell you this? I tell you for your own good. So stop it!"

Do you know anyone like that? They're always shaping you up for your own good. They're irritated by other people all day long: "How can anyone *breathe* so loud? That annoys me."

What happens when you have a parent, teacher, or supervisor who has dozens of restrictive zones? They think, "I'm the boss now. I'm going to shape everybody up. From now on, everyone toes the mark. I'm instituting some very serious rules. To begin with, no long hair and no short skirts. And don't let me catch you using pencils instead of pens. Everybody signs in when they arrive, and out when they leave."

See, now that you're the boss, you'll do to your employees exactly what your parents, teachers, and supervisors did to you—try to force conformity to restrictive zones that have nothing to do with the tasks at hand. In fact, the cause of many employee strikes is not that employees aren't getting enough benefits, but that some rigid, dictatorial, dogmatic bosses have many restrictive zones which they feel compelled to pass along to everyone else. They're not happy at their jobs; they irritate them. So they decide to shape *you* up or ship *you* out.

Don't Change *Them*, Change *You*

Please face a simple fact about people: you can't shape *them* up, so why not shape *you* up? Change your restrictive zones, and try being more relaxed, comfortable, pleasant.

To become aware of your own restrictive zones, consider your habits and attitudes and ask yourself: "In what ways do I act *compulsively?* Does that behavior make much sense?" For example, suppose you're compulsively punctual. How did you get that way? Probably through fear feedback: "I can't be late or else." Maybe when you were young, your parents trained you to always be on time by scolding or spanking you whenever you were late. When that didn't work, they grounded you socially for a month. What did you learn? "If I'm late, awful things happen."

So now you're 38 or 48 years old, and you're running a little late. You start to think, "Man, I can't be late!" You don't think, "Or else Dad will punish me." All you know is "I can't be late or else." That compulsive, restrictive behavior prevents you from acting sensibly and realizing your potential, because it limits your behavior to a conditioned, *or else* response.

Punctuality compulsion can cause you to do irrational things. For example, if you're a compulsively punctual person and you're running late for an appointment, you may be driving along and see a train about to head you off at a crossing. You get the feedback "I can't be late!"—

so you race the train to the crossing. Recklessly, you risk your own life and the lives of everyone else in the car, just because you fear being late. And if the train *beats* you to the crossing, you act crazy: "It's *illegal* for a train to take this long at a crossing! I'll report this to the authorities!" You are so annoyed, you can't think straight. When the train passes, you get even more compulsive, more reckless. You may drive 75 in a 35 mph zone. And if the other party is late, you're livid. "Can't you be on time?" *Anybody's* lateness can drive you almost to distraction.

If you have some definite restrictive zones, you won't place yourself into environments that bother you. You'll stay with people who are like you, people who won't upset you.

Are some restrictive zones okay? Sure, you want some safeguards. You should feel upset if someone tries to steal from you. But you don't want the job of policing the world: "Stop slurping your soup. Get your hands away from your face." You're always picking on people, trying to shape them up.

Your kids know what bothers you and when they're mad at you, the best way to get back at you is to do what they know bothers you. So they violate your restrictive zones constantly. I used to yell at my kids, "Don't slam the door. I've told you a hundred times."

They remembered, of course, and on a cold winter day, when I was watching a football game, they'd leave the door open. So I'd yell from my easy chair: "Shut the door."

Then they'd slam the door shut. I'd yell, "Don't slam the door."
"Sorry, Dad. The wind got it."

They know what bothers you. And the more restrictive zones you have, the crazier they can drive you.

You don't need to feel accountable for everybody else's behavior. You don't need to allow other people to make you feel miserable and ruin your day.

First ask yourself, "What rules are necessary here?" Examine the way you conduct your family life, your career, and your social life. Identify rules you enforce that exist for no other reason than to make you feel good.

Why bother? Because if you don't change your restrictive zones, you won't develop your full potential as a human being—and you may inadvertently block someone you love from using theirs.

When we adopted children and had foster kids, I wanted all of them to feel happy and loving around me. But I would come into the living room with all the kids there, and somebody would violate one of my restrictive zones. I would scold, "Get your feet off the couch!" "Get the dog out of here!" "Don't eat ice cream in that chair!"

The kids would start filtering out of that room one at a time: "I think I'll take out the garbage, Dad." "And I'll help him, Dad." "Gee, I almost forgot, Dad. It's my turn to mow the lawn." I'd say, "No, it isn't. And anyhow, it's *raining!*" See, they suddenly got very creative at finding things to do. Soon, I'd be sitting there alone, wanting to be a loving father but feeling that everyone *hated* me. To justify myself, I'd say, "That's just the consequence of being a good father."

Indeed, there are consequences when you impose your will upon someone else, especially when you try to imprison them in your restrictive zone. What happens in a marriage when you argue over restrictive zones? You start off loving each other, and you end up trying to strangle each other. "Don't let me catch you squeezing the toothpaste in the middle!" and "Don't chew that ice around me!" are unnecessary restrictive rules that can break up marriages. Think about all the silly things you fight over. Why do they upset you in the first place? Your parents passed on some of these prohibitions to you. Be assured, unless you are aware you have them, you will pass them on to others.

We sometimes retaliate against people who violate our restrictive zones. In the days of the *Wild West*, when people felt hostile, they could solve the problem by taking out a six-gun and shooting. In medieval Europe, they could express their hostility by wielding a sword: "Off with their heads!" But in our very sophisticated, modern society, we've gone into the banking business to vent our hostility. We build up *IOU* accounts. When people irritate us, we tell ourselves, "I won't let that bother me." But, subconsciously, every time we think about it, we make a deposit in our *IOU* account: "I owe you one for that." And soon, when our account gets full, it's time to start paying people back what we owe them.

One way you do that is to find out what upsets them, and then do it. "I didn't know that bothered you, dear. Heh-heh-heh. I'm sorry." No, you're not. Husbands and wives know how to irritate each other, kids and parents know how, employers and employees know how. It's a safe way of paying someone back for upsetting you.

A friend of mine is a warden in a federal penitentiary. He told me that in the old days, convicts had to keep the top button of their uniforms buttoned at all times. He said if a convict ever wanted to annoy a guard, all he had to do was get up early in the morning, rip the top button off his uniform, and throw it away. The guard would spot the wide-open collar before breakfast, and he'd get upset: *"Button your button!"* The convict would say, "Can't. Lost it." The guard would get so mad, he'd stomp around muttering all day long. The cons would keep it up all year. Now, can you imagine torturing yourself every day over *"Button your button"*? Some of us do that.

Another hostile response to the imposition of someone else's restrictive zones is *withholding*. When you make people feel hostile, they find out what you want or need, and they withhold it from you. Little kids withhold their toys or their cooperation. Grown-ups withhold their knowledge and experience.

In companies, when one department gets mad at another department, its people withhold cooperation. People who are habitually late to business meetings could very well be hostile people withholding their very presence from the meetings.

I once worked with a National Basketball Association team which started a season with a great surge, but finished with a crash. I called the coach and asked him, "What happened?" He said, "A few players thought some of their teammates were getting too much publicity, so they stopped passing them the ball. They'd just say, 'I didn't see him.'" In other words, they withheld.

So, how is it on your team, in your family, at your work? Do you see why it's important to dissolve your restrictive zones? You can have the best superstars on your team, but if they develop hostility they will start violating each other's restrictive zones—which only compounds the problem and creates a mess.

Unless you see the underlying causes of anger and hostility, you won't know how to treat the problems. You might fall back on ineffective *remedies* like divorce, firing people, benching them, *pushing* them back, withholding, or imposing more rules. Unless you recognize some things that are bothering you and reprogram yourself inside, you'll keep producing unhealthy conditions.

Start setting your goals on a *want to, choose to, like to, get to* basis. Visualize the profitability in the goal and why it will be advantageous for you and others. It's not just a matter of looking forward to something; it's *how* you look forward that makes a difference. You don't want to look forward with trepidation and fear. That's worrying—or negative goal setting. Even if you have unappealing choices, try to see the advantages, and tell yourself why it's in your best interest to go that way. Then move aggressively into it. Focus on the *value*. Placing your life on a value-oriented basis creates drive and innovation; it's what makes life a grand adventure.

Working Together: Constructive Zones

Mother Teresa once said, "I can do what you can't do, and you can do what I can't do; together we can do great things."

To get from *here* to *there*, you'll need to recruit around you people who share the same vision, mission, and values. One person can't do it alone. You need to be supported by people who keep their drive alive and move forward.

You've got to create a critical mass around you of people who, in their own way, do whatever they need to do to build the community or environment toward a shared ideal. It takes a complementary team of people. Not everyone can be in the limelight. Not everybody has to be doing the same thing or playing the same role. Teams and companies are merely groups of people who band together to meet goals. Teams and groups have comfort zones. Groups have an efficacy level. Groups get intimidated. Groups have self-talk. Groups have pressures. Groups respond negatively or positively. Groups have fears.

Around the world, organizations are full of people who sit and say "management will do this or do that." And so they sit and wait. Nations and corporations have cultural norms, their own beliefs and attitudes that they've assimilated. They don't even know they have them. The culture can cause a lack of personal growth, a lack of empowerment. Some cultures want unempowered people. For example, in the past, the ruling parties of South Africa wanted an unempowered black population—not now. Likewise, some corporations wanted people to be put on hold and stuck. Now they need them to grow.

Japan is facing that problem now. We once hosted a group of Japanese people who work with American Family Life Assurance Corporation (AFLAC), the largest and most profitable American company in Japan. The Japanese have a challenge with self-efficacy. They don't accept personal credit or acclaim for accomplishment. All of the credit goes back to the team. Paul Otaki, the president of AFLAC Japan, has grown beyond that norm. But he has a large sales staff, thousands of people selling the same product, and they don't seem to rise above the level of the group. And if they do, they give the credit back. This has become a real problem for them. They are plateauing, not only as a company, but as a nation. They can't break through that mental barrier to reflect on personal success, and then to set new standards, new goals, new levels of success.

Environmental Comfort Zones

Take a hard look at the environment you've created in your business. If you have a department store, restaurant, bank, or business that attracts people to you, where people must walk in, then you must ask if the comfort zone or environment that you've created keeps certain people out—people you might have been trying to attract.

For example, suppose you're a department store and you have women's fashions. What people, what clothes, what advertising do you set up? What environment? If you have an environment with ladies who look very fashionable and petite like models, in sizes 7, 8 and 9, and you have other women who wear a size 14, 16 or 18, they may feel out of their comfort zone coming into your department. If they do come in, you ask them, "Can I help you?" "No thanks, just looking." And out they go.

A client of ours in Australia established a comfort zone for women who wear sizes 12 to 22. And they would advertise for those women. In their stores, they would have salespeople who are those sizes wearing very fashionable dresses. And women would feel comfortable coming into that shop.

Have you ever gone into a restaurant and felt that they set the environment up for the help instead of for the clients? You wonder, "How can they be playing background music like that?" Well, the employees are having a great time. They have to work there, and so they select the music and direct the whole thing, not for the benefit of clients. They drive the clients away; the music is there for their own comfort.

You need to ask,"What business are we in and what is our environment set up to attract and repel?" Since it's hard to create an environment where everyone feels at home, you might decide, "In this particular area, our store can't be too nice, or they won't come in." Create the environmental comfort zone appropriate for the clientele you're trying to draw.

A client of ours in Los Angeles was a large children's hospital. When they learned about environmental comfort zones, they looked at their lobby. The lobby wasn't at all for the clients, the little kids who came in frightened to death, the moms and dads who were worried, and the brothers and sisters there. The lobby only had pictures of the donors, high-back couches—very formal.

So, they decided they would put a giant Big Bird in one lobby and a Ronald McDonald in another lobby to create the comfort zone for the people with whom they're doing business. Then they rearranged their emergency wards so that mothers would no longer be torn apart from their children for the good of the technician, not the child. So, take a look at how you want things to be. And you create your business environment accordingly.

Shifting Corporate Attitudes

When leaders start talking about visions and goals to meet, saying "Oh, we're going to get there," they've got people with all kinds of attitudes who are working against the process of moving toward that goal.

Effective leaders teach a critical mass of people who they can rely on to change corporate attitudes. Until these people set a goal, they don't even know what attitudes they individually need to change, and then the restrictive attitudes will jump out at them on the journey. The leadership team must model the change in attitude. Otherwise, people will complain, find fault with, sabotage, and tell you why you shouldn't grow. They will work against accomplishing the goal.

Once I met with people inside the United Auto Workers and Ford Motor Company. What were their attitudes? Members of United Auto Workers thought they worked for the United Auto Workers union, not for Ford. One person came up during the break and said, "You're talking about Ford; you ought to bring up United Auto Workers." I said, "I thought you worked for Ford." "No, no, no." At the end I asked members of the United Auto Workers, "What do you suppose happens if Ford goes broke? What are you going to build and work on? Where are you employed?" But union has this attitude about management.

In turn, Ford management has this attitude toward union. For them to work harmoniously, both need to change attitudes. Then they can get inventive and creative as to how to solve problems together instead of withholding, instead of trying to figure out how to sabotage each other or try to manipulate each other. You've got to change the attitude and then you solve problems.

I said to the union members: "You have a very vital role to play. Your role seems to be different today, and we ought to look at this whole process differently. Your purpose is to protect the dignity of the worker, from recruitment through retirement. You see that injustice and hostile working conditions threaten personal dignity and that having the right wage causes people to have dignity and enables them to raise their families. When you see injustice, your role is to intervene courageously and make the change. It's that simple."

These words brought tears to their eyes. They had been adversarial, attitudinal, working against each other, withholding, trying to get more. "No, your role is to protect the dignity of the work force. They have a right to dignity in youth, dignity in work, dignity in wage, dignity in working environment, and they need dignity when they retire. Now let's get together and let's get after world competition. Let's build our future together."

Union and company managers each have their own point of view and can't see past it to the other point of view. So they shut the place down and do all kinds of dumb things to get after each other, when they're working for the same goals—dignity in the workplace, decent wages, and protection against injustice. But they fight among themselves instead of fighting the opposition, the competition. When you get them to see their scotomas, they say, "I'll be damned." After that, they know that they can work together.

My premise is that all the problems are solvable. All the problems in school are solvable. All the problems in labor are solvable. All these problems are solvable. We are creative geniuses. We just need to figure out what's blocking the solutions. What's keeping us from getting there?

Every culture, country, and organization has some scotomas. Subcultures live with walls between them. They see the world from their own points of view, wondering why the other *idiots* can't see. They're full of scotomas. Until you help them see. Then they say, "Well, look at that." You don't do it to embarrass them. You say, "I wonder if we're leaving something else out."

In many places, people are raised in an environment where they *know how people are,* and they will not see another difference. "There is no other way." And when you tie those scotomas with hate and fear, you harden. Your way becomes the truth, and you act like the truth. You build scotomas when you sit in your office and lose touch with your clients on the outside. People who never leave *home* create their own scotomas. And they wonder why they run into problems with reality.

They start with the premise that there are no solutions to community problems. Of course there aren't, especially if you start with that premise. But try starting with a different premise—that you can improve the quality of life for people by tackling the job in your own companies and communities, breaking down barriers and solving problems.

Where you find no hope, you come in and show them hope. When they find it, they change their point of view, change the way they look at the world, change the way they solve problems.

As you expand your comfort zone in organizations, you affect more people. Whatever you're doing in your church, your hospitals, your community, or for that one person, can be expanded. You can do it on a larger scale, especially when you work with a team.

c h a p t e r   1 7

WHO-SAID OF THE GREATEST MAGNITUDE

REMEMBER the story of *The Wizard of Oz?* Dorothy had the misfortune of being blown out of town, and the house dropped on a wicked witch who had some fancy shoes. Not knowing any better, Dorothy put the shoes on, which made the Wicked Witch's sister mad, and so she had to get out of town.

But Dorothy didn't know how to get out of town, and so the Good Witch, Glinda, showed up on the scene and said, "The only way to get back to Kansas is to go see the Wizard, the wonderful Wizard of Oz. He's got the touch. He's the *Who-Said of the Greatest Magnitude* with all the power."

And so Dorothy was off to see the Wizard, the wonderful Wizard of Oz. She was off to see the Wizard, because of the wonderful things he could do.

Now on her way, Dorothy ran into somebody without heart, somebody without courage, and somebody without brains. But being a very optimistic person, she fought off all the bad things that would occur—and she arrived at the Wizard's home. He was such a fake that he had to hide behind a curtain.

But the belief that Dorothy and her companions had in the Wizard made the difference. When the wizard asked the Cowardly Lion, "Well, what do you want?" the lion said, "I'm afraid of everything." He said, "Well, I can understand why. Every brave person has a medal, and I notice you're not wearing a medal. By the power vested in me, the great Wizard of Oz, I give you a medal, and now you've got courage." Through a rite of passage, a one-time affirmation, the Wizard changed the belief system of the lion. He now believed that he had courage, even though the lion had always had it.

Scarecrow's head was full of stuffing, so he felt dumb and couldn't think. So the Wizard said, "I can understand why. Every smart person has a diploma. I notice you don't have a diploma. All you need is a diploma, and so by the power vested in me, for all the smart things you did for Dorothy and Toto, I give you a diploma. Now you've got brains, so go act like it." You see what happens to many people? "Oh, I don't have a diploma, I don't have a degree, I couldn't do that." Yes, you can.

And the Tin Man didn't have a heart, so the Wizard said, "Oh, I can understand the problem." So he gave him a clock so he could hear the clock tick. "Now you've got heart; go act like it."

Dorothy and Toto, the Tin Man, the Cowardly Lion and the Scarecrow all went to see a positive Wizard who gave them courage and heart and brains.

Over the years, you run into wizards, coaches, teachers, employers, and people who try to take your guts away or take your brains away. They tell you what you can't do because of your color, race, sex, or aptitude. And you often fall for it.

The Wizard of Oz story teaches us the importance of making positive affirmations to ourselves and other people. Rites of passage and powerful one-time affirmations and vows can result in dramatic behavior changes.

Who-Saids and Rites of Passage

A *Who-Said* can be anyone you admire and respect, anyone whose words have the power to influence how you think and act. "Who said so?" "Well, *they* did." "Oh, then it must be so." It could be your parents, boss, supervisor, spouse, or someone you've never met: "I read it in the paper. Dr. Expert said so." It could even be something impersonal: "The *Farmer's Almanac* said so," "The encyclopedia said so," "The horoscope said so."

A rite of passage is a ritual associated with a change in status—a formal ceremony presided over by a *Who-Said of the Greatest Magnitude*. Consider a wedding ceremony. A minister, priest, rabbi, or judge is the presiding *Who-Said*. So, two people come in knowing they're single, and acting single. Then this *Who-Said* says, "Do you take this man (or woman) to be—?" And with just one statement of fact, the woman (or man) vows or affirms, "I do." Then *Who-Said* proclaims, "By the power vested in me, I now pronounce you man and wife." Now the couple believes they're married. Think about that. See how simple it is? You come in acting single, a *Who-Said* proclaims you married, and you go out acting married!

If the marriage doesn't work out, a judge puts the couple through another rite of passage: "By the power vested in me, I hereby dissolve this marriage." Now they go out and act single again! Isn't it amazing? All it takes is *words* in a one-time affirmation by a *Who-Said of the Greatest Magnitude.* The belief is changed, and so is the behavior. Because whether you believe you're single or married, you don't need to consciously remember. You will act like the person you believe yourself to be.

The military knows this. Suppose you're a soldier, and you don't believe you're brave. They put you through some rugged training, and then have a ceremony with pomp and circumstance, in front of a lot of *Who-Saids of the Greatest Magnitude.* They give you medals and proclaim you brave. Suddenly, you *feel* brave. You didn't before, but now you do. So what happens? You leave there acting brave: "They say I'm brave. It must be so."

That's what graduation ceremonies are all about. Somebody studies for seven years to become a surgeon. They're called an *intern.* The day before graduation, they can't operate on anyone because, in most states, it would be illegal—and you wouldn't think of letting them cut *you* open, right? You'd say, "No way. You don't have a diploma. You're not a doctor yet!"

But the next day, they go through graduation ceremony, with caps and gowns and pomp and circumstance, and they march down a carpeted aisle to a stage. Onstage is the dean of the medical school in his robes and tasseled cap. And this *Who-Said of the Greatest Magnitude* proclaims, "By the power vested in me, I grant you a doctor's degree." *Now* you'd let them do an operation on you, right? Because now you believe in them. As soon as they have their diploma, you say,"Oh, then it must be so."

Yesterday, they couldn't. Today, they can. What changed? Only the *belief.* They went through a rite of passage with a one-time affirmation by a *Who-Said of the Greatest Magnitude*—and now they have the power to change your life. Just *words!*

Of course, not just anything that anyone says has that power. It has to come from someone you believe in. And the circumstances and spirit of intent behind the words are essential, too. For example, two people meet in a bar for the first time and, after a few minutes of conversation, the guy says, "Oh, I love you." And the woman says, "Well, yes, I love you, too." The bartender says, "And I pronounce you man and wife." That won't work, will it? It's the same words, but the bartender isn't a *Who-Said,* and the circumstance and spirit of intent are different.

Do you see how powerful belief is, and how powerful the *Who-Saids* in your life can be? But the truth is: *Who-Saids* don't possess the power. It's *you* who grants it to them. *Who-Saids* have power partly because we've been conditioned to need someone else's blessing, approval, or permission. So, you're always waiting for other people to give you permission, or to affirm that you're capable of doing what you already know you're capable of doing: "Here's your football letter. Now you're an official member of the team." "Oh, thank you. I've played two years, but I didn't know I was an official member of the team until you gave me this letter." "Here's your pilot's license. You're officially a pilot." "Oh, thank you. I've only flown 60 hours. I didn't know I was a pilot until you gave me this license."

Breaking Self-Defeating Beliefs

Now, I'm not saying, "Fly without a license" or "Break any laws that you don't make yourself." I'm simply saying that when you grant other people undue influence over what you think and do, you give up accountability for your own life. Somebody tells you, "Okay, you're ready now," and you say, "I *am*? Oh, thank you. I wouldn't have known if you hadn't told me." But you do know. You just won't let yourself believe it.

It's like the placebo effect. The power isn't in the pill, it's in your acceptance of the doctor's affirmations that "This pill will get you well." It's the *belief* that makes you well. But belief can also make you sick. It's a matter of what you tell yourself—or what someone else tells you—that you believe.

Throughout your life, people will give you negative placebos that will make you feel sick. They may tell you, "Ain't it awful?" and "There's no hope" and "You can't get that job" and "It's a waste of time." Beware, because your subconscious can't distinguish between positive or negative placebos, happy or depressing thoughts, healthy or harmful beliefs. It doesn't care if you're happy or sad, healthy or sick. It simply accepts whatever you tell it. So, you can talk yourself *into* or *out of* self-limiting, denigrating beliefs. You can talk yourself *into* or *out of* excellence.

Become aware of the affirmations you tell yourself and your team members, and the affirmations that others give you, because you're constantly acting and making decisions based on their false, irrelevant information.

You and I must stop affirming things that can ruin our future happiness and success. You accomplish that by being careful who you listen to, controlling your self-talk and team talk, writing affirmations, and visualizing what you want. Successful, high-performance people *choose* whom they listen to. They build blind spots to the junk. When they want to try something new, instead of thinking *fear*, they think *challenge*."

Even a one-time affirmation by another person can alter your behavior drastically: "You're a troublemaker," "You're just like your sister, and she wasn't bright either," "You'll never be a doctor—you don't have the aptitude," "You're too awkward to be a athlete." In the past, you affirmed these proclamations from people you regarded as authorities.

Who are the *Who-Saids* in your life? Whose opinions have you sanctioned as "the truth." How do *they* know "the truth"? What did they tell you about yourself that you didn't already know? Why do you need them?

Every good leader is a genius at positively affirming other people. One time, I was traveling to an army base (Fort Bragg) where they develop America's elite soldiers. I was met at the airport by a general, two helicopter pilots, and two bodyguards in camouflage fatigues. The general (Bernard Loeffke) said, "I'm here to escort you to the base." As we talked, I noticed he had a star on his shoulder, which indicated he was a brigadier general. He said, "Excuse my two bodyguards. I'm a great target for the KGB." And I thought, "What am I doing with this guy?"

When we got in the helicopter, he said, "We're doing some very important exercises here, and I could be captured." He explained why our enemies would be interested in him. He had five silver stars, four bronze stars. He was a graduate of West Point. He'd served four terms in Vietnam, and he could speak Russian, Chinese, French, Spanish, and Portuguese. He had a doctorate degree in foreign relations, a master's degree in Russian. He was head of the Inter-American Defense Board.

That night, at dinner in the officers club, this General and I were engrossed in conversation. As we were talking, a Colonel (Nick Roe) walked by. The general reached out, grabbed the Colonel by the arm, and introduced him to me this way: "*This is the bravest man I know in the world.* He spent five years in solitary confinement as a P.O.W. in North Vietnam. He escaped in his fifth year. He's here to teach us how to be brave and how to survive." Then he let the Colonel go.

The General used me to affirm to the Colonel how much he admired him, and how brave he thought he was. But he couldn't just throw his arms around him and tell him. So he told the Colonel by telling *me*. He did that continually over my 24-hour stay. He was a master at third-person affirmation. And it was never flattery—it was always something sincerely great about the person.

Just before we left, a young officer saluted us as we got in the car. The General stuck his own foot in the door to keep it open. He pointed at the officer and said to me, "One day, this man will be the finest special forces officer in America, and I'll tell you why." He told me about that kid, and then he let him close the door. That officer saluted us again, proudly.

Why did he believe this guy? Because everyone knew that if *the General* said something, it must be so. By continually third-person affirming in this manner, the General showed that he was a *Who-Said of the Greatest Magnitude*—a master at building positive belief in others. He knew that people self-regulate around their self-image, and so he was constantly elevating the standard.

You can do the same thing by catching people around you in the act of doing things well, and either talk to them directly or talk to another person about them and affirm their worth.

For example, if you are managing a quality program, you've got to raise the standard on the inside of your people, or your quality will be artificial and temporary. They will always go back to the old way when you leave the environment. You have got to change the internal standard of people by affirming and helping them grow.

Sometimes, you do that for your children. You brag about them, in their presence, to somebody else. Physicians do that when they want someone to get well. They'll stand at the patient's bedside and tell an intern that the patient is doing well and will be leaving soon. The doctor can't tell certain patients directly because they won't believe it. Yet, when they overhear it being said to a third party, they believe it.

Learn to use the tremendous power you've got to help people become what they are truly capable of becoming.

But beware. You can also be a very negative wizard when you devalue, belittle, or criticize someone negatively. Once they believe you, they will act like what you've affirmed. What do you think happens when a father tells his son in Little League, "Don't strike out"? When the kid comes up to bat, he strikes out. The father says, "Why can't you hit? I taught you everything I know, but you can't do it." I wonder why. When the kid goes up to hit, I wonder if his subconscious says, "You can't hit. Your *dad* said so. It must be true." Is that kid going to hit? He might when he realizes his dad is a Negative Wizard of the Greatest Magnitude, and then takes back the power.

Do you do this in your family, your marriage, or in your social and business relationships? Who are the negative people you listen to? Stop letting other people feed you negative junk. Be in charge of your own life by taking back accountability.

Too often we let other people see us for us. "Tell me, what do you think of me?" "Tell me, what do you think I can do?" Sometimes they tell you things that are very limited, and if you absorb and accept the input, you behave like it, even though it may not be true. Often a *Who-Said* only gives you the permission to be, to act, to have what you already have the potential to be, do, or have. When you have the ability, but not the sanction, you restrict yourself from using your potential.

Imagine how many smart people never went to college or held themselves back because they didn't give themselves or weren't given permission by some wizard.

Free yourself from and avoid being restricted by negative wizards. You, your children and your team members will run into negative wizards who may say you don't have any heart, you don't have any courage, you don't have any brains, you don't have the aptitude. You don't have what it takes to be in this business. If you absorb that from somebody who is an inadequate manager, from a teacher who shouldn't be teaching, from a disgruntled grandparent, or from a frustrated little league coach, you absorb it as reality. You give too much sanction, too much credit, to what you perceive as an authority.

You don't realize at the time how powerful those negative wizards are in restricting the use of your potential. When they tell you where you are inadequate or no good or not capable and where you believe them, you hold back. Your tremendous ability and potential is held back by the powerful beliefs that you hold.

So please be aware of your role as a positive or negative wizard to the people around you. See, they think, for the most part, that you've got the power. There are people at work, and people in your family, who believe you're an authority. So, you need be a very uplifting, constructive, and positive influence, giving them heart and giving them courage. Be careful of your caustic, devaluative, belittling remarks. Because even though you may not mean them, or think that you've got that much influence, you never know.

Remember the song, "We're Off to See the Wizard"? Change the words a bit: "I'm off to *be* the Wizard." You can be a wonderful wizard if you have the affirmative touch. You don't have the touch for everybody, but you have the touch for those people who believe that you've got the power, so use it wisely.

Affirming and Empowering Others

When I was young, I wanted to be a high school football coach when I grew up. And so that was my goal. I didn't want to teach, but I had to teach to be a coach. Have you ever had a teacher like that? As long as you kept your mouth shut and watched the movie while I worked on my football plays, everything would go all right.

On the last day of school at the end of my first year of teaching, I was walking down the hall and was met by one of my students, a girl named Bev Woodward. She said, "Mr. Tice, I was waiting until now to tell you—you are the worst teacher I have ever had in my life."

Well, I couldn't get mad at her, because it was true. I didn't care if I taught. At the time, her comment went right by me, but a couple of days later I said, "I don't want to be like that." And I remember making a vow: "Nobody will ever say that to me again. I'll be the best teacher my students will ever have."

One way I tried to make good on that positive vow was to positively affirm the worth and ability of my students and athletes. I still try to do that. I do that, for example, with my granddaughter, Tiffany.

When Tiffany comes into our home or office, I'll say, "Oh, Tiffany's here." I'll make a big deal of it. And then I'll say, "Tiffany always smiles when she sees her grandpa." And I'll hope that she'll smile for me. When she smiles, I say, "I knew you'd smile for me." Okay. But other people don't know, so they think, "Oh, what a happy kid."

Next time I see Tiffany, I'll say, "Oh, Tiffany is here. She always smiles when she sees her grandpa." I'll reach out and smile, and she'll smile back. And I'll say, "See?"

Soon others will say, "She smiles for everybody." "She was just born happy." "She has a natural, positive disposition."

Now, everybody expects her to be happy.

What if you always treated people around you in a very positive, affirming, constructive way, seeing the best in them; helping them see it in themselves? Suppose you repeated your positive affirmations several times. Each time you saw them, you'd tell them again, in another way. You'd continually affirm their worth and their ability. If you are that kind of a mentor or leader at work or at home, you will watch the people grow around you—and their growth will be spectacular.

That is the way the best generals, coaches, teachers, executives, and parents are. And this doesn't mean that they are soft or let people walk on them. They are very firm about what they want done, but they are very constructive, positive, and supportive of you and your way of doing it.

Building Credibility

The reason that General Loeffke could have such influence with Colonel Roe is that Loeffke had tremendous credibility. I could have said the same thing: "I think that you are the bravest man I ever met." Same words, no power, because Roe would not perceive me as credible. But he knew that Bernie was highly credible, and so if Bernie said he was brave, he was.

You greatly improve your chances of having positive influence with people when you have credibility in their eyes, and you affirm them in connection to their contribution to a purpose or cause or campaign. You can light that spark. You can make a difference. Don't you get the feeling that you could and should?

Many parents wonder, "How I can work with my children now?" Many managers seek change now. It doesn't make any difference what area of your life you apply these principles, all parts of your life will be improved.

If you want to get your people to grow, you have got to be perceived as credible in their eyes. You have got to constantly work to enhance your credibility. When you have credibility, you can affirm people with great power.

Credibility is part of your self-efficacy. You need to persuade others to join you in your effort. And they're always looking to see why they should do what you ask them to do.

They ask, "Why should I act on what you're telling me?" They want to know if you're credible. So they ask, "Why should I listen to you?" They look for three things.

• *Similarity.* The first thing they ask is, "How are you similar to me?" So credibility comes when people perceive you as having something in common with them. That's important to them. "Have you ever done something similar?"

• *Competence.* "If you have done something similar, were you good at it?" Now, even if you were never an expert in a similar area, you could still have credibility with me if you ever coached, managed, or mentored anybody like me to be successful. So you don't need to be a doer as long as you are a maker of doers. For example, Angelo Dundee, the fight manager of heavyweight champ, Muhammad Ali, could not beat up anybody. How could he manage a world champion fighter? Why would a boxer want to go to him? Because he had coached people like Ali, and he had a great ability to bring the best out of people. So he had immense credibility.

• *Knowledge.* You'll also have credibility if you know what you're talking about. Do you have the knowledge?

When you have all three—similarity, competence, and knowledge—you'll have tremendous power to influence and lead people. They'll act on what you say.

Constantly develop your credibility in areas where you want to make changes in your community, family, or profession. You've got to be perceived as credible, not because you want acclaim but because you want others to be effective when they take action.

Setting Group Goals

Members of an organization are like members of a symphony orchestra. In a symphony, there are many individuals who play different instruments.

Suppose that you're the conductor, and you need to elevate the performance of the orchestra. Simply affirming that everybody's performance is elevated isn't going to do it. But if you involve all members in setting the new standard, then, once all members agree to it, you can ask them to improve their individual performance. To have a better symphony, those who play the oboe or violin must improve the quality of their playing. And their playing must fit in harmoniously into the overall performance.

As the conductor, you need to lead out in setting group goals. Remember to apply the basic principles of goal setting in groups to ensure that you still have followers.

1. *Get the big picture.* See your organization as a whole entity. If you only set goals in one area, you may run obsessively after one goal, focusing all your energy and creativity in one direction or department while frustrating all others. So look at what makes up the whole of the way you run your business. Look for models of healthy organizations and ask questions like "How are they structured? How does manufacturing work with marketing? How do they maintain good relationships with customers and suppliers? How do they create an environment for growth?" If you set goals in one area, you'll drive in that direction, but it may throw everything else out of order. This balanced goal-setting process will take some real thought on your part and the part of the people you're working with. What makes up the whole? Where are we presently? What would be ideal? What is the way we want it? How can we grow?

2. *Put the pieces into sequential order.* Ask your team, "What is imperative? What is essential to keep this organization viable and alive?" An imperative is that without which your organization will fall apart. What are your priorities? You can't do them all at one time. You might work on 15 goals at the same time, but not all in one area. You want to work with some balance, but which ones are you going to choose? Take time to figure out what is most important to you, and put those things into a sequential order. That's where you set your goals and you let the rest of that drop to the side or take a back seat.

3. *Involve people meaningfully.* If you just tell people what to do, their goals become a *have to*. There's no sense of shared ownership. So sell the value in the goal or vision that you want to achieve, instead of announcing, "All right, folks, here's where we're going to go, come on, move it." Believe me, your goal won't be a "move it" with them. So, ask yourself, "How do we weave the new fabric into the old? If I want the organization to grow, how can I show somebody else the value for them in achieving this aim or this end? Not everybody works for the same reason. How can I prove to them that we all need each other; that if they meet the group goal, and we'll all benefit and be successful?"

4. *Create constructive images.* Often, we try to motivate people with fear by telling them what we don't want. We talk about survival, about loss of business, or about all the bad things that may happen. Let's talk in the positive vein about what we do want. Remember, you move toward what you think about. If you're thinking about survival, that's all you're going to get. If you're thinking about loss of market share, that's what you're going to work toward. Instead of focusing on what you don't want, list those things you do want as a group.

5. *Share accountability.* As the leader, you can't just sit down and say, "Well, why don't they do something about this?" because what we do in our organizations is push all accountability to the top to keep control when we need to push accountability down and make everybody wake up.

Suppose that you and a companion are invited to a party in an area of town where you don't know your way around. Your companion is doing the driving and has a map and instructions on how to get there, and you're just along for the ride. Your friend has some trouble finding the address, but you finally arrive at the party. You have a good time, and now you want to go home. But your friend says, "I want to stay a little longer. You take the car; I'll get a ride home with somebody else."

Remember, you didn't drive. But you take the keys, and start driving in the direction you think will lead you home. The next morning, your friends asks, "How did it go last night?"

I guarantee you'll say, "I got lost, thanks to you, because I didn't know where I was going."

"But you came right with me."

"I know, but I didn't watch where we were going because I thought you were going to drive home."

You shut off your awareness when you give up accountability.

6. *Avoid imposing time limits.* Often people put time limits or deadlines on their goals when they set them. Sometimes that's necessary. But suppose that your teams sets a time frame based upon present resources, or present know-how, or current technology. You then lock yourself into a budget and schedule. Suppose your time line is two years, but you could have done the task in six months had you known about or heard about some resource when you set the goal. Once you lock on to some time limit, you tend to reject that it could be done faster. So, I suggest that you keep yourself free of time restrictions, wherever possible.

Naturally, you need to have sequence and order, but many managers use deadlines to create motivation. But when you put time limits to make people do something, people push back, as the work becomes a *have to, or else.* And so you get into procrastination, slovenly work and creative avoidance. Then you think you need more discipline, and so you impose more rules and fall back to a command-and-control style. But this only works against your system. If you keep yourself free of time restrictions and focus on improving the process for getting work done, you will sharply reduce the cycle time.

7. *See your goals as done.* Write your group goals in present tense, as if they are already accomplished, and then affirm, "The building is done; the game is won; the business is mine; the book is written; the change is made." As with individual goals, the discrepancy between your affirmation and current reality will cause the creativity, energy, and urgency needed for resolution. The discipline of seeing yourself through the event, the crisis, the change, allows you to work effectively during the process, without feeling all uptight and stressed out.

8. *Respect confidentiality.* If you announce a goal or surprise people with a sudden change, many people will likely work against you because all the emotional stress hits them at once. You need to sell the dream, and give them the chance to visualize it. In early stages, you only share your goals with your partner or spouse in areas that will help both of you grow together.

9. *Make ongoing modifications.* Once a group meets a goal, members tend to flatten out and have down time. So if you want continuous improvement and growth, don't wait until you achieve the goal; as you approach it, see past your original goal and set and assimilate a new one way out here. This will drive you through the goal. Of course, you'll still celebrate the achievement, but you won't stop. You keep your organization moving because you're now chasing a bigger goal.

10. *Write and affirm your group goals properly.* If you are serious about growing an organization, you will learn how to write and group goals that meet the following criteria.

• *Personal.* You need to change your organization, not another. Write your group goals to trigger imagery in first-person plural form ("we") so that you see yourselves doing it.

• *Positive.* Always trigger the picture of what you are trying to become, not what you are leaving behind. Being positive means affirming the attribute you want to acquire.

• *Present tense.* Write all your goals in the now, as if you already have the characteristic or acquisition before you ever do. Because, you are assimilating into your mind the desired behavior, as if you have already done it, you already are—present tense.

• *Achievement-oriented.* Indicate achievement, not ability. Don't say, "We *can be* the market leader." Sure, you have the potential to be, but you need to say, "We are the market leader," even though right now you're not. When you say, "We are" when you're not, you're creating a healthy tension. When you affirm you are, then you behave that way.

• *No comparisons.* Don't compare your organization to others; if you want to grow fast, focus on what you want to do, where you want to grow, how you plan to improve quality. Your hang-up is you. If you look around, you'll always find companies that are better or worse. So what?

• *Action words.* Write your goals and affirmations using action words. Make the picture a moving picture: "We smoothly, we quickly..." "Put in words that would cause your pictures to move.

• *Emotion words.* The more emotion, the faster the change. "We joyously...we happily...we proudly...." Put in words that will give you the emotion that you wish to absorb into your system.

• *Accuracy.* Be specific and accurate. The clearer the picture, the faster the change. Say exactly how you want to change. Otherwise, you'll be vague: "We're going to be a lot better this year." How much better? "Just better." Don't give yourself an out; be specific. That way, you get better feedback. You can then measure yourself against your vision.

• *Balance.* Set goals in a variety of areas—personal growth, family growth, financial growth, spiritual growth, social growth. Choose areas where you may want to expand or grow because you know you have a lot of potential in those areas.

• *Realistic.* If you can see your group doing it, the goal is realistic for you. Don't worry about where the material or people or information is coming from, and don't worry about not knowing how at the present moment. Affirm and imprint what you want, using pictures, words and feelings.

You, the conductor, might affirm, "We are this, and we are that," but that doesn't cause any accountable action on my part. To inspire people to progress beyond their present capability, you need to look for ways to affirm each member of the team. For example, if you can get the president of an organization to make affirmations not only to upgrade his or her leadership performance but also to enhance the skills of all members of the team, then team performance will rise. You may affirm the shared ideals, mission, and goals, and assimilate that into your system: "This is the way it is." And yet some individuals in the company don't care about the overall picture; all they care about and affirm is their piece of it, their growth, their department.

As a leader, you need to get everybody aligned. If you see there's selfishness or withholding or people working against each other, you can't affirm, "We work in harmony, cooperation, and love." You might say those words, but nothing will happen.

You need to affirm: "I cause the harmony, the team effort. I cause it by the way that I talk, nurture people, and build trust in the organization." You can't affirm for me. In a team or family affirmation, you might get several people focusing on the same affirmation. But in your affirmations, you still use first person: "Because of my leadership, the members of this organization are," and then go on to affirm what you want.

If you affirm "we are," it has no influence on me; however, you can influence the group or team by the way that you perform your piece of the action. The group will change based upon the leadership, inspiration, direction, or encouragement that you provide. If you want to elicit something out of a team, you can say "we," but to make a change, you must say "I" and "me." Affirming the "we" won't make much difference. Everybody can see the main mission and goal, and everybody ought to affirm those ends, but then it breaks down to that personal accountability. Each person must be accountable to grow and enhance his or her individual performance.

So, when you make group or team affirmations, always add your own personal part, your accountability for causing the action and the growth. Otherwise, you're wasting effort to affirm the "we." Use your own words, because different words have different meaning for different people.

If you try to push an affirmation on your team or family, you say to them, "Here, you need this." They're going to push it right back: "I'll tell you what you need." Remember: your team and family members are affirming something all the time in their self-talk. As a team leader, you can influence their affirmations. The question is: will you inspire them to be positive and constructive, leading in the direction you want to go, or allow careless team talk to affirm a different direction?

So, how do you get people to expand and grow? You encourage your team members to take charge of their own futures. You might try the following activities to get them involved.

1. When you have people who don't want to affirm or aren't involved in the written part of the affirmations, put the affirmations on signs and post them on the refrigerator, bedrooms, locker room, or boardroom. As team members come and go each day, they read these posters and assimilate the affirmations.

2. Play music that is uplifting, positive, constructive, and supportive of your team affirmations.

3. Read and recommend articles, books, and poems that paint a vivid image of the qualities and characteristics you would want assimilated by your team members.

4. At the end of a daily practice session, briefly talk about how things went, asking "What did you enjoy today? What was the most fun, the most exciting, the best thing that happened to you today?" Allow team members to express a positive feeling or experience, and then ask them, "And what are you looking forward to tomorrow?" So, you take them from a fun, warm emotion of today and drop them into a positive expectancy for tomorrow. High-performance people always have a positive expectancy of things occurring in the future. You, too, can develop that habit.

5. You might say to them: "I've set some goals myself lately. And I know how I want things to end up. This is the way I see things happening for us this year." What you're doing is getting them to project themselves into the future, in the way they choose to have things go, with strong emotion and clarity to the picture.

6. At mealtimes and other times you're together, be aware of what you talk about and how you talk. You can direct the conversation and project it into a constructive event in the future. You can affirm: "I see you as being...." You need to affirm people constantly into that future state.

7. Identify areas where you feel your team members need to grow and then affirm them into that state. Make affirmations to build their esteem and teach skills to build their confidence in those areas. Write personal affirmations about how you are going to influence their development.

8. Schedule special activities and near-term events that they can look forward to with great anticipation. People care about making affirmations if they care about having a successful date, ballgame, test, or presentation. Just ask, "How do you want the event to come off? How do you want the party to be? How would you like to perform at that event? Let's write how we want it to be."

You get them to describe it and write it out, and then read it back to them again and again, saying, "Let's see if we can add to this. Tell me a little more. Let's write that down so we don't forget it." What you're doing is assisting them to meet a challenge, and then you go on to face another one, and another one. If your team stays together for a while, you can get team members in the habit of planning the way they want events in their life to occur. After they get into this habit, you can say, "What else? What more can we do?"

You and your team members will care about making affirmations when those affirmations are tied to results you really care about. Encourage them to make a *shopping list* of what they want things to be like and what they'd like to have. On a personal level, maybe that's earning a better living, getting a better job, being popular, looking good, having new clothes, driving a new car. Use the natural things that they desire and show them how they can obtain those things as a natural consequence of obtaining the team goals. Help them see that if they want to achieve their long-term goal, "here's what you need to do this week." In a natural way, enhance the way they're doing things now; and before you know it, they'll be setting their own stretch goals, affirming them, assimilating them, and achieving them on their own.

chapter 1 8

BOOSTING TEAM ESTEEM

ONCE when I was coaching high school football, I had a very talented punter. But in a crucial game, he kept booting the ball off the side of his foot. His first punt went only 10 yards before slicing out of bounds—not at all the way I wanted it. So when the kid came to the sideline, I grabbed him and said, "Hey, stupid! You're kicking the ball off the side of your foot! Go sit down and think about it."

So the kid sat down and visualized kicking the ball off the side of his foot, over and over again. And, no doubt, he felt that awful, sinking sensation in his stomach, too.

Later in the game, the same kid had another chance to get us out of a hole with a good long kick. But he shanked another short kick off the side of his foot. It made me madder than the dickens. Hadn't I told that kid what he was doing wrong?

I grabbed him when he came out of the game and said, "Hey, you did it again! You didn't pay attention to me, did you? Go sit down again and think about it."

The same kid kicked three more off the side of his foot in that game. When he came off the field the last time, he tried to hide. But I found him, grabbed his shirt, and said, "You did the same dumb thing five straight times! You're not playing for the rest of the game! You may not play for the rest of your *life!*" I was serious. I added, "Besides that, you don't even get good *grades!*"

Now, who should have been benched? The player was doing exactly what he was being coached to do. And he was being berated and belittled for doing it.

I know now that I should have told him calmly, "That's not like you. You're better than that. Next time, drop the ball with the nose up." The job of the coach is to tell players what he *wants* them to do, and how to do it *right*. That creates a positive feedback loop—a positive way to manage people. You recognize that everybody has scotomas to their faults, but they see the right thing to do if it's pointed out to them.

When coaches use game films to point out their players' mistakes, even slow down the film to focus on *everything the players do wrong*, they not only reinforce the mistake but they also reduce team esteem. When the player makes the same mistake, the coach says, "You don't listen! I'd be a great coach if it weren't for these players."

Ask yourself, "Am I leading people toward success and excellence? Do I visualize what I want and then clearly describe to them what I want them to do? Do I build or destroy individual and team esteem?"

When you, as a team leader, say negative, sarcastic, cynical, or caustic words to your team members, you damage their esteem.

Suppose you have two water buckets representing a positive-negative esteem balance. You start most seasons and ventures with nothing in either bucket. But if you put most of the weight in the right bucket, soon it gets so heavy that you lean in that direction; eventually, you may topple over. The same thing will happen if you put most of the weight in the left bucket. You will lean, and then topple, to the left.

Every time you make a positive affirmation—a positive statement of belief or fact—to your team, imagine that it adds weight to the right bucket. Conversely, every negative, destructive affirmation you make adds weight to the left bucket. If you accumulate more weight in the left bucket, your team will lean in the negative direction. If you accumulate more weight in the right bucket, you'll lean in the positive direction.

When you build beliefs and attitudes through smart team talk, you lean toward the positive. Of course, you must always monitor your lean and learn how to redistribute the weight if necessary.

By using two statements—*that's like us* and t*hat's not like us*—you constantly affirm the future positively for your team. As you add positive weights to your balance scale and update the *truth* about your team, you change the direction in which you lean, and start using more of your collective potential.

When a member of your team makes a mistake, you don't beat the person up or run yourself down. You manage the negative emotion by laughing and saying, *that's not like you,* and then looking forward to *the next time.* Affirm what is *right* with you and your team. Imprint competence and high performance by affirming *"That's just like us"* until every team member believes it inside.

Team Talk and Team Esteem

Teams, groups, and organizations have self-talk. I call it team talk.

Smart team talk is positive, affirmative talk. It's smart because it builds team esteem. If your team talk is negative, your team performance reflects it.

And yet in your social and professional groups, you will hear negative talk constantly around you: "Ain't it terrible?" "Things can't get much worse, can they?" When people start faultfinding and complaining, you must learn to say, "Stop it. I don't buy that." Otherwise their self-talk could overwhelm your own.

As a teacher, coach, leader, or manager, you need to understand that to have high-performance teams and organizations, you've got to elevate the image, standards, and esteem of your members. Rule one in your organization ought to be *constructive feedback*, yes, but no cheap shots, no negative backbiting, no belittling, no sarcasm, no cynicism.

What's it like now in your organization? Are people running it down, always pointing out what's wrong? Low-performance organizations have a constant stream of negative self-talk going through them. Most of us tend to tell the people we care about the most everything that's wrong with them, pointing out their faults constantly. And if we think and communicate in pictures, they're thinking and recording pictures that we don't want. In a sense, we're like the coach who videos the games and shows the players their mistakes over and over until they get them down good. Then we wonder why they don't perform better. We run our people down, and then tell them to go out and win.

Effective leaders treat people with dignity and respect; they see and build potential in them. Leaders speak to people as they see them—as if they already are what they are supposed to be. The male child of royalty is treated royally because some day that kid will be king. You don't run him down, beat him up, and then tell him to go out and act like a king. You affirm his greatness.

In the military, they sing affirmations: "Off we go into the wild blue yonder, flying high into the sun. Down we dive, zooming to meet their thunder. Atta boy, give 'em the gun."

Listen to this one. "We live in fame or go down in flame. Nothing will stop the Army Air Corps." Such songs use the power of affirmation, and strong emotion, to unite peers in a noble cause.

General Bernie Loeffke once shared with me four simple keys he uses to influence people in different countries: he learns their names; he learns their songs; he learns something of their language, history, and culture; and he shares a joke or a laugh with them. All of this is very affirming.

Paradoxically, we might be very successful at launching many campaigns and influencing millions of people worldwide, and still have problems with our own children. You can imagine how disappointed Diane and I have been with some of our kids, and how sad we've been because of the tragedies some have gone through. But you know, there's a way of looking and taking about the failures of our families and teams that lifts the spirit so you don't quit, give up, or make yourself a mess. You can't live in a world of gloom and doom and pessimism and do great work. You need to boost team and family esteem. But how do you correct yourself and others, so that you keep moving on instead of damaging your self-image and self-esteem and getting overwhelmed by disappointment and grief?

Again, it gets back to *smart self-talk* and *smart team talk*. You can control your self-talk to the point that it doesn't matter whether your spouse gives you positive reinforcement or whether your boss says you're doing a good job. Of course, it's much easier when you get it. But don't become dependent on the positive affirmation of another to affect how you're going to grow. When you do get it from others, it will help you grow much faster. If you sit around and wait for people to praise you, you won't even begin to reach your potential.

When people do applaud you or praise you in a constructive way, learn to say, "thank you." Learn to accept compliments graciously. Learn to accept praise. You've been taught to be humble. But humility doesn't mean pushing away praise: "Ah, we're no good; it was nothing." You give credit to God and to people who have helped you. If you have anything to do with it, you must say "thank you," and then affirm to yourself, "I'm good."

Smart self-talk and *smart team talk* will elevate your team image and esteem. I work with athletes and teams who struggle with negative self-talk. When they understood the importance of self-talk, they make great strides. Young athletes tend to show emotion quickly when they perform badly. But when they perform well, they often deny that they've performed well. They may perform well all day and make just one mistake, but then they focus on it. They may even deny that they're any good and put themselves or their team down. Now, they may need to handle it that way on the outside, but on the inside, they need to reaffirm their worth, potential, and positive performance.

Team-Esteem and Performance

If you lack the self-assurance, you'll find it hard to reach the next plateau because you think, "I can't make it. I'm no good. I don't have what it takes. Why even *try?*"

You may feel devalued, insignificant, powerless to control what happens to you. But you can boost your self-esteem the same way you can improve your self-image: through your own self-talk. ***Remember: We limit ourselves*** *by the way that we think.*

If your team talk is negative and limiting, you limit your ability to change and grow. Your team will move toward and become what you think and talk about. If you dwell on being powerless and insignificant, your team members will say, "Okay, coach, whatever you say." They will start leaning toward a negative, locked-on, limiting view of themselves as ineffective and powerless.

High-performance teams have high team esteem. Team esteem is your collective confidence and respect. It's how *good* you all feel about being you; it's your positive feeling of dignity and worth. And it affects what you can achieve. The better you feel about yourself, the better you perform and behave. So you can talk yourself into being very positive, strong, firm, committed, powerful, and assured. You can talk yourself into taking risks, trying new adventures, learning new skills, extending yourself to new people, and new places. In fact, everything you do corresponds to your self-esteem.

Occasionally we all run into negative wizards who load us down with heavy weights. Bosses with low self-esteem themselves chip away at their employees' self-respect and self-worth. These people then block themselves with careless, negative self-talk simply because they believe the observations of someone else.

If you continue that pattern in your organization, you'll find it difficult to compete, because you don't respect your own products or opinions. You need applause, approval, compliments, and reassurance from the outside: "Please tell us: Do we look all right?" "Do you think we can do that job?" "Are we doing the right thing?" You only sanction what some person or group on the outside says to you, which further damages team esteem.

If you have high team esteem, you have a healthy *can-do* attitude and respect your own opinions and products. Many of us have a mistaken idea about humility. We are raised to believe that thinking well of ourselves is wrong. We were taught, "Don't get a swelled head. Nobody likes a braggart." In other words, "If you start thinking you're good, I'll point out 100 things that are wrong with you." As a result, we tend to reject what's good in us. We accept and then affirm, "We're lousy." Even if we affirm "We only excel at one thing," we tend to improve our performance in all other areas. Our subconscious picks up the *positive* message, too.

In high-performance teams, humility simply means *credit where credit is due.* If somebody helps you to succeed, give them credit. If you succeed on your own, give *yourself* credit.

I once worked with the staff in a federal penitentiary, and I met a young man who had been behind bars for a long time, but who was scheduled to be released. I asked him, "What kind of job will you get?" He said, *"Anything."* In his mind, he was saying, "I've been in prison. I'm a bad person. I don't deserve a good job." I said, "How much do you think you ought to get paid?" He said, *"Whatever."* He'd been beaten down by so many people in his life, and for so long in prison, that he'd lost his own self-worth. So he told himself, "Whatever people are willing to pay me is all I deserve."

I said, "You'll probably be looking for a car to get around in, right?" He said, "Yeah, probably." I said, "What kind of car?" He said, *"Just some wheels."* In other words, "Any old junker is good enough for me." Do you see what can happen when you have a diminished sense of self-esteem in your family or on your team ? *Anything* will be good enough. Then I said, "Someday, you'll want to find a girl and get married, won't you?" He said, "I suppose so." I said, "What kind of a girl are you hoping to find?" You can guess his answer. He said, "Anything." It's sad and tragic. What kind of girl would most likely be drawn to him? A girl looking for "anything," too.

Prison is full of people with low-self-esteem. Out in the yard, at meals, even in the cell blocks, they rip and tear and devalue. You rarely hear a good word said about anybody. If you have low esteem, you belittle others. A husband with low self-esteem can't stand to have a wife who thinks highly of herself. If she has a job that he considers better than his, he might say to her, "You'll never hold that job. You can't even organize the house." In other words, "Get back down where you belong." Parents with low self-esteem won't allow their children to rise above them. They'll say to their child, "What makes you think you're so good? You can't even do your chores right at home." Low self-esteem managers are faultfinding, sarcastic, belittling, angry managers who are threatened by employees with high self-esteem. Teachers with low self-esteem won't let kids in their classroom think better of themselves than they do of the teacher: "Don't be a know-it-all. If I need your help, I'll ask for it."

Be aware of conditions in your family, at your job, in your relationships, in your community, because the self-esteem of those around you can also have a profound effect on you.

We draw ourselves into the relationships, the jobs, the teams, the incomes that we feel worthy of receiving. That's why you need to work at building your self-esteem, your team esteem, your family esteem. For example, you can continually upgrade your children's self-esteem by telling them, "You're a good person." "You're a brave swimmer." "You're nice to your sister." "You're smart." But beware. They will go out to the playground and the streets, and somebody else will tell them they aren't worth anything, and they might get careless with their self-talk: "They're right. I'm not worth very much." Other people will try to take away their heart, their brains, and their guts. As a leader, you must stay strong and constructive, and continue to bolster team esteem. Of course, to do that, you need to build high self-esteem in yourself and others with Smart Talk.

Not Ready for Rejection

People with low self-esteem are frightened of change and risk. They wait for somebody else to step out first, and then maybe they'll follow their footsteps.

Diane and I have traveled to some of the world's finest resorts, and we've observed the children there. The high self-esteem kids are out having fun, experiencing adventures and meeting new friends. The low self-esteem kids spend days sitting in front of the television. Their parents say, "Why don't you go to the pool and meet some other kids?" the kids respond with, "No, I want to watch this program." Those kids are thinking, "Who would want to play with me? Nobody likes me at home, so who would want to be my friend here?"

Even if people want to meet new friends, they think, "I can't. My self-image is so soft that one more blow will kill me. If I go out and you tell me I'm not worthy, I can't take the hit. So I'll stay here and protect myself."

You'll find people in your companies, in your offices, on your teams, who think and act like that. They say, "I could've taken on that other company, but I didn't want to. They aren't worth my time." "I could have told the boss about the new product, but I didn't want to. She wouldn't care." "I could've played with that team on the weekend, but I didn't want to. They're a lousy team."

The real reason—and they won't say this out loud—is, "I'm frightened to death." So instead, you may see them criticizing those who *do* take risks and try the new. That's because people with low self-esteem are threatened by people with high self-esteem. They need to rip and tear at them to put them in their place. And where is that? *"Below me!"*

How far can you lead other people? No further than you can get them to see themselves doing it. You, as the leader, may be able to see yourself doing it, but if they can't see themselves doing it, they'll lag behind. You can't get them to participate because they can't see it. You may then resort to intimidation or force or bullying, trying to push people to where you think they belong.

"Send Us Anywhere!"

If you have high team esteem, you're not afraid to take risks, to venture out of your comfort zone, and to attack life as an *adventure*.

Suppose someone tells a high self-esteem team, "You can't do it. You don't have the skill."

They'll respond, "Maybe not now, but we'll learn it."

"You've never even done it before."

"Yes, but it'll be fun learning how."

"Look at the competition—they'll eat you alive."

"We don't even think about the competition."

High self-esteem people don't consider situations as *risks*. They think they can handle anything, an attitude that helps them build scotomas to risk.

In doing some research on high-performance thinking, I had the chance to spend time with some of America's elite commandos. I helped debrief some of them when they came back from the Vietnam war. I was interested in knowing, "How do they *think?*"

Learning how these people are trained was a revelation to me. My concept of military training was people being bullied, belittled, embarrassed, demeaned. In fact, that's the way I used to coach football. I'd run my players down, tell them how wimpy and cowardly they were, hoping to motivate them—and then I'd say, "Now go out and win!" I'd humiliate them all week, and then on Saturday, they'd go out and perform in the game like the humiliated wimps they *believed* they were. That was the team esteem I inspired. I was ignorant of how to train high-performance people.

When I dealt with our commandos, I found out for the first time that when they're in training, no one ever devalues, criticizes negatively, belittles, or demeans them. Their goal is to elevate self-esteem in the individual and in the group. So they instill pride, worthiness, excellence, capability, and success. To these commandos, no assignment is too tough. They think they can do anything they're asked to do. Because of their exceptionally positive training, these elite commandos were willing to take risks commensurate with their high self-esteem. The better they felt about themselves, the more risk they were comfortable with.

As a result of their training, elite commandos come to expect the highest performance out of their equipment, the utmost support from their staff, and continual success from themselves. They have the self-assurance and high team esteem: "We're the best."

People around those commandos are constantly putting them up, positively affirming and re-affirming, "You are the world's finest. You've got what it takes." So these people think, "We can do anything. Send us anywhere!"

Hopefully, this story will give you an idea of how to treat your spouse, your children, your employees, your teammates. Think about it:

Are your people treated like wimps or like elite commandos? Do they expect excellence from themselves? Are they willing to take risks? Whom do you surround yourself with—people with high self-esteem or people whose self-esteem is lower than yours? Do your family or team members think, "We can do anything"? Do they attack conflicts and problems like elite commandos? Or do they believe they're outer-directed and dependent on "lucky breaks"?

You can raise your self-esteem, and the esteem of others, by controlling your self-talk and your team talk. Look for ways to affirm yourself with your self-talk, and to catch your people in the act of doing things right. From now on, tell them, "Hey, you're good. You're one of the best. I like the way you do things." By positively affirming them, you become a powerful, significant, positive wizard to the people around you.

Your team esteem is challenged when you get away from the familiar and tackle new situations. If you're not careful, you might succumb to negative criticism. And then self-doubt brings on hesitation, which can bring on failure.

When you're feeling vulnerable, you build scotomas to the positive about yourself and your team. "We're no better or different." You constantly bolster your team esteem so that whenever you move into something unique, you're thinking like elite commandos: "We can do it. Send us anywhere!"

Don't dwell on the negative things that happen, but think about your successes, especially when you set new goals. To build your group efficacy, you need to reflect on your success, which causes you to assimilate it, and then project it into the future.

When you train your team, ask them to reflect on their accomplishments, and then guide their forethought into the future with the same emotion. Ask them, "What did we do today that we're proud of? What are we looking forward to tomorrow?" That's how you establish the new reality.

One way to build your team resiliency is to make a list of 10 things that went wrong in your business—a bankruptcy, a goal that you set and failed to meet, a product failure, a service snafu, a relationship failure—and then to review that list and remember how *well* you recovered from those events. Then take that same emotion forward into your new aspiration, and say, "We'll do great; and even if it doesn't come off as planned, we'll recover from that, too." You lead and communicate better with people when you remind them of the difficulties or trials they've been through, and overcome. "We came back; we're tough. So give us another one. And if we don't do it? It'll hurt, but we'll bounce back."

Also, ask your team members to make a list of 10 things that they've done well. Let them go back in time and record and assimilate their successes so they can repeat and build on them.

Celebrate your team success. Don't pass too lightly and too quickly on to something else. Get into the fun habit of going back and using past events to create future success. Take time to enjoy your accomplishments. If you pass too quickly and too lightly over your team successes and recoveries, you and your team members won't assimilate them to add to your efficacy. In your family, teams, and organizations, you need to assimilate those positive qualities and accomplishments through affirmation.

Create Happiness-Producing Events

Recently, I was talking to my youngest daughter, who is now a wife and mother of three children. I was suggesting how she could help Alix, her daughter, to have a happiness-producing environment. I said, "Have her make some pancakes for her four-year-old brother. She'll feel a sense of accomplishment, and her brother will also feel great." That's a happiness-producing event.

Or, I said, "help Alix bake cookies, and take them to a neighbor. She will be happy to serve; you will be happy with her accomplishment; and the neighbor will be happy with the gift."

These happiness-producing events don't need to be something done in faraway places or at the top of the cost scale.

I said, "Or, Alix could paint a picture and take it to great-grandmother. Great-grandmother will be thrilled with the picture; she'll put the picture on the wall. It will mean happiness for great-grandma, happiness for Alix, and happiness for you."

You can sit and wait for somebody to invite you to a party or make a party. Do good things happen from the outside or do you cause them? Am I the only one that causes parties? No. If somebody throws a better one, I go. But if they don't throw one, I plan one myself. Every day is a happiness-producing event for me. Diane and I create them all over the place.

In your teams and organizations, create happiness-producing events, in addition to whatever else you do. In your social and professional interaction with other people, exchange constructive ideas and positive suggestions. Such talk creates a positive feedback loop that has the power of stopping dysfunctional and negative behaviors.

Suppose you have an obnoxious 13-year-old who's driving you nuts. He's profane, uncooperative, irresponsible. If you affirm: "I can't get along with this kid—nobody can," you perpetuate the reality you see today. If your verbal and nonverbal feedback to the kid is negative—"You can't get along with anybody! You're irresponsible!"—the kid will perpetuate those same problems.

So, if you have an obnoxious 13-year-old, you must visualize not what the kid is, but what you want the kid to become: a happy, successful, responsible, cooperative, mature, 25-year-old. Then, when the kid acts like an obnoxious 13-year-old, you say, "Stop it! I won't tolerate that. You're much better than that. You're a much nicer person. I see you as —" and then you describe the way you imagine him to be.

See the difference? You establish a positive feedback loop; you feed back not what the kid is, but what you envision him capable of being in the future. You already see him as a nicer, more mature, 25-year-old. The kid will reflect back on the spirit and the power of your affirmation, visualize it, and, hopefully, move toward it. In effect, you deny the kid's present reality and shut it off—even if it's true—and create a new reality. In other words, "You are cooperative. You are responsible. You are a nice person. You are pleasant to have around. You are mature—and I will not accept less from you anymore." You can do the same with employees or anyone else you manage and lead.

Why do you and I sometimes treat the people we love the worst? How do you treat your siblings? How do you treat your spouse? How do you treat your parents? How do you treat your closest friends, your closest business associates—the people you absolutely rely on the most? Do you communicate to them: "What's the matter with you anyway? How can you be so dense?" Almost like you expect them to raise their hand and say, "I was hoping you'd ask me that. I never thought you'd give me the chance to tell you." See how dumb that is? But we do it anyway: "I've been meaning to tell you what an irresponsible person I am. I'm sure glad you brought it up again."

Those closest to us are most vulnerable because they love us. We have their attention, and we know their flaws. If you tell your seven-year-old, "You're the messiest kid I've ever seen!" what's that picture look like when you're seven? What will the kid affirm with his own self-talk? Cleanliness? Order? No: "I'm the messiest kid he's ever seen. My dad says so. It must be so." And what's the kid going to continue to affirm? "It's like me. I am messy. Everybody says so."

Once that *takes,* they act like the person they believe themselves to be. So now they've got to throw their clothes on the floor, or else they'll feel crazy. Then you come in and you see the clothes scattered all over the place, and you think, "There they are again!" You get the kid and say, "Look at those clothes! This proves it; this is the biggest mess I've ever seen!" And the kid thinks, "I know. I'm good at it. You've been telling me I'm the greatest at it for years!"

Because you have tremendous potential, you must become very aware of the power of words and the spirit of intent behind them. Words trigger pictures that bring about emotions. What pictures are we painting when we bring up how incompetent we think somebody is? Does it trigger the constructive change we want in that person or the constructive zone we want in the organization? Absolutely not. It triggers the exact image for tomorrow that we want to move away from today.

Every minute you spend describing to your children, your spouse, your friends and associates, what you don't want in them, without knowing it you're helping them perpetuate those very things, especially if they consider you to be the great wizard.

You can set great aspirations and goals, but you need the help and cooperation of others to realize them. The key question is not "How many people do I know?" it's " How many people can I get to help or join me?" Do you know anybody who's efficacious who will help you? Developing your credibility, personality, character, and relationships increases the size of your aspiration because you say, "I don't know how, but I know someone who does, and I can get him or her to help on this one."

You collect capability around you to bring about end results in places you want to make a difference. As you increase the size of the goal you set, you can't do it all, but now you have a bunch of people around you who know how.

As you get bigger and better and stronger and bolder, soon you'll see opportunities in your PTA, your community, your political leadership, your church, or wherever you happen to be. You'll seek to make a very significant difference.

Team Vision
If you don't have a clear team vision, you need to involve team members in creating one. As a variation of the concept I mentioned earlier, imagine taking a few people and saying, "Okay, I'll give you each $1,000 if you put this thousand-piece jigsaw puzzle together."

They say, "Okay, no problem."

You then dump the pieces out on a table in front of them, and say, "You've got to put this puzzle together in two hours."

They look at each other and say, "No problem."

You then take the box top with the picture on it with you as you walk away, saying, "It's all yours. Good luck in putting it together."

Have you ever tried to put a jigsaw puzzle together without the box top? It's not easy. But suppose that somehow, your great team pulls it off. When you come back two hours later, they have the puzzle solved.

And so you say, "I knew you were really good. Now I have a new challenge for you—a bigger puzzle.

This time you dump three thousand-piece jigsaw puzzles on the table, and say, "This one is three times bigger than the last one. Do you think you can do it?"

Your team nods, "Sure, if you leave us the box with the picture on it."

So you put one box with a picture in front of them. But then you call each person out individually and show them a similar but different box top. You leave them saying, "You've got six hours on this one. Good luck."

Now, when you come back, you find that your team members are trying to choke each other and beat each other up. They are yelling, "That's not right, you idiot. Can't you see?"

Sometimes we do the same thing with our team and family members. Everybody has a similar but different picture or vision.

You might say, "The closer we can come to sharing the same vision, the better off we are. So let's put our heads together and get clear on what we're building here so that everybody can get behind it."

Once you focus on a team vision, it becomes your team affirmation. It clearly defines, "This is what we're building. This is what we're all about. We can use everybody's energy to achieve the goal."

Creating a team vision is like creating your own vision, except there's more of you. You need to come to agreement. You talk about what this team, nation, church, family, department, or company is all about. The vision is a blend of diverse wants and desires.

When I was coaching football in high school, our team vision was to be the best in the state, to be undefeated. But we had several players who were playing for other reasons. They didn't really care about being the best in the state or going undefeated. Some were playing to impress their girlfriends. Others were playing to get their pictures in the local paper. Some were playing to get a scholarship to college. Others just wanted to play for the fun of it. Everybody had his own reasons for playing.

Admittedly, as the coach, I also had my *other* reasons. I wanted to make a living. I wanted to be successful. I wanted to gain respect. There is never just one reason why people work as a team.

I was always trying to figure out what I could say or do to inspire these kids. One day I thought, "I'm coaching at Kennedy High School, a Catholic high school. If I talk to them about playing for God, I can't get any higher motive than that."

So, I talked to my players about going out and beating those heathen schools. "We are on a crusade," I would say.

Well, that didn't even wake them up. They didn't care about playing for God. So I started talking about playing for the school. Their response: "Who cares about the school?" And so I talked about playing for the coach. That almost made them throw up. They weren't motivated by my reasons. I couldn't get them to play for God, the school, or me. So one day I just asked them, "What are you guys playing for?"

They came up with some of the worst reasons—the picture in the paper, the girlfriend, the scholarship, the fun. I said, "You must have higher reasons than that." They didn't. So I said, "Okay, will you impress your girlfriend even more if we win? Will your picture in the paper look better if you're scoring a touchdown? Will your chances of getting a scholarship improve if you make a contribution that wins a game?" They finally got the message. Our vision was to win—and win we did.

The reasons why people are playing on your team are diverse. But if you can align your reasons if you have the attitude, "I need you, and you need me, and we all need each other to achieve the goals and ends that we want." By creating the vision, agreeing on it, and committing to it, you will get out of life what you want and I'll get out of it what I want. We both win. Our vision is to win, and we describe what that win looks like, and how many wins we want.

Here at The Pacific Institute, we have a vision: To help people enhance the quality of their lives so that they can then improve their families, their community, their organizations. Some people choose to work with corrections, some with military, education, health care, and so on. We have different areas of emphasis, but we're all aligned behind our overall vision. And we know that it takes us all, working together in harmony, to achieve our goals.

In like manner, you can work on a vision with your team or family. What is the purpose for your family? Why are you bonded together? For emotional support, for care and feeding, for financial support, for health? Create a wonderful motto or picture or vision or mission with which every member of the family can identify, and then get aligned in moving in that direction.

Otherwise you have an organization of individuals who, like cats, head off in their own direction. You can have a family with a father going one way, a mother going another way, a child going this way, and a child going that way. You still have a family, but it's dysfunctional.

You can have a functional, happy family and team spirit when you get synergy and alignment behind a shared vision, mission, and goal. One image, one goal. Otherwise, there's little purpose for being a family, or having a company.

Who creates the team vision? The leader may have the vision, but every member needs to buy into it. Otherwise, you get second-hand values, second-hand morality, and second-hand goals. With second-hand values, your children might behave exactly as you wish them to behave in your presence, but the moment you leave town, things change fast. They go back to living their values and their life in *their* style.

Likewise, some folks in your company might profess the same mission or goal and say and do the right things around the boss, but in the bathroom or over a drink, they talk about what they really mean. You might as well get everybody together and invite those who have a different vision and mission and who choose not to be there to go and do their thing some other place. If you're not all working on a *want to* and *choose to* basis on the same goal, you won't have the energy and synergy you need to get from where you are now to where you want to go as a group.

Why Quality Programs Don't Work

When you look at models and *benchmarks,* you see what other people are doing. But you won't change a bit unless you identify with it and change your inner picture of what's possible for you and your team.

Most quality programs don't work because they don't change the expectations or internal standards of the people doing the work. You impose external motivation, expectation, and standards when you say, "Go after the Baldrige Award." Even if you win the award, you will likely fall backward fast, unless in the process of pursuing the award, people internalize the standards.

My experience suggests that when people go after something for some reason outside themselves, they don't change the standard on the inside. Hence, they don't sustain the improvement.

So, how do you continuously improve yourself? How do you continuously improve others? How do you get people to become more creative and accountable? How do you get them to solve problems?

You help them to change themselves from the inside using visualization, affirmation, goal setting, assimilation, practice, and performance. You help them to see themselves differently, and then their performance will improve naturally and continuously.

Families, teams, groups, companies, cities, and nations also have images—the collective idea of "how good we are." Often these images need to be changed; otherwise, your organization keeps itself as it sees itself.

When people come into your business, they will act toward your business as they see your business. And how do they see your business?

Often they see it through their experience with the person who's right in front of them.

For example, for many years, I would travel once a month to a resort where we presented leadership seminars. One time I arrived early to make sure that everything was prepared correctly and noticed that a light was burned out right above where I would be standing and speaking.

I asked a young man who was working there, "Could you please replace this light."

He replied, "I doubt it."

"Why do you doubt it?" I asked.

He said, "Well, it's not my job. And I already told management about it three or four days ago, and they haven't done anything about it yet."

I was left with the impression, "Ah, their service is falling down." I started thinking that they were not attentive, that they didn't care about me. I picked up this image from one employee.

I knew the top executive of the resort, but when I was setting up for my seminar I was dealing with one employee. All day, I was saying, "The service here has really fallen off." All weekend I found many other things wrong—the paint, the food, the sound system. And, when I returned to my office I said, "We've got to change sites; their service doesn't meet our standards any more."

How are you seen by your customers and other stakeholders? How do you want to be seen? Is your vision shared by others? Do you affirm it? And has it changed the internal standards of everyone involved? If not, your quality won't improve much.

Effective Leaders Affirm People

One time I was working with the leaders of the Boys' Clubs of America in California. I told them about a friend of mine, Fred Akers, who was then head football coach at the University of Texas. He had a player named Russell Erkslaven, who kicked a field goal 62 yards, the NCAA record at the time. I got on the phone and called Fred and said, "Fred, I want to congratulate you for Russell's field goal."

He said, "Why congratulate me? I didn't kick it."

I said, "I know, Fred, but if you didn't believe that Russell could kick it, you would not have allowed him in the game. You believed in your player, and you gave him the chance to perform."

Even though the potential is there, many coaches and managers don't see it; and if they don't see it, they won't allow their people to develop it and use it.

After I told this story, one of the leaders of the Boys' Clubs raised his hand and said, "Once I worked at a camp for children who were blind or had arms or legs amputated. But the camp rule was that every child at camp needed to participate in the activities—ride a horse, swim, clean up the kitchen, set the table. We were teaching them, *You can do it.*

"One night my job was to cook dinner for everybody, and I had a little spastic girl helping me. We were cooking roast beef, and when it was done, I put it on a tray. Now this little girl stood up with this tray and wanted to carry the roast beef into the dining room. Being spastic, she had trouble with her coordination, and so she was wobbling around as she started off for the dining room with the roast on the tray. I said to myself, 'My God, that's our dinner, and if she drops it we don't eat.' It seemed like it took her forever to get to the dining room, but when she got there everybody whistled, applauded and cheered her accomplishment.

"In retrospect," he said, "it isn't so remarkable that she carried the tray without dumping the roast beef on the floor; the most remarkable thing was that neither I nor anyone else took it away from her."

The esteem of individuals, teams, companies, and nations rises and falls based upon Smart Talk. To the degree your self-talk is constructive, you feel good about yourself. Esteem building is, in large part, a do-it-yourself project. But master mentors and effective coaches, teachers, parents, and bosses can make a major assist, if they believe in themselves and those they lead.

Here are two basic self-affirmations for leaders.

1. Important people listen to me when I talk, because I have something of value to say. Make this affirmation over and over to boost your esteem as a leader. If you don't keep increasing your own esteem, you won't raise your aspirations and expectations of others. Reflect on times when important people listened to you. As you reflect, you cause your esteem to rise. You can then reverse the affirmation: "I listen carefully to other people because they have something of value to say." You will then pay closer attention when your children or colleagues are talking. You won't just be there in body; you'll get genuinely caught up in what they are saying—not necessarily for what they are saying, but for who they are and what they mean to you.

2. I am an important and valuable person, worthy of the respect of people who are important to me. I have made this one for years. I can't be important to the billions of people in the world. I can be important, though, to people who are important to me.

When you know that you are a person of value, you feel worthy of the respect of others. You carry yourself in a way that says, "I'm worthy of respect." And people will send that same message back to you.

You get back what you send. As you respect yourself more, people treat you with more respect.

Unfortunately, the opposite is also true. One of our adopted children had been very badly abused before we got him. And when we sent him to first grade, the kids picked on him. Every year the kids picked on him. We put him into a new junior high school where nobody knew him, and still people picked on him. He went to a new high school where nobody knew him, but people picked on him. He went into the military, and the sergeant picked on him. He got a job but lost it because people picked on him.

We bought him a tow truck and set him up in a small business. He came home a few weeks later and said, "I quit."

I said, "How come?"

He said, "Bill (his office manager) is picking on me."

I said, "You can't quit. You own the business."

You see, if you think in your own mind, "I'm not worthy," you set yourself up to be picked on.

I said to him, "If you don't change how you feel about yourself on the inside, this cycle will not change. You set yourself up for a string of bad luck."

He just grinned. But he still has his *bad luck.*

As a parent, coach or leader, you may see your people in an ideal state way out into the future, but you've got to speak to them with goals that they can connect with. If you talk too far out, they get intimidated by it; or they can't imagine it. For example, you don't talk to a five-year-old about going to a university. You want to trigger imagery that the kid can connect with. So you talk about the first grade. You talk where they can connect in a constructive way and make it exciting. If you only talk to the vision "out there," which is a mistake I've made many times, you may be talking to people who can't even imagine it, and so they just grin at you. They won't connect with it or buy in.

In this book, I sincerely hope that I've connected with you. I know you can make a major difference in your company and community. I don't care if you're "a leader" right now. That isn't important. Leadership can come from almost anywhere. As you progress—and as you keep your heart right—you will see places where you can make a difference. It doesn't need to be a big splash to start with. What matters is that you turn and face the problem and make a personal contribution toward the solution.

I can hardly wait to hear what you do. Diane and I enjoy hearing from people we've touched. We look forward to learning what you're doing, all the magnificent differences that you're making, because of your Smart Talk, and your Smart Walk. Please, keep in touch.

P o s t s c r i p t

I want to ask for your help—not to help me, but to help others. My friend Alec Dixon, whom the Peace Corps was modeled after, died last year. I asked him to be my mentor three years ago. He said, "The race that you're running is too exhausting. If you sprint the whole distance, you'll kill yourself. It's a relay race. You've got to run your leg of the race as hard and fast as you can, and then pass the baton."

I'm writing this book to *pass the baton*. I want to pass the baton to you so that you can run your leg of the race for love—in your community, your work, your family, or your church.

I can't do it all myself. You can't do it all yourself. But you and I can start getting little things done all over the place. And the little things will get bigger and bigger.

I want you to pass the baton to the people around you. I want the people around you to ask, "How can I be like you?" And you tell them, "This is how." Many people will want to model you.

That was difficult for me because I was not willing to be admired. It was almost like, "If you only knew who I was in the past, you wouldn't bother." But they didn't know. They just saw me as I am now. And so I needed to allow people to admire me. So will you as you do great things.

I once asked Jim Wright, the ex-Speaker of the House who served under at least eight U.S. presidents, "Would you give me the one quality or characteristic that stands out most in each of them?"

He gave me the list, and said, "Each one who was great was willing to be admired." He added, "You need to develop the willingness to be admired. You need to be willing to let your sons, daughters, children, and the people around you admire you. Not because you need the admiration, but because they need the model."

I needed to develop that ability. I wasn't allowing that. People would come and say, "You've changed my life. You've helped me." And with my body language, I'd reject them. I must have made many people feel like fools. I didn't intend to, but I pushed them away. Can you imagine saying, "Mister, you're so dumb to think that. Why would you ever admire me? You can't be very smart." I must have been sending that message. I needed to change my attitude.

General Cal Waller, a three-star general who served as deputy commander of Desert Storm, once came to me and said, "Some of the high-potential people we have in the service do something stupid to sabotage their success. After their very competitive selection to general officer, they do something to blow their opportunities." He said, "I also see that in professional athletes who suddenly rise to the top. They have abundance of money. All of a sudden they're on drugs, and they do the dumbest things to blow their success." He was very concerned about how to get this information across so that high-potential people would stop self-sabotaging.

This is why I want you to pass this baton. I want you to get this message out into the hospitals, to people working with abused children. I want you to get it out to people who are chronically unemployed. I want you to get it out to people in ghettos, I want you to get it out to potential leaders so they understand they don't need to keep sabotaging their success.

I'm confident you will surpass what Diane and I have done with our lives.

Some time ago, I saw a poster that showed two people walking in the distance, and it said something like this: "Don't walk behind me, I may not be leading; and don't walk in front of me, because I may not choose to follow you. Just walk beside me, and be my friend." That is what I would close with. I'm not asking you to follow me. And I'm certainly not going to follow you. But Diane and I would ask you to be empowered and to walk beside us and just be our friends.

Index

About the Author

He may have started out as a high school teacher and football coach, but a belief in "no limits" has led **Lou Tice** to become one of the most highly respected educators in the world today. His singular style of teaching – taking the complex concepts and current research results from the fields of cognitive psychology and social learning theory, and making them easy to understand and even easier to use – has brought him students from all over the globe.

Lou's ability as a consummate teacher and mentor has brought him to some of the world's hot spots: to the leaders of Northern Ireland, where he has worked since the mid-80's; to Guatemala, where he has worked since the signing of the Peace Accords in 1995; and to South Africa, from before the end of the era of apartheid to this very day. In 2004, he brought his considerable talents to bear in an on-going partnership with University of California head football coach, Pete Carroll, to make a positive difference in South Los Angeles.

Born and raised in Seattle, Washington where he and Diane, his wife, still make their home, Lou received his bachelor's degree from Seattle University. He went on to earn an MA in Education from the University of Washington, with a major focus in the mental health sciences. Lou is the internationally recognized author of the popular books, *Smart Talk for Achieving Your Potential* and *Personal Coaching for Results*. He is co-author of *Leadership is a Performance Art* with USC Head Football Coach Pete Carroll, and co-editor with Dr. Glenn Terrell, President Emeritus of Washington State University, of *Cultures of Excellence*.

About The Pacific Institute

The Pacific Institute was founded by Lou and Diane Tice, in 1971. Since then, the company has expanded onto six continents and into over 60 countries, and its programs have been translated into a multitude of languages. It has developed a reputation for offering the most practical and enlightening programs ever to come out of the fields of cognitive and self-image psychology and high-achiever research. International headquarters for The Pacific Institute is in Seattle, Washington.

The guiding principle of The Pacific Institute is that individuals have a virtually unlimited capacity for growth, change and creativity, and can adapt readily to the tremendous changes taking place in this fast-paced, technological age. Central to this is that individuals are responsible for their own actions, and can regulate their behavior through a structured process that includes goal-setting, self-reflection and self-evaluation, among other things.

By applying The Pacific Institute's education, people are able to develop their potential by changing their habits, attitudes, beliefs and expectations. This, in turn, allows individuals in an organizational setting to achieve higher levels of growth and productivity, as well as shifting the collective behavior. This shift leads to more constructive organizational cultures, and healthier, higher performing workplaces.

Solidly grounded in the latest research coming out of the fields of cognitive psychology and social learning theory, documented results clearly show measurable increases in organizational effectiveness and productivity after applying The Pacific Institute concepts.

- Over 60% of the Fortune 1000, as well as top businesses in Europe, the Americas, Africa and Asia, have used the Institute's varied resources to create corporate excellence.

- Adult and juvenile justice systems employ specialized curricula to combat recidivism, and to return parolees to their communities as positive contributors.

- Public and private schools and school systems use the Institute's educational curricula to improve student learning and retention, teacher satisfaction and district-wide efficacy.

- Social service agencies return higher wage earners to the workforce, with the attitudes desired by employers.

- All levels of government, as well as the military, employ the Institute's curricula to improve and enhance efficiencies and effectiveness.

Throughout the year, The Pacific Institute offers a wide variety of seminars and conferences that showcase the "best practice" applications of its education and services: the Cascade Forums, "Taking It to the Next Level" weekend seminars taught by Lou Tice "live and in person," as well as the annual Global Conference. On a daily basis is the free email service, the Winner's Circle, from Lou.

Lou Tice is in great demand as a speaker and consultant for organizations seeking to become more effective and achieve lasting, measurable results. The Pacific Institute continues to expand the scope of its activities around the world. For updated news and further information, please log on to our website at www.thepacificinstitute.com or contact us at:

The Pacific Institute
1709 Harbor Ave. S. W.
Seattle, WA 98126
800.426.3660 (U.S. and Canada)
206.628.4800 Direct
206.587.6007 Fax